The Dynamics of Industrial Collaboration

The Dynamics of Industrial Collaboration

A Diversity of Theories and Empirical Approaches

Edited by

Anne Plunket
Assistant Professor, Université Paris Sud, France

Colette Voisin
Professor, Université Paris Sud, France

Bertrand Bellon
Professor, Université Paris Sud, France

Edward Elgar
Cheltenham, UK • Northampton, MA, USA

Published by
Edward Elgar Publishing Limited
Glensanda House
Montpellier Parade
Cheltenham
Glos GL50 1UA
UK

Edward Elgar Publishing, Inc.
ᴍᴋ 136 West Street
Suite 202
Northampton
Massachusetts 01060
USA

A catalogue record for this book
is available from the British Library

Library of Congress Cataloguing in Publication Data
The dynamics of industrial collaboration : a diversity of theories and empirical
approaches / edited by Anne Plunket, Colette Voisin, Bertrand Bellon.
    p. cm.
  Includes bibliographical references and index.
  1. Strategic alliances (Business) 2. Business networks. I. Plunket, Anne,
  1970– II. Voisin, Colette. III. Bellon, Bertrand.

HD69.S8 D96 2002
338.8'7—dc21   2001053221

ISBN 1 84064 582 2
Printed and bound in Great Britain by MPG Books Ltd, Bodmin, Cornwall

Contents

PART II. PROCESS AND EVOLUTION OF COOPERATION

PART III. INDUSTRIAL AND RESEARCH NETWORKS

Figures

Tables

Contributors

Bertrand Bellon, ADIS, University Paris-Sud.

Didier Bréchemier, KMPG Consulting France.

Cécile Borzeda, ROSES-CNRS, Université de Paris-I.

Maurice Cassier, CERMES, CNRS, Paris, France.

Massimo G. Colombo, Università di Pavia and CIRET-Politecnico di Milano.

Godefroy Dang-Nguyen, ENST Bretagne, France.

Marco Delmastro, Università di Pavia and CIRET-Politecnico di Milano.

Joëlle Farchy, ADIS, University of Paris 11.

Dominique Foray, Institut pour le Management de la Recherche et de l'Innovation (IMRI, CNRS), University of Paris-Dauphine, Paris, France.

Corine Genet, Laboratoire INRA/SERD, Grenoble, France.

Vincent Giard, University of Panthéon-Sorbonne, IAE in Paris.

John Hagedoorn, Department of Management Sciences at the University of Maastricht.

Preben Sander Kristensen, Ike Group, Aalborg, Druid-Disko.

Sarianna Lundan, Department of Management Sciences at the University of Maastricht.

Jean-Charles Monateri, IREPD, University of Grenoble..

Thierry Pénard, University of Rennes, France.

Anne Plunket, ADIS, University of Paris Sud.

Joël Thomas Ravix, Idefi-Latapses, CNRS, University of Nice – Sophia Antipolis, France.

Yorgos Rizopoulos, CRIISEA, Université de Picardie, France.

Fabrice Rochelandet, ADIS, University of Paris 11.

Michel Sapina, IREPD, University of Grenoble, France.

Stéphane Saussier, ADIS, University of Paris XI Sceaux and ATOM-University of Paris I, Sorbonne.

Pier Paolo Saviotti INRA, Université Pierre Mendés-France, France.

Anker Lund Vinding, Ike Group, Aalborg, Druid-Disko.

Colette Voisin, ADIS-PESOR, University of Paris Sud, France.

Preface

Like the former ADIS (Research Center of the Faculté Jean Monnet, University Paris Sud) publications, *The Dynamics of Industrial Collaboration* is the result of a collective work. Research material was gathered over two years from various horizons. It was first presented at *The Industrial cooperation: diversity and synthesis* Conference on May 3 and 4, 1999. This collaborative work between scholars and professionals has also resulted in an other book *La coopération industrielle*, in French, which was published by Economica, Paris.

The books could not have been published without the financial support of the "Ministère de l'éducation Nationale, de la recherche et de la technologie", the European Commission's DG XII, the Faculté Jean Monnet and the Université of Paris Sud.

Many thanks are due to Francoise Segers and Sylvie Duarte for their help with the organization of the conference.

Bernard Offerle, Senior lecturer in English for economics, must also be thanked for his precious help in checking the proofs.

ADIS
Faculté Jean Monnet
54, Boulevard Desgranges
92331 Sceaux Cedex
France

D21

L24

Introduction: Research on Inter-firm Collaboration, Evolution and Perspectives

Anne Plunket, Colette Voisin and Bertrand Bellon

1. THE NATURE OF COOPERATION: THEORIES AND EMPIRICAL EVIDENCE

Inter-firm collaboration has represented one of the major organizational mutations over last two decades. This strategic issue has quickly become a theoretical question for scholars of economics and management. If inter-firms cooperation is not a recent phenomenon as such, its contemporary form is quite new and dates back to the end of the 1970s; its rapid evolution has taken a variety of forms such as joint ventures, contractual relations and various forms of networks.

Despite the amount of work done in this field, many questions remain open. For example, how may we explain that cooperative behavior, which sheds a new light on the issue of the firm's boundaries? How, at the same time, may we account for the complexity of its forms, its objectives and the changes it has introduced in firms and industries?

Analytically, the rapid growth of inter-firm relationships has coincided with the revival of the theory of the firm. Partly for this reason, cooperation has been defined in comparison with the nature of the firm. In particular, the theory of transaction cost defined cooperation as a hybrid form between the hierarchy and the market. But these approaches have proven insufficient; they have therefore prompted the conclusion that inter-firm cooperation is of a distinct nature from the firm and the market. In consequence, more recent studies have gone further to explain the dynamic boundaries of the firm; they integrate the characteristics of technology and the constraints of innovation and the creation and diffusion of new knowledge (Colombo and Delmastro, Chapter 1). Thus, the treatment of these questions is growingly based on the development of the evolutionary and resource-based approaches.

Whereas scholars have focused on the rather static approaches that kept process questions almost underdeveloped, more recent studies, mainly under the impact of evolutionary theory, have raised the fundamental need for more dynamic accounts of governance structure and agreements. They aimed at finding an endogenous explanation not only of the emergence but also the evolution of inter-firm cooperation.

Empirically, the first works were mostly concerned with the forms of collaboration (joint ventures, equity versus non-equity ventures) and the problems of instability (Kogut, 1989; Gomes-Casseres, 1987; Ho Park and Russo, 1996). They suggested explanations of failure and success rates. Among the possible cooperative forms that may be chosen by firms, joint ventures, once the most popular, are often less preferred than non-equity and contractual partnerships, in particular in R&D (Hagedoorn and Lundan, Chapter 5). Since then, the cooperative relationships have evolved towards various forms of collaboration such as research consortia (Cassier and Foray, Chapter 11; Saviotti, Chapter 10) but also more complex network-firms as shown by Giard (Chapter 12). Saviotti discusses the importance of innovation networks and the fact that they have become stable components of industrial organization. He shows that these networks are based on three types of actors, namely large diversified firms, small new technology firms and public research institutions. In particular, the stability of these networks is explained by the dual role played by these small new technology firms which both contribute to understanding the technology and communicating it to the large diversified firms. Cassier and Foray emphasize another aspect of research networks, that is, the role played by collective invention in opposition to the privatization of knowledge: "R&D consortia are producing a new economic category of knowledge, called collective or pooled data, which is shared among participants during the period of research and has a hybrid nature, between public and private goods". Finally, the developments in information technology and New Economics have given rise to new forms of cooperation as shown by Dang-Nguyen and Pénart (Chapter 3) and Farchy and Rochelandet (Chapter 4).

From a supposedly temporary phenomenon, inter-firm collaboration has now become a standard organizational form. This point can be mainly explained through the tight link between the formation of strategic alliances and technology. Agreements are not all technological; this aspect nevertheless remains a key element in a majority of them. Among the major reasons for the growth of this organizational form since the seventies, one finds the globalization of markets, the speed, complexity and uncertainty of technological developments, the increase in R&D costs, the need for firms to manage an increasingly broad spectrum of different technologies, access new markets and competencies in various technological regimes and industries (Hagedoorn, 1990, pp. 19-20).

Like any other social activity, industrial collaboration is a complex phenomenon, which can hardly be grasped through a unique theoretical framework. Our motivation for organizing the "Industrial Cooperation: Diversity and Synthesis" conference in Paris was to try and draw the line between what we already know and what still wants implementing. We wanted confrontation on an interdisciplinary basis so as to offer the opportunity to revisit and reformulate some of the theoretical and empirical issues raised by this phenomenon. This book is one of the spin-offs of this conference; it offers some of the latest research on industrial cooperation.

In the introduction, we intended to give an overview of the literature on inter-firm cooperation. We raise some of the controversies, which put the various theoretical approaches face to face with their explanatory capacity and their limits. On a micro-economic level, four theoretical perspectives are particularly significant when explaining inter-firm or inter-institutional collaboration: the theory of transaction costs and contracts, the evolutionary theory and the resource-based view. Most of these approaches concern the theories of the firm and their dynamic boundaries but not, strictly speaking, the theories of cooperation as such. As shown in this book, none of these approaches are dominant and the new perspectives suggest that scholars find it fruitful to integrate some of these theories. In fact, there is an increasing acceptance that the theoretical account for this phenomenon belongs somewhere in between a transaction cost, an agency issue and an evolutionary and resource-based view that integrate both incentives and cognitive issues. Yet, this integration is not so easy to achieve because of the tensions and even the incompatibilities of the assumptions underlying in the major explanations.

2. THE VARIOUS FORMS OF COOPERATION

The Role of Opportunism Versus the Creation of Knowledge

The rationales and forms of inter-firm agreements have been one of the first issues raised by the theory. Transaction cost theory, originally developed to account for integration, gradually included inter-firm cooperation as an intermediate form between the market and the hierarchy. By focusing on the assumptions of limited rationality and opportunistic behavior, Williamson (1985) emphasized that the economic agents are not able to anticipate all the states of nature, nor write complete contracts. This is particularly relevant when the transactions are based on investments in specific assets to the transaction, that is, assets, which can barely be or cannot at all be redeployable in other activities. Consequently, if there is a risk of opportunism, agents may find it beneficial to choose modes of organization and coordination for their transactions – the structure of governance – which limit the transaction costs.

If this approach is indeed partly validated empirically (Pisano, 1990; Hennart, 1991; Saussier, 1999; Masten and Saussier, 2000), it is above all a theory of vertical integration, and thus remains limited when studying the cooperation without combining it with other theories (Saussier, 2000; Saussier and Brechemier, Chapter 1; Colombo and Delmastro, Chapter 2; Plunket, 1999). Nevertheless, this approach has raised some criticisms such as the problem of the measurability of transaction costs by firms (Buckley and Chapman, 1997) or the way uncertainty is considered and treated by the theory, namely whether the issue of technology is included or not (Barney and Lee, 1998). In fact, empirical studies show that a high degree of uncertainty (mostly due to technological risks) does not necessarily lead to integration but may favor collaboration.

The evolutionary theory associated to the resource-based view offer an explanation for this paradox (Colombo and Delmastro, Chapter 2). Choosing to carry out an activity in-house or externally matters insofar as the resources invested and created involve irreversibilities (Gaffard, 1989). In other words, governance structures are not perfectly substitutable (Foray, 1991). In fact, the trade-off between these organizational forms does not only depend on transaction costs but also on whether the resources and competencies are readily available or need to be created by the firms. Thus, the resource-based view is particularly adapted to the analysis of the formation of alliances as a way for firms to access the tangible and intangible resources that are specific to some firms but cannot be exchanged on the market because they would be too costly or even difficult to develop in-house. These resources represent a hierarchy of tangible and intangible assets (Praest, 1999). Tangible assets include financial, technological assets such as equipment, etc. Intangible assets represent the knowledge base of the firm, including patent rights. This knowledge base consists of the competences and the capabilities, which define a set of know how (Carlsson and Eliasson, 1994) based on routines (Nelson and Winter, 1982; Cohen et al. 1996; Cohen and Bacdayan, 1994). Among these, the dynamic capabilities enable the firm to face environmental changes, to adapt to them and modify the organizational competences (Teece, and Pisano, 1994). The characteristics of knowledge and resources creation play a major role in the formation of collaborative ventures; they are dependent on some conditions, which characterize the technological environments of firms. Three conditions are particularly emphasized by Malerba and Orsenigo (1993). First, there is appropriability, that is, the easiness of imitation (Teece, 1992, Pisano, 1990, 1991): if approapriability is low, then the knowledge base will be less tacit and thus easier to imitate. In this case, property rights may be less efficient to protect the firms' innovations. The second feature is what Malerba and Orsenigo call pervasiveness, that is, the possibility of applying the results of some research to a variety of products and markets. The third significant aspect is related to the type of assets, which are developed in the agreement. The development of specialized assets creates unilateral dependence, which is a source of vulnerability (Teece, 1992) in some cases, but may also become a major incentive to implement long-lasting relations (Borzeda and Rizopoulos, Chapter 8).

Multiplicity and Integration of Complementary Theories

Recent studies suggest that the integration of various theories and their stylized facts give a better understanding of the tradeoffs underlying the choice of cooperation versus other forms such as hierarchy (Foss and Mahnke, 2000). Saussier and Bréchemier (Chapter 2) show that incomplete contract theory does not permit the analysis of inter-firm agreements when internal organization is not retained. They show the need to complement the theory of incomplete contracts with the theory of transaction costs, when studying the decision to cooperate or not, and the contractual practices when the integration solution is not retained. This comes from the fact that the theory of incomplete contracts more or less ignores the role of asset specificity and focuses on the role of non-contractibility, whereas the theory of transaction cost emphasizes the role of asset specificity. "The integration of both theories gets important when analyzing the contractual practices such as the various types of ground services of four European airway companies where (i) several crucial dimensions of the transaction are non-contractible and (ii) specific investments appear to be present only at low levels" (Saussier and Bréchemier, Chapter 2).

Regarding the appropriate form of strategic and technological alliances, Colombo and Delmastro (Chapter 1) show that one must go beyond transaction cost theory and integrate the considerations inspired by the competence-based theories of the firm, "which emphasize the role of alliances as learning-oriented, capability-building devices". In fact, a majority of firms choose non-equity bilateral arrangements when their relations concern R&D and other technology-related activities. In the latter case, their findings do not support the view advocating more formal forms as suggested by transaction cost economics.

In the integration of transaction cost and evolutionary theory some major issues introduce tensions, even incompatibilities. On the one hand, opportunism is considered as a constant in most contractual approaches. It should instead be regarded as a variable (Noorderhaven, 1995) and evolve to leave room for a cumulative process of learning and trust (Lazaric and Lorenz, 1998), and thus help to model the partners' incentives to cooperate. There is *a priori* no incompatibility between the concept of opportunism and the bases of the evolutionary theory. Indeed, if opportunism is a key variable of the economic agent's behavior, it is not incompatible with trust (Noorderhaven, 1995); in the contractual analysis opportunism does not imply that the firms cannot but adopt the attitude of a predator. On the other hand, if some conditions change within or outside the firm, it may be that the cooperation appears ex post not to be a good solution any more, and in this case, the firms can decide to stop the agreement or terminate certain commitments as shown by Plunket (Chapter 9). Finally, maximizing rationality is incompatible with the rationality of the evolutionary models because it is based on a rationality, which is indeed procedural, and yet mainly limited. In fact, when taking their decisions, economic agents face problems of competencies (Heiner, 1983) and information (Dosi and Egidi, 1991). Lack of competencies arises when the agents have difficulties in treating a complex problem. Lack of information arises when considering all the states of nature is impossible. For these two reasons, at least, agents, just like the firms, are not able to maximize objective functions. The cognitive approaches on which the evolutionary theory is based show that agents do not maximize but choose "satisficing" solutions while following rules and routines, which were elaborated in former experiments, through learning processes. Thus routines have a dual nature. On the one hand, they guide action, which consists of applying the same answers to similar situations since none of the decisions that are to be taken are completely new. On the other hand, they constitute models of problem resolution: agents will tackle and solve the questions by applying the modes of resolution, which were developed in the past and have proven the most effective (Cohen et al., 1996). Consequently, the rationality of the agents in the evolutionary theory is not based on maximization behavior, but consists in following rules, " *the rule-following behavior*" (Vanberg, 1993; Plunket, 2000).

3. THE PROCESS OF COOPERATION: AN EVOLUTIONARY PERSPECTIVE

Mainly under the impact of the evolutionary approaches and the rise of the resource-based view of the firm, an increasing part of research has focused on the study of the evolution of inter-firm agreements. A large majority of these studies are based on surveys and case studies and therefore takes a longitudinal perspective. Two issues are particularly emphasized throughout the literature. First, initial conditions, such as prior commitments and cooperative incentives and also the design of property rights, help to explain the outcome of agreements. Second, interactive learning and knowledge creation are major driving forces behind the evolution of agreements: they contribute to the stability and success of collaboration.

The Role of Initial Conditions: Commitments and Intentions

Cooperation begins with the negotiation of the conditions to implement and manage the agreement. These include the definition of common aims, the resources allocated by each partner, the division of labor, the way information is exchanged as well as the conditions of monitoring, and finally the definition of property rights settlement. Usually firms also negotiate efficiency conditions and advancement schedules that enable them to assess the relevance and the future of the agreement. Favoring some convergence of views may seem most important, as it will help prevent conflicts. Similarly, defining ways to manage conflicts from the start may help in securing the agreement's outcome (Ring and Van de Ven, 1994).

Cooperations not only face uncertainty regarding their future states, they also face the problem of not knowing the partner's real intentions towards the alliance. This concern has been emphasized throughout economics, management and sociology. Thus, one of the first concerns, more particularly in game theory (Axelrod, 1984 and Gulati et al. 1994), has been to find ways to undermine the fatal conclusion of the prisoner's dilemma and favor a cooperative outcome. As long as agreements are used as instruments of passive flexibility (Wolff, 1995) in a attitude "wait and see", or as a substitution of merger or acquisition, the agreement is likely to be unstable because of the suspicion and the lack of commitment relating to the latter. As a consequence, firms may concede unilateral or bilateral commitments, thus revealing their real intentions cooperative or opportunistic. These commitments are, usually, investments in tangible or intangible assets, which may be more or less specific to the transaction. Williamson (1983) has called these investments "hostages" because, they tend to make the commitments irreversible to a certain extent and thus place the partner, who initiated them, in a vulnerable situation. This may appear somewhat paradoxical: on the one hand, it is required of them that they should secure themselves from opportunism, and on the other hand, they should deliberately place themselves in a vulnerable situation! The apparent contradiction can be resolved because the two issues are not necessarily exclusive of each other. However, in game theory, this behavior (that is, hostages) is equivalent to a shift in the prisoner's dilemma game whereby the expected defection is changed into the possibility of a longer collaboration (Gulati et al., 1994). Borzeda and Rizopoulos (Chapter 8) discuss the role of interdependencies in building long-lasting relations. They distinguish four generic types of long-lasting relations according to their density, complexity and degree of mutual dependence of actors. They also emphasize the role played by trust in the development of these interdependencies. These commitments and investments appear to be the first necessary conditions for the evolution of cooperation. Over time they may be modified by the advancement of the project: the achievements of the common work may place collaboration in a new light giving major importance to the project, or part of it, and thus requiring higher investments.

The Evolution of Cooperation: Knowledge Creation and Institutionalization

Inter-firm agreements evolve through the partner's interaction; this creates cooperation and becomes a source of added value. Evolutionary theory lays particular emphasis on learning as a driving force of organizational dynamic. There is a widespread acceptance that without commitments there cannot be any learning and without learning the continuation and efficiency of the relation can be questioned. Lazaric and Lorenz (1998) show that inter-firm alliances depend on the association of two different frameworks through the creation of a common organizational entity, and on trust which reduces the intrinsic uncertainty and risk of opportunism in such cooperation. The interactive learning process is the result of a more pro-active behavior characterized by the emergence of common communication, language standards and routines (Lundvall, 1985; Cohen et al., 1996). Genet (Chapter 7) discusses the role played by informal links in the genesis of collaboration between SMEs and public laboratories. She shows the role played by informal interactions in the emergent phase as in the evolution of cooperation through the reduction of uncertainty and risks inherent in any relationship. Trust generates privileged modes of cooperation. Also, firms should give preference to the partners with whom they have already collaborated or to the collaboration partners they expect to be important in the long run (Kristensen and Vinding, Chapter 6). Ciborra (1991) has described the learning processes that take place during alliances:

"The alliance brings into corporation new expertise concerning products marketing strategies, organizational know how, new tacit and explicit knowledge. New management systems, operating procedures and modifications of products are typical outcomes of such a process of incremental learning. A firm can learn how to set up and fine-tune alliances *per se*. The result of such learning is the institutionalization of the organization's rules and routines aimed at managing alliances".

Thus routines structure the behavior of organizations (even in the interactive setting of a cooperative agreement). They emerge through repetition and get crystallized in experiences (Nonaka, 1994). Thus organizational learning is the process by which knowledge is acquired, accumulated and memorized in a firm. It is the process by which the agreement becomes an organizational entity *per se* with its own rules, routines and modes of conflict resolution. The establishment of coordination rules for structuring durable and complementary relationships between firms is particularly well illustrated by synchronous production in the car industry. Because of continuous organizational and production innovation, firms must cooperate to ensure proper coordination in operations management, as well as in contractual and complementary investments (Sapina and Monateri, Chapter 13). The authors show how firms need to coordinate both hybrid contractual forms and complementary investment policies in order to reduce uncertainty and stabilize contractual relationships, profitability of production and coordination of their investments. Also based on Richardson and Penrose's work on different types of activities, Ravix (Chapter 14) adopts a cross-industrial view of French industrial collaboration and sheds a different light on industrial organization. He shows that all industries are not structured in the same way. Arrangements depend on the role played by cooperation or market transaction in the organization of production.

Though cooperation is usually chosen for its apparent flexibility (Nooteboom, 1992), it is paradoxical that cooperation gains its actual efficacy through a process creating irreversibilities, based on the specialization of the knowledge base and assets. Three types of assets (technological, relational and organizational) may be created through cooperation, thus creating three complementary sources of irreversibility (Lazaric and Marengo, 2000). First, irreversibility may be organizational through the emergence of routines and common memories: the relation sets its own rules of managing the relation and transferring information. Irreversibility may be technological as parties may be locked-in because of the technological path chosen and because efficacy means specialization, which may lead to non-redeployable investments. Finally, organizational and technological assets are based on relational assets, namely, on investments for building up trust and communication schemes enabling the partners to work together and, in particular, share tacit knowledge.

Finally, the evolution of inter-firm alliances may be considered through the impact of the external environment of the agreement, for example, the external shocks that affect the agreement's goals and results but also each partner's environment corporate and internal situation. Plunket (Chapter 9) shows that if the learning process is a necessary condition of the agreement's success, the evolution of the agreement depends on the modification of each partner's corporate situation such as changes in corporate governance or strategy, even though the economic viability of the agreement has not changed.

The book is in three parts: forms of collaboration, process and evolution of cooperation and industrial and research networks. The various chapters give an overview of the lastest research developed on these questions. A dual approach along both theoretical and empirical lines was given priority. The primary objective was to give a precise idea of the diversity of forms in existence and of the processes, which underlie these relationships. Second, it has seemed fruitful to confront these results with the existing dominant theories. In fact, the confrontation of theory with empirics and the confrontation of various theoretical approaches helps to extend and broaden our understanding of this phenomenon. It appears that the theories of transaction costs and contracts are more robust in explaining the conflicts at the start and the end of cooperation when it comes to sharing the results. The evolutionary and resource-based view seems more convincing to explain the cooperative process and show how agreements create resources and added value. Once again, it appears that the integration of theories can be seen as an alternative approach leading to a theory which discusses both the initial and final conditions as well as the process perspectives and how they may interact and lead to the outcome of cooperation.

REFERENCES

Axelrod, R. (1984), *The Evolution of Cooperation*, BasicBooks.
Barney, J.B. and Lee, W. (1998), "Governance Under Uncertainty: Transaction Costs, Real Options, Learning, and Property Rights" Druid summer Conference, 9-11 June, Bornholm, Denmark.
Buckley, P.J. and Chapman M. (1997), "The perception and measurement of transaction costs", *Cambridge Journal of Economics*, **21**, 127-145.

Carlsson, B. and Eliasson G. (1994), "The nature and Importance of Economic Competence", *Industrial and Corporate Change*, **3** (3), 687-711.

Ciborra, C. (1991), "Alliances as learning experiments: cooperation, competition and change in hightech industries", L.K. Mytelka (ed), *Strategic Partnerships, States, Firms and International competition*, Pinter Publishers, London.

Cohen, C.D. and Bacdayan, P. (1994), "Organizational routines are stored as procedural memory: Evidence from a laboratory study", *Organization Science,* **5** (4).

Cohen, M.D., Burkhart, R., Dosi, G., Egidi, M., Marengo, L., Warglien, M. and Winter, S. (1996), "Routines and other recurring action patterns of organizations: contemporary research issues", *Industrial Corporate Change,* **5** (3), 653-698.

Dosi, G. and Egidi, M. (1991), "Substantive and procedural uncertainty, an exploration of economic behaviours in changing environments", *Journal of Evolutionary Economics,* 145-168.

Foss, N. and Mahnke, V. (2000), "Advancing research on competence, governance, and entrepreneurship", in N. Foss and V. Mahnke (eds), *Competence, Governance, and Entrepreneurship*, Oxford University Press.

Foray, D. (1991), "Repères pour une économie des organisations de recherche – développement", *Revue d'économie politique* **101** (5).

Gaffard, J-L. (1989), "Marchés et organisation dans les stratégies technologiques des firmes industrielles", *Revued d'Economie Industrielle,* **48**, 2e trimestre, 35-51.

Gomes-Casseres, B (1987), "Joint venture instability: is it a problem? " *Columbia Journal of World Business*, Summer 1987, 97-102.

Gulati, R. Khanna, T. Nohria, N. (1994), "Unilateral commitments and the importance of process in alliances", *Sloan Management Review,* Spring 1994.

Hagedoorn, J. (1990), "Organizational modes of inter-firm co-operation and technology transfer", *Technovation*, **10** (1), 17-30.

Heiner R. A. (1983), "The origin of predictable behaviour", *The American Economic Review*, **73** (4), 560-595.

Hennart, J-F. (1991), "The transaction costs theory of joint ventures: an empirical study of Japanese subsidiaries in the United States", *Management Science,* **37**(4), 483-497.

Ho Park and S. Russo, M.V. (1996), "When competition eclipses cooperation: an event history analysis of joint venture failure", *Management Science*, 42 (6), 875-890.

Kogut, B. (1989), "The stability of joint ventures: reciprocity and competitive rivalry", *The Journal of Industrial Economics*, **XXXVIII**, december, 183-199.

Lazaric, N. and Lorenz, E. (1998), "Trust and organizational learning during inter-firm cooperation", in N. Lazaric and E. Lorenz (eds), *Trust and Economic Learning*, Edward Elgar.

Lazaric, N. and Marengo L. (2000), "Towards a characterization of knowledge and assets created in technological agreements: some empirical evidence in the automobile-robotics sector", *Industrial and Corporate Change*, **9** (1), 53-86.

Lundvall, B Å. (1985), *Product Innovation and User-Producer Interaction*, Aalborg University Press, Aalborg.

Malerba, F. and Orsenigo, L. (1993), "Technological regimes and firm behavior", *Industrial and Corporate Change*, **2** (1).

Masten, S.E. and Saussier, S. (2000), "Econometrics of contracts : an assessment of developments in the empirical literature of contracting", *Revue d'Economie Industrielle*, **92**, 215-236.

Nelson, R.R. and Winter S.G. (1982), *An Evolutionary Theory of Economic Change*, Cambridge University Press.

Noorderhaven, N.G. (1995), "The argumentational texture of transaction cost economics", *Organization Studies*, 16 (4), 605-623.

Nooteboom, B. (1992), "Towards a dynamic theory of transactions", *Journal of Evolutionary Economics* 2, 281-299.

Nonaka, I. (1994), "A dynamic theory of organizational knowledge creation", *Organization Science*, **5**, 1, 14-37.

Pisano, G. (1990), "The R&D boundaries of the firm: an empirical analysis", *Administrative Science Quraterly*, **35**, 153-176.

Pisano, G. (1991), "The governance of innovation: vertical integration and collaborative arrangements in the biotechnology industry", *Research Policy*, **20**, 237-249.

Plunket, A. (1999), "Evolution de la coopération : contribution à l'étude des déterminants des processus d'évolution et de sélection de la coopération technologique", thèse en sciences économiques, ADIS, Université Paris Sud.

Plunket, A. (2000), " Les règles d'évaluation et de décision dans l'évolution de la coopération technologique", in C. Voisin, A. Plunket, B. Bellon (eds), *La Coopération Industrielle*, Economica.

Praest, M. (1999), "Demarcation of Technological Competence Groups: Methods, Problems, and Future Opportunities". Accepted for publication in Sanchez and Heene (1999): *Advances in Applied Business Strategy*. JAI Press.

Ring, P. and Van de Ven, A. (1994), "Developmental processes of cooperative interorganizational relationships", *Academy of Management Review*, **19**, 1, 90-118.

Saussier S. (1999), "Transaction Cost Economics and Contract Duration", *Louvain Economic Research*, **65**, 3-21.

Saussier, S. (2000), "When incomplete contract theory meets transaction cost economics: a test", in C. Ménard (ed) *Institutions, Contracts and Organizations: Perspectives from New Institutional Economics*, Edward Elgar, 376-399.

Teece, D. (1992), "Competition, cooperation, and innovation: Organisation arrangements for regimes of rapid technological progress", *Journal of Economic Behavior and Organization*, **18**, 1-25.

Teece D., Pisano G. (1994), "The dynamic capabilities of the firms: an introduction", *Industrial and Corporate Change*, **3** (3).

Vanberg, V. (1993), "Rational choice, rule following and institutions, an evolutionary perspective", in U. Mäki., B. Gustafsson and C. Knudsen, (eds.), *Rationality, Institution and Economic Methodology*, Routledge, London and New York, 171-193.

Williamson, O. (1983), "Credible commitments: using hostages to support exchange", *The American Economic Review*, **73**,(4), 519-540.

Williamson, O. (1985), *The Economic Institutions of Capitalism*, Free Press, New York.

Wolff S. (1995), "Accords inter-entreprises, apprentissage et flexibilité dans le secteur des télécommunications", in N. Lazaric, J-M. Monnier (eds), *Coordination Economique et Apprentissages des Firmes*, Economica.

PART I

Forms of Collaboration: Theories and Trends

D23 O32
(Italy)
L24 D45

1. The Choice of the Form of Strategic Alliances: Transaction Cost Economics and Beyond

Massimo G. Colombo and Marco Delmastro

1. INTRODUCTION

From the second half of the 1980s, in the economic and managerial literature there has been growing interest in strategic alliances between firms, partly as a result of the availability of large data sets such as the CATI database set up at MERIT (see Hagedoorn, 1991). Theoretical and empirical studies have focused on various issues, among which the following ones figure prominently: the factors that lead firms to establish cooperative agreements (Mariti and Smiley 1982; Arora and Gambardella, 1990; Colombo 1995); the choice of joint ventures as opposed to acquisitions and establishment of autonomous subsidiaries, especially as a mechanism to enter into foreign markets (Balakrishna and Koza, 1993; Hennart and Reddy, 1998; Mutinelli and Piscitello, 1998); the mutual relations between external collaborations notably in the technological sphere, and firms' internal R&D investments (Berg et al. 1982; Pisano, 1990; Kleinknecht and Reijnen, 1992; Colombo and Garrone, 1996 and 1998; Veugelers 1997); and the implications of collaborative arrangements for market structure and industrial policy, with special emphasis being placed on R&D consortia.[1]

On the contrary, less attention has been devoted to the organizational form of strategic alliances. An exception is given by a few empirical studies, mainly inspired by the transaction cost economics (TCE) paradigm (see Williamson, 1985) and other contractual approaches. Such studies (see Pisano, 1989; Gulati 1995; Garcia Canal, 1996; Oxley 1997) generally analyze the choice between equity forms (that is, joint ventures and acquisitions of minority shareholdings) and contractual (that is, non-equity) arrangements, such as licenses, customer-supplier relations, joint collaborations in research, marketing or distribution, and adopt the view that firms resort to equity agreements in order to economize on transaction costs when there is a non-negligible risk of opportunism, but not so much as to mandate hierarchical internalization.

In this chapter, we try to go beyond the contractual perspective on the organizational form of strategic alliances and to integrate it with considerations inspired by competence-based theories of the firm, which emphasize the role of alliances as learning-oriented, capability-building devices. We do so by providing new empirical evidence based on the estimates of a multinomial logit model on the use of equity joint ventures and non-equity unilateral agreements as opposed to contractual bilateral arrangements on the part of a sample composed of 67 out of the world's largest enterprises in information technology (IT) sectors. The findings of the empirical analysis confirm some of the arguments of TCE; in particular, complex relations are found to be prevalently governed through equity forms. They also illustrate some shortcomings of the approaches based on a contractual perspective on the theory of the firm. Notably, when collaborations have a technological component bilateral contractual modes turn out to be more likely than both equity joint ventures and unilateral quasi-market arrangements. In addition, empirical support is provided for the role played by interactive learning and firms' distinctive capabilities in the choice of the governance mode of alliances: the probability that a technological collaboration be a joint venture rather than a bilateral contractual form is shown to decrease with the degree of overlapping of firms' patterns of technological specialization. In this sense, the results of this chapter are complementary to recent empirical works on the relation between the establishment of alliances and the evolution of firms' competencies (Mowery et al. 1998. Cantwell and Colombo, 2000).

The chapter is organized as follows. In section 2 the data set is presented. In section 3 the econometric model is specified, the explanatory variables are described in detail, and expectations as to the signs of such variables are discussed. Section 4 contains the empirical findings. Section 5 concludes the chapter.

2. DATA

The data on alliances used in this paper are provided by the ARPA database developed at Politecnico di Milano. ARPA surveyed agreements in Information Technology industries (that is, semiconductor, data processing, and telecommunications) over the 1980-1986 period. Information contained in ARPA was gathered from the international financial press, technical magazines and specialist studies. Coverage of local sources of information for all three most developed areas (US, Europe and Japan) allowed controlling for geographic biases in a quite satisfactory way. ARPA covers a total of 2,014 cooperative agreements; they involve 1,574 partners that belong to 1,177 different autonomous entities. As to governance modes, equity agreements (mainly joint ventures), non-equity joint collaborations and licenses are the most prominent categories, with a 29.2%, 24.6% and 20.8% share respectively. [2]

In this chapter, we consider equity joint ventures, non-equity joint (that is bilateral) collaborations and non-equity quasi-market (that is unilateral) agreements involving only firms that belong to a sample composed of 67 large North American, European and Japanese industrial groups from the largest 150 ones in the world's IT industries. For reasons which will be explained later, we confine attention to alliances concluded between 1983 and 1986. Selection of the firms was based on two criteria. First, data were needed on firm-specific characteristics (for example size, profits, degree of internationalization, R&D expenses) over the entire period under consideration. Such data were obtained from various sources: specialized magazines such as *Datamation* and *Electronic Business*, sector studies (*Benn Electronic File Directory* and *Gartner Group Top 100 Almanac*), firms' annual reports and other directories (such as the *Japan Company Handbook*). Considerable effort was devoted to checking the coherence of the various sources. Availability of such data restricted the sample to 100 firms (see Colombo, 1995). Second, we obtained access to the dataset on the patent activity in the US of the world's largest firms during the period 1969-1995 set up at the University of Reading. The Reading dataset includes information on 784 firms, which account for over 46% of all patents granted in the US between 1969 and 1995. Each patent is assigned to one of 56 technological sectors according to the type of technological activity with which it is primarily associated. Out of the 100 above-mentioned firms, 67 were comprised in the Reading database.

The final sample can be regarded as representative of the world's largest firms in IT industries. It is composed of 34 North American, 20 European and 13 Japanese enterprises. In our view, coverage of all three areas of the "triad" represents a significant improvement with respect to previous empirical studies on the issue at hand. In the period 1983-1986 ARPA has surveyed 278 alliances between the sample firms. Equity joint ventures, non-equity bilateral collaborations, non-equity unilateral arrangements and acquisitions of a minority interest accounted for 19.4%, 30.9%, 47.1% and 2.5%, respectively. Due to a "small number" problem, this latter category was excluded from the empirical analysis.

3. THE ECONOMETRIC MODEL

The Specification of the Model

The empirical analysis is based on the estimates of a multinomial logit model. Its purpose is to explain what factors influence the relative probability that a collaboration be governed through an equity joint venture (EJOV), a non-equity unilateral form (NEQMA), or a non-equity bilateral form (NEJC). The model is specified as follows. Let us consider a cooperative relation i between two or more firms ($i = 1,...,271$). For the sake of simplicity, let us code with 0, 1 and 2 the choice of an NEJC, an EJOV, and an NEQMA, respectively. Let V_i^j be the benefits accruing to partner firms if organizational form j is chosen ($j=0,1,2$). V_i^j will depend on the characteristics of both the collaboration and the partners. Such characteristics include: (a) the complexity of the collaboration, described by the vector of variables COMPL; (b) a variable (TECH) indicating whether the collaboration has a technological component or not; (c) a vector of variables (SECT) that distinguish whether the partners of the collaboration compete in the same sector(s) or not; (d) partners' experience of prior collaborations, both in general (EXPALL) and between each other (PREALL); (e) a variable (CTS) capturing how similar partners' collections of distinctive technological capabilities are; and (f) a vector X_i reflecting other firm-specific characteristics. For reasons which will be evident later, we assume:

$$V_i^j = \beta_0^j + \beta_1^j \cdot COMPL_i + \beta_2^j \cdot PREALL_i + \beta_3^j \cdot EXPALL_i + \beta_4^j \cdot SECT_i + \beta_5^j \cdot TECH_i + \beta_6^j \cdot TECH_i \cdot CTS_i + \beta_7^j \cdot CTS_i + \beta_8^j \cdot X_i + u_i^j \quad j = 0,1,2, \qquad (1.1)$$

with u_i^j ($j=0,1,2$) being the error terms. Furthermore, let us assume that the organizational form j chosen by partner firms from the choice set J is the one yielding the maximum expected benefits. Let d_i^j ($j = 0,1,2$) be a random variable that equals 1 if alternative j is chosen and 0 if it is not. It results:

$$d_i^j = 1 \text{ if } V_i^j > V_i^k, \ \forall \ k \neq j; \text{ otherwise } d_i^j = 0, \quad j = 0,1,2.$$

As is usual in this kind of settings, the assumption is made that the disturbances u_i^j are independently and identically distributed with Weibull distribution. Then, the model for the choice of the organizational form is:

$$Prob \ (d_i^j=1) = exp \ (\beta_0^j + \beta_1^{j'} \cdot COMPL_i + \beta_2^j \cdot PREALL_i + \beta_3^j \cdot EXPALL_i + \beta_4^{j'} \cdot SECT_i + \beta_5^{j} \cdot TECH_i + \beta_6^j \cdot TECH_i \cdot CTS_i + \beta_7^j \cdot CTS_i + \beta_8^{j'} \cdot X_i) \ / \ \Sigma_j \ exp \ (\beta_0^j + $$

$\beta_1^{j} \cdot COMPL_i + \beta_2^{j} \cdot PREALL_i + \beta_3^{j} \cdot EXPALL_i + \beta_4^{j} \cdot SECT_i + \beta_5^{j} \cdot TECH_i + \beta_6^{j} \cdot TECH_i \cdot CTS_i + \beta_7^{j} \cdot CTS_i + \beta_8^{j} \cdot X_i) \quad j=0,1,2.$ (1.2)

In order for model (1.2) to be identified, the coefficients of one of the alternatives have to be set to 0. With no loss of generality, we set $\beta_k^0=0$, $k=1,....,8$; that is, the NEJC category was taken as the baseline in the econometric estimates. Model (1.2) was then estimated by maximum likelihood using the following log-likelihood function:

$$L = \Sigma_i \, \Sigma_j \, d_i^{j} \cdot \ln Prob \, (d_i^{j}=1) \, . \qquad (1.3)$$

The Independent Variables of the Model

As was suggested in the former section, the independent variables can be subdivided into six categories (see Table 1.1 for definitions and Table 1.2 for descriptive statistics).

The first group includes variables, which reflect the complexity of transactions. We considered the number of partners (NPARTNERS), the number of functional activities involved in a collaborative relation (NFCONTENTS), with a distinction being made between technological activities, production, and marketing and distribution, the geographic scope captured by the number of geographical areas (that is, North America, Europe and Japan) to which the partners belong (NGEOAREAS), and the sectoral scope. As to this latter aspect, the dummy variable SPECTASK equals 1 if a cooperation has a unique specific task and 0 if it has a broadly defined sectoral scope or it embraces a variety of narrowly defined tasks.[3] In accordance with TCE, we expect a positive impact of NPARTNERS, NFCONTENTS and NGEOAREAS on the likelihood of a relation being an equity joint venture, due to the need for more hierarchical forms to govern complex transactions; for the same reason, we predict a negative sign for SPECTASK. In addition, note that licenses account for the overwhelming majority of non-equity quasi-market agreements. Since they represent a typical mechanism to enter into foreign markets, we also expect a positive correlation between NGEOAREAS and the choice of a non-equity unilateral arrangement as opposed to a bilateral one.

The second category is composed of variables which intend to capture the "shadow of the past" effect. PREALL is defined as the ratio between the number of prior alliances that link the partners of a given collaboration to each other and were concluded in the previous three years[4] and the maximum number of possible linkages between them. Such number increases with the number N of firms in the alliance as $N(N - 1)/2$. According to the contention of game theoretic and sociological contributions (see Parkhe, 1993; Gulati, 1995), the estimated coefficients of PREALL in the EJOV estimates should be negative. A similar reasoning applies to EXPALL, which is defined as the average number of previous agreements established by the partners of an alliance with both firms that are included in the sample and firms which do not belong to it. As more expert firms should be able to monitor the behavior of their partners more effectively, they would preferably resort to non-equity forms.[5] Nonetheless, one should acknowledge that the underlying content of a newly established alliance may be influenced by the "shadow of the past" in a way which is not entirely reflected by other explanatory variables. If the threat of opportunism is reduced, partners may turn to more ambitious, large-scale collaborative ventures; with everything else being equal, this would increase the probability that an equity form be chosen. In addition, firms may be willing to enter into arrangements as costly as an equity joint venture only if they are confident about partners' competence and trustworthiness. Such an argument implies that recourse to equity forms is more likely if firms have prior experience of successful collaborations between each other. Failure to take into due account the above mentioned effects may lead to mixed results as to the signs of PREALL and EXPALL.

Table 1.1. The explanatory variables of the econometric model

Variable	Definition
SPECTASK	Dummy variable: it equals 1 for alliances that have a narrow sectoral scope; otherwise it equals 0.
NFCONTENTS	Number of functional activities involved by an alliance.
NPARTNERS	Number of partners of an alliance.
NGEOAREAS	Number of geographical areas (*i.e.* North America, Europe, Japan) from which the partners of a collaborations originate.
TECH	Dummy variable: it equals 1 for alliances that involve R&D and/or design and/or engineering components; otherwise it equals 0.
PREALL	Ratio between the number of prior alliances that link the partners of an alliance to each other and were concluded in the previous three years and the maximum number of possible linkages between them.[a]
EXPALL	Average number of previous alliances established by the partners of a collaboration.
CTS	Average value of the correlation indices between the distributions of the revealed technological advantages[b] of any pairwise combination of the partners of an alliance across 31 technological fields related to Information Technologies.
MAINSECT	Dummy variable: it equals 1 if all partners of an alliance have the same primary sector of activity in Information Technologies; otherwise it equals 0.
COMMONSECT	Dummy variable: it equals 1 if (a) all partners of a collaboration are in one or more common sectors in IT and (b) MAINSECT equals 0; otherwise it equals 0.

DATE	Year in which an alliance was established.
SIZE	Average value of total sales of the partners of an alliance in the year in which the alliance was established (billion US $, 1980 prices).
INTERNAT	Average value of the ratio of international sales to total sales of the partners of an alliance in the year in which the alliance was established.
ROS	Average value of the returns on sales of the partners of an alliance in the year in which the alliance was established.
R&D	Average value of the R&D to sales ratio of the partners of an alliance in the year in which the alliance was established.
DIVERSIF	Average value of the Utton diversification index (two-digit SIC classification) of the partners of an alliance in the year in which the alliance was established.
SCOPE	Average value of the Utton diversification index within I T (semiconductor, data processing, and telecommunication) of the partners of an alliance in the year in which the alliance was established.
SIZEGAP	Ratio between the value of total sales of the smallest firm and that of the largest firm in an alliance in the year in which the alliance was established.
INTERDIFF	Largest difference between the ratios of international sales to total sales of the partners of an alliance in the year in which the alliance was established.
ROSDIFF	Largest difference between the returns on sales of the partners of an alliance in the year in which the alliance was established.
R&DDIFF	Largest difference between the R&D to sales ratio of the partners of an alliance in the year in which the alliance was established.
DIVEDIFF	Ratio of the difference between the largest and the smallest value taken by the Utton diversification index (two-digit SIC classification) of the partners of an alliance to the sum of such values in the year in which the alliance was established.
SCOPEDIFF	Ratio of the difference between the largest and the smallest value taken by the Utton diversification index within Information Technologies (semiconductor, data processing, and telecommunication) of the partners of an alliance to the sum of such values in the year in which the alliance was established.

Notes
(a) The maximum number of individual linkages between the partners of an alliance equals $N(N-1)/2$, with N being the number of partners.
(b) The revealed technological advantage (RTA_{ij}) of firm i in technological class j is calculated as follows. Let P_{ij} be the number of US patents granted to firm i in technological class j over the period 1969-'95. Then $RTA_{ij} = (P_{ij}/\Sigma_j P_{ij})/(\Sigma_i P_{ij}/\Sigma_{ij} P_{ij})$, i=1,....,67; j=1,....,31.

The third group of variables considers the influence that the sectors to which partner firms belong exert upon the choice of the organizational form of a collaboration. More precisely, two dummy variables were defined. MAINSECT is set to 1 when all partners in a given relation have the same primary sector of activity, with a distinction being made between semiconductor, data processing, and telecommunications. [6] COMMONSECT equals 1 if the following conditions apply: (a) all partners are in one or more common sectors and (b) MAINSECT is equal to 0.

The fourth group of variables includes only the TECH dummy. This variable distinguishes collaborations which involve R&D and/or design and/or engineering components from other ventures, which concentrate on production, marketing and distribution, or both. TCE suggests a positive effect of such a variable on the relative probability of resorting to an equity joint venture as opposed to a contractual bilateral relation. However, when uncertainty is radical, aversion towards commitment of non-recoverable investments and the desire to preserve an exploration-oriented approach may lead firms to choose a more flexible, less hierarchical form, with opposite implications as to the sign of the coefficient of TECH. As regards non-equity quasi-market arrangements, competence-base theories suggest that such forms are a rather inefficient learning device, even though they may be instrumental to transferring codified and component-embodied knowledge. Hence, we predict a negative coefficient for TECH also in the estimates relating to this category of agreements.

In view of the objectives of the present chapter, the fifth category deserves special attention. It also includes just one variable (CTS) which aims to capture similarity of technological capabilities among partner firms. CTS is defined as follows (see Cantwell and Barrera, 1998; Cantwell and Colombo, 2000). Let RTA_{ij} be the revealed technological advantage of firm i in technological class j. Denoting by P_{ij} the number of US patents granted to firm i in technological field j over the period 1969-1995, RTA_{ij} is given by the following expression:

$$RTA_{ij} = (P_{ij}/\Sigma_j P_{ij}) \; / \; (\Sigma_i P_{ij}/\Sigma_{ij} P_{ij}) \; .$$

Only 31 technological fields associated with IT sectors were considered. In other words, RTA_{ij} coincides with the ratio of the share accounted for by a given technological class out of the number of US patents in IT granted to the firm under consideration, to the share of the same technological class out of the total number of US patents in IT granted to all sample firms. RTA_{ij} varies around one, with values greater than one suggesting that a firm is comparatively specialized in the activity in question. We then calculated the Pearson's correlation coefficient r_{ik} between the RTA distributions of any pairwise combination of firms i and k across the 31 technological fields. Such index measures the (positive or negative) correlation between the patterns of technological specialization of firms, as were reflected in the RTA values; it can then be regarded as a proxy of the degree of overlapping of the technological capabilities of firms. The value of CTS for a given alliance is given by the average value of r_{ik} calculated across all pairs of firms i and k involved in the alliance.

We claim that ease of learning from each other is greater for firms with similar patterns of technological specialization. Consequently, when a collaboration includes R&D and other technology-based activities (that is, TECH equals 1) and is thus likely to be oriented towards the development of *new* capabilities, we expect a negative impact of CTS upon the probability of firms resorting to an equity joint venture as opposed to a contractual bilateral form.[7] Instead, CTS should not exhibit any discriminating power for productive and commercial alliances (that is when TECH equals 0), as such alliances more often are instrumental to gaining access in a cost effective way to the services of partners' *existing* capabilities and interactive learning plays a minor role. We also expect CTS not to have any significant effect in the NEQMA estimates. In fact, in addition to hindering interactive learning processes, lack of an overlapping knowledge base may also be a serious impediment to quasi-market arrangements aimed at unilateral transfer of knowledge, due to the absence of an adequate absorptive capacity by the recipient firm.

Table 1.2. The explanatory variables: descriptive statistics

	Type	Mean	Std. Dev.	Min.	Max.
SPECTASK	Binary	0.675	0.469	0	1
NFCONTENTS	Discrete	1.646	0.730	1	3
NPARTNERS	Discrete	2.199	0.885	2	11
NGEOAREAS	Discrete	1.649	0.478	1	2
TECH	Binary	0.472	0.500	0	1
PREALL	Continuous	1.074	1.258	0	5
EXPALL	Discrete	28.209	15.942	2	89
CTS	Continuous	-0.002	0.272	-0.583	0.916
MAINSECT	Binary	0.373	0.484	0	1
COMMONSECT	Binary	0.782	0.413	0	1
DATE	Discrete	84.697	1.101	83	86
SIZE (bl. US $ at 1980 prices)	Continuous	7.301	7.138	0.905	33.177
INTERNAT	Continuous	0.374	0.149	0.025	0.819
ROS	Continuous	0.034	0.041	-0.241	0.119
R&D	Continuous	0.077	0.021	0.026	0.130
DIVERSIF	Continuous	1.593	0.583	1.000	3.818
SCOPE	Continuous	1.656	0.452	1.000	2.672
SIZEGAP	Continuous	0.411	0.290	0.005	0.986
INTERDIFF	Continuous	0.234	0.185	0.002	0.937
ROSDIFF	Continuous	0.049	0.053	0.000	0.442
R&DDIFF	Continuous	0.037	0.030	0.001	0.127
DIVEDIFF	Continuous	0.215	0.169	0.000	0.633
SCOPEDIFF	Continuous	0.191	0.141	0.000	0.486

Furthermore, we introduced into the model a series of firm-specific control variables. SIZE, INTERNAT, ROS, R&D, DIVERS and SCOPE measure average size, given by the average value of the turnover of the partners of an alliance in the year in which the alliance was established (in US $ at 1980 prices), degree of internationalization, proxied by the share of total sales realized in foreign markets, returns on sales, R&D to sales ratio and diversification (in general and within the IT industries, respectively; in both case the Utton diversification index was used).[8] SIZEGAP is the ratio between the value of the turnover of the smallest firm in a given alliance and that of the largest firm; it is greater than zero and smaller than 1, with values near 1 indicating alliances between rather similarly sized firms. INTERDIFF, ROSDIFF and R&DDIFF are given by the largest difference of degree of internationalization, returns on sales and R&D intensity between partner firms. DIVERSDIFF and SCOPEDIFF reflect differences in diversification patterns between firms; both of them were calculated as the ratio of the difference between the largest and the smallest values taken by the Utton index in a collaboration to the sum of such values.

For all these variables but SIZEGAP, larger values are associated with greater structural and behavioral differences between the parties of an alliance. Lastly, TIME indicates the year in which an alliance was concluded; it controls for time-specific patterns.

In accordance with the evidence provided by previous studies inspired by TCE, the empirical findings show that firms tend to resort to equity collaborations for complex relations. NPARTNERS and NFCONTENTS have positive and statistically significant (at 99%) coefficients in the EJOV estimates. The coefficient of NGEOAREAS is also positive though only marginally significant (at 90%). Only SPECTASK takes the wrong sign, but is not significant; the reason may be that recourse to a standardized classification for the definition of the sectoral scope of a transaction does not allow to reveal its underlying complexity.

4. THE EMPIRICAL FINDINGS

The results of the econometric estimates are illustrated in Table 1.3. The first two columns refer to the unrestricted model, which includes all explanatory variables described in the previous section. The third and fourth columns report the findings relating to a model, which was obtained through subsequent nested restrictions; at each stage the null hypothesis that the coefficients of the dropped variables are not statistically different from 0 was checked through a χ^2 LR test. The table shows the estimated values of the coefficients of the explanatory variables, their standard errors and significance levels, and the results of a series of χ^2 LR tests of hypothesis.

Table 1.3. Estimates of a multinomial logit model

		Unrestricted		Restricted	
		EJOV	NEQMA	EJOV	NEQMA
B_0	Constant	19.327 (48.820)	47.230 (38.664)	-6.24 (1.95)* **	23.990 (19.098)
B_1	SPECTASK	.301 (.798)	.334 (.557)		
B_2	NFCONTENTS	2.612 (.612) ***	-0.250 (.452)	2.355 (.41) ***	
B_3	NPARTNERS	1.548 (.45) ***	-0.319 (.687)	1.414 (.28) ***	
B_4	NGEOAREAS	1.327 (.752) *	1.458 (.574) **	1.011 (.588) *	1.43 (.405) ***
B_5	TECH	-4.05 (1.07) ***	-3.34 (0.60) ***	-3.87 (.791) ***	-3.32 (.440) ***
B_6	CTS	.091 (2.982)	1.671 (2.321)		
B_7	TECH*CTS	-6.134 (4.293)	-2.805 (2.744)	-4.833 (2.26) **	
B_8	PREALL	.480 (.306)	-.085 (.283)	.489 (.183) ***	
B_9	EXPALL	.066 (.061)	.054 (.036)	.039 (.018) **	.035 (.017) **
B_{10}	MAINSECT	.78 (1.093)	.514 (.670)		
B_{11}	COMMONSECT	-1.024 (1.535)	.058 (.840)		
B_{12}	DATE	-.325 (.582)	-.57 (.455)	-.302 (.230)	
B_{13}	SIZE	-.0124 (.132)	.007 (.053)		
B_{14}	INTERNAT	-.77 (2.972)	2.582 (2.159)		2.455 (1.290) *
B_{15}	ROS	-4.375 (12.554)	-8.378 (9.019)		
B_{16}	R&D	-26.60 (19.738)	-5.598 (15.806)	-31.5 (13.40) **	
B_{17}	DIVERSIF	.576 (.653)	-.021 (.633)		
B_{18}	SCOPE	-2.191 (1.211) *	-.149 (.977)	-1.608 (.703) **	
B_{19}	SIZEGAP	2.763 (1.564) *	.002 (1.238)	2.739 (1.02) ***	
B_{20}	INTERDIFF	4.29 (2.465) *	1.274 (2.044)	2.345 (1.21) *	
B_{21}	ROSDIFF	-12.662 (12.95)	-5.786 (6.059)		
B_{22}	R&DDIFF	2.046 (12.926)	5.456 (9.127)		
B_{23}	DIVEDIFF	-0.755 (2.496)	-1.735 (2.059)		-1.857 (1.053) *
B_{24}	SCOPEDIFF	3.305 (2.774)	1.356 (1.898)		
	Log-likelihood	-147.41		-159.17	
	N. of observations	271		271	
	LR test	267.26 (48) ***		243.74(24) ***	
	LR tests:				
	$B_7^{EJOV} = 0$	5.52 (1) **		8.46 (1) ***	
	$B_6^{EJOV} = B_7^{EJOV} = 0$	10.40 (2) ***			
	$B_7^{NEQMA} = 0$	2.78 (1) *			
	$B_6^{NEQMA} = B_7^{NEQMA} = 0$	2.78 (2)			
	$B_6^{EJOV} = B_7^{EJOV} = B_6^{NEQMA} = B_7^{NEQMA} = 0$	12.88 (4) **			

Notes
* p>0.9; ** p>0.95; *** p>0.99. Standard errors or degrees of freedom between parentheses.
EJOV: equity joint ventures. NEQMA: non-equity quasi-market agreements.

Generally speaking, the econometric results are quite robust. As is illustrated in Table 1.4, the unrestricted and restricted models correctly predict the governance mode of 80.1% and 76.7% of the sample collaborations, respectively. As to GEOAREAS, it is interesting to note that in the NEQMA estimates this variable exhibits a positive, highly significant coefficient. This result is in line with the popularity of licenses as a mechanism to enter into foreign markets.

Table 1.4. Classification tables of the multinomial logit model

Actual	Unrestricted model Predicted			
	EJOV	**NEJC**	**NEQMA**	**Total**
EJOV	42	7	5	54
NEJC	8	62	16	86
NEQMA	2	16	113	131
Total	52	85	134	
% of cases correctly predicted: 80.1%				

Actual	Restricted model Predicted			
	EJOV	**NEJC**	**NEQMA**	**Total**
EJOV	37	6	11	54
NEJC	8	61	17	86
NEQMA	1	20	110	131
Total	46	87	138	
% of cases correctly predicted: 76.7%				

EJOV: equity joint ventures.
NEJC: non-equity bilateral joint collaborations.
NEQMA: non-equity quasi-market agreements.

On the contrary, neither the arguments proposed by studies informed by game-theoretic and sociological approaches, which emphasize the impact of the "shadow of the past" upon alliance form, nor those of mainstream industrial organization studies, which are concerned with the role of market structure variables, are supported by our empirical findings. On the one hand, PREALL and EXPALL have a positive coefficient in the EJOV estimates, significant at conventional levels in the restricted model. The greater the number of previous alliances established by the firms involved in a collaboration, both between each other and with other firms, the higher the likelihood that they will resort to an equity organizational form. This result may be explained by failure to take into due account modifications in the underlying characteristics of newly established collaborations engendered by prior alliances. In this regard, information on the amount of resources committed by the parties to a collaboration (for example value of tangible assets, number and professional characteristics of employees) would be very helpful to shed new light on this issue. Unfortunately, such information is usually not available in this kind of studies. On the other hand, there is no evidence that firms which are in the same sector of activity are more inclined towards equity collaborations. MAINSECT has a positive, though not significant, coefficient in the EJOV estimates; the coefficient of COMMONSECT is negative and not significant.

As was mentioned earlier, firms included in our sample quite infrequently turn to an equity arrangement for collaborations in the technological sphere. The same holds true for non-equity quasi-market arrangements. Namely, the estimated coefficient of TECH takes a negative, statistically significant at 99% sign in both the EJOV and NEQMA estimates. Differences between our findings and some previous studies may be explained by the finer classification of the forms of cooperative agreements adopted in this chapter, which distinguishes bilateral from unilateral non-equity arrangements. Actually, agreements of this latter category quite rarely extend to R&D, even though they may involve technology transfer activities; thus placing them in the contractual agreement category along with bilateral joint collaborations may have biased previous results. Of course, such differences might also partially be explained by industry biases. The characteristics of technology do differ across industries as to aspects such as the degree of tacitness and appropriability hazards (see for instance Levin et al., 1987), which may influence the relative appeal of different governance modes. Unfortunately, our data are limited to IT industries. Additional evidence relating to other industries would be very useful to get further insights into the impact of technological factors on the organizational form of alliances.

One of the main concerns of this study was with the role played by firms' distinctive capabilities. The findings of the regressions clearly support the argument inspired by the capability perspective that the likelihood of choosing an equity mode for a technological agreement increases with the diversity of the collection of technological competencies developed by partners. When TECH equals 1, CTS, which reflects similarity of the patterns of technological specialization between the firms engaged in a cooperative relation, has a negative coefficient in the EJOV estimates of both the restricted and unrestricted models. The null hypothesis that this variable has no significant effect can be rejected, as is apparent from the χ^2 LR tests reported at the bottom of Table 1.3. The χ^2 statistics equal 10.40 (with two degrees of freedom) and 8.46 (with one degree of freedom) in the unrestricted and restricted models, respectively; both values are significant at

99%. When we turn attention to non-equity unilateral agreements as opposed to bilateral ones, CTS loses its explanatory power. It has a positive coefficient when an alliance focuses on production and/or marketing and a negative one for technological collaborations. However, the χ^2 LR tests show that such effects are not statistically robust.

Finally, let us consider control variables. Their overall explanatory power is rather modest, especially as regards the NEQMA estimates. As to this latter category of agreements, none of the control variables is statistically significant at conventional levels, with the exception of DIVEDIFF, which captures diversity in the degree of diversification between the partners of an alliance. As regards equity forms, they seem to be more likely if firms have low innovative intensity and a focused sectoral scope within IT, are of similar size but have different propensities towards international activities.

5. CONCLUDING REMARKS

In this chapter, we have analyzed the choice by firms of the organizational form of strategic alliances. We have contrasted approaches variously inspired by contractual theories of the firm, which rely on static efficiency considerations and transaction cost minimization, with arguments suggested by the capability perspective, which instead emphasizes the role of alliances as interactive learning devices oriented towards innovation and the development of new capabilities.

We have considered a sample composed of 271 alliances which were concluded by 67 out of the world's largest enterprises in IT industries between each other over the period 1983-1986. A multinomial logit model has been estimated, providing new insights into the use of equity joint ventures and non-equity unilateral agreements as opposed to non-equity bilateral ones.

The findings of the empirical analysis confirm the evidence provided by previous studies inspired by TCE that equity modes are more frequently used to govern complex transactions. The likelihood that such an organizational form be chosen clearly increases with the functional span of an alliance, the number of partners and to a lesser extent the number of regional areas from which they originate. However, our findings do not support the view suggested by TCE that such forms are suitable to relations concerning R&D and other technology-related activities; the overwhelming majority of alliances that include a technological component turns out to be governed through non-equity bilateral arrangements. Nor are the empirical results consistent with the proposition set forth by game-theoretic managerial contributions and sociological approaches that due to the "shadow of the past", firms that are involved in a network of prior alliances are more likely to resort to non-equity arrangements, as the threat of opportunism is less severe. On the contrary, evidence is provided that the probability of a collaboration being an equity joint venture increases with the number of prior alliances established by partner firms, both between each other and with other firms. This may indicate an omitted variable problem, which is common in these kinds of studies, due to failure to properly control for modifications over time in the underlying content of newly established alliances. We also did not find any support for the view proposed in the industrial organization literature that the sector of activity of the partners of an alliance exerts an influence on their decisions as to the organizational form.

Even more interestingly, the empirical analysis shows that in accordance with competence-based theories of the firm, the characteristics of the collection of technological capabilities possessed by firms have a considerable impact on the form of their alliances. More precisely, if we confine attention to technological alliances, firms with overlapping patterns of technological specialization much more frequently resort to non-equity bilateral forms than firms characterized by divergent technological capabilities. For these latter firms, the need to set up a more intense relation and to create an environment more conducive to interactive learning plays a key role in orienting their choice towards equity forms.

NOTES

1. A reach stream of the industrial organization literature has pointed out that collaborative arrangements may serve the purpose of internalizing the externality associated with R&D spillovers, with positive implications for social welfare. See for instance Katz and Ordover (1990). For a review of such studies see De Bondt (1996). For a view on this issue informed by heterodox theories of the firm, see Jorde and Teece (1990).
2. For a detailed description of the ARPA database see Cainarca et al. (1992).
3. An example of the former category is provided by a cooperative agreement confined to dynamic random access memories (DRAM); examples of the latter category are given by a collaboration in semiconductor and by one that embraces DRAM and microprocessors.
4. As data on alliances are available from 1980, this is the reason why in this study attention is confined to the analysis of the form of alliances that were established by sample firms after 1982.
5. We are aware of the likely collinearity between this variable and time. However, we also share Oxley's (1997) view that such variable nicely reflects the growth of the alliance-related experience of the sample firms over the 1980s.
6. Actually, the main sector of activity is defined as the sector out of the three considered in this study which accounts for the largest share of a firm's turnover.

7. As CTS is calculated over the period 1969-1995, endogeneity problems may arise. In other words, the choice of the governance mode of alliances may influence the subsequent evolution of firms' capabilities. Our decision not to limit to the 1969-1979 period in calculating CTS was mainly determined by the desire to avoid "small numbers" problems. Note however that a preliminary investigation showed that the patterns of technological specialization of sample firms are quite stable over time (on this topic see also Patel and Pavitt, 1997). In addition, the findings of previous studies on the impact of the governance mode of alliances upon firms' technological capabilities provide mixed evidence (see for instance Nakamura et al. 1996; Mowery et al. 1998). Lastly, if the choice of an equity form would result in an increase of the degree of similarity between partners' technological specialization due to more profitable interaction as is suggested by the aforementioned literature, our results would be reinforced.

8. See Colombo (1995) for a more detailed description of such variables and their alleged effects upon the likelihood of establishing an alliance.

REFERENCES

Arora, A. and Gambardella, A. (1990), "Complementarity and external linkages: the strategies of the large firms in biotechnology", *The Journal of Industrial Economics*, **38**, 361-379.

Balakrishna, S. and Koza, M.P. (1993), "Information asymmetry, adverse selection, and joint ventures", *Journal of Economic Behavior and Organization*, **20**, 99-117.

Berg, S.V., Duncan, J. and Friedman, P. (1982), *Joint Venture Strategies and Corporate Innovation*, Oelgeschlager, Gunn & Hain Publishers Inc., Cambridge, Mass.

Cainarca, G.C., Colombo, M.G. and Mariotti, S. (1992), "Agreements between firms and the technological life cycle model", *Research Policy*, **21**, 45-62.

Cantwell, J.A. and Barrera, M.P. (1998), "The localization of corporate technological trajectories in the interwar cartels: cooperative learning versus an exchange of knowledge", *Economics of Innovation and New Technology*, **5**, 257-290.

Cantwell, J. and Colombo, M.G. (2000), "Technological and output complementarities, and interfirm cooperation in information technology ventures", *Journal of Management and Governance*, forthcoming.

Colombo, M.G. (1995) "Firm size and cooperation: the determinants of cooperative agreements in information technology industries", *International Journal of the Economics of Business*, **2**, 3-29.

Colombo, M.G. and Garrone, P. (1996), "Technological cooperative agreements and firms' R&D intensity. A note on causality relations", *Research Policy*, **25**, 923-932.

Colombo, M.G. and Garrone, P. (1998), "A simultaneous equations model of technological agreements and infra-mural R&D", in M.G. Colombo (ed) *The Changing Boundaries of the Firm*, Routledge, London and New York.

De Bondt, R. (1996), "Spillovers and innovative activities", *International Journal of Industrial Organization*, **15**, 1-28.

Garcia Canal, E. (1996) "Contractual form in domestic and international strategic alliances", *Organization Studies*, **17**, 773-794.

Gulati, R. (1995), "Does familiarity breeds trust? The implications of repeated ties for contractual choice in alliances", *Academy of Management Journal*, **38**, 85-112.

Hagedoorn J. (1991), "Changing patterns of interfirm strategic technology alliances in information technologies and telecommunications", WIK, mimeo, **72**.

Hennart, J-F. and Reddy, S. (1998), "The choice between mergers/acquisitions and joint ventures: the case of japanese investors in the united states", *Strategic Management Journal*, **18**, 1-12.

Jorde, T.M. and Teece, D.J. (1990), "Innovation and cooperation: implications for competition and antitrust", *Journal of Economic Perspectives*, **4**, 75-96.

Katz, M.L. and Ordover, J.A. (1990), "R&D cooperation and competition", *Brookings Papers on Economic Activity*, **6**, 137-203.

Kleinknecht, A., and Reijnen, J.O.N. (1992), "Why do firms cooperate in R&D? An empirical study", *Research Policy*, **21**, 347-360.

Levin, R., Klevorick, A., Nelson, R. and Winter, S. (1987), "Appropriating the returns from industrial research and development", Brookings Papers on Economic Activity, **3**, 783-820.

Mariti, P. and Smiley, R.H. (1982), "Cooperation agreements and the organization of industry", *The Journal of Industrial Economics*, **4**, 437-451.

Mowery, D.C., Oxley, J.E. and Silverman, B.S. (1998) "Technological Overlap and Interfirm Cooperation: Implications for the Resource-based View of the Firm", *Research Policy*, **27**, 507-523.

Mutinelli, M. and Piscitello, L. (1998) "The entry mode choice of MNEs: an evolutionary approach", *Research Policy*, **27**, 491-506.

Nakamura, M., Shaver, J.M. and Yeung, B. (1996) "An empirical investigation of joint venture dynamics: evidence from US-Japan joint ventures", *International Journal of Industrial Organization*, **14**, 521-541.

Oxley, J.E. (1997) "Appropriability hazards and governance in strategic alliances: a Transaction cost approach", *Journal of Law, Economics, and Organization*, **13**, 387-409.

Parkhe, A. (1993) "Strategic alliance structuring: a game theoretic and transaction cost examination of interfirm cooperation", *Academy of Management Journal*, **36**, 794-829.

Patel, P. and Pavitt, K. (1997) "The technological competences of the world's largest firms: complex and path-dependent, but not much variety", *Research Policy*, **26**, 141-156.

Pisano, G.P. (1989) "Using equity participation to support exchange: evidence form the biotechnology industry", *Journal of Law, Economics, and Organization*, **5**, 109-126.

Pisano, G.P. (1990) "The R&D boundaries of the firm: an empirical analysis", *Administrative Science Quarterly*, **35**, 153-176.

Veugelers, R. (1997) "Internal R&D expenditures and external technology sourcing", *Research Policy*, **26**, 303-315.

Williamson, O.E. (1985) *The Economic Institutions of Capitalism*, The Free Press, New York.

2. What Governance Structure for Non-contractible Services? An Empirical Analysis[1]

Didier Bréchemier and Stéphane Saussier

1. INTRODUCTION

When they wrote their fundamental article concerning incomplete contract theory, Grossman and Hart made explicit reference to transaction cost economics (Grossman and Hart, 1986). As shown elsewhere, they failed to completely formalize the transaction cost theory (Tirole, 1999; Kreps, 1996; Fares and Saussier, 1998; Masten, 1999; Saussier, 2000b). However, they succeeded in focusing on one important dimension of transactions: non-contractibility. On the one hand, the transaction cost theory focused on the asset specificity needed to realize a transaction and the uncertainty level surrounding the transaction to explain contractual relationships (Williamson, 1996). On the other hand, the incomplete contract theory argues that when crucial dimensions of a transaction are non-contractible, this could lead to integration. Asset specificity is no longer the central argument (Hart, 1995, Hart et al., 1997).

In this chapter, we use the incomplete contract theory and transaction cost theory frameworks as complementary tools to analyze contractual practices in various types of services where (i) several crucial dimensions of the transaction are non-contractible and (ii) specific investments appear to be present only at low levels.

Starting with incomplete contract modeling, we put forth propositions concerning the make or buy decisions. Even if this theoretical framework made advances in the last decade, it does not appear as an "empirical success story". Very few empirical tests exist concerning incomplete contract theory's propositions. We perform such a test on ground services realized for airway companies in several countries. As far as we know, it is one of the first econometrical tests of this theoretical framework. Data is collected through questionnaires. Results show that even without any high level of specific investments, vertical integration may be chosen to avoid opportunistic behavior when crucial dimensions of the service are non-contractible. This chapter concludes that non-contractibility may be a crucial determinant for organizational structures, as important as uncertainty or specific investments. Nevertheless, we believe that a transaction cost analysis is necessary to complete the picture in order to understand the decision to cooperate or not, and contractual practices when the integration solution is not retained. The idea of "probity hazard" developed recently (Williamson, 1999) may be a way to fill the gap between the two theoretical frameworks.

The chapter is organized as follows: we first come back to the main propositions with regard to the make or buy decision following the incomplete contract theory in section 2, before testing them in section 3. An extension using transaction cost economics is proposed in order to refine the propositions and extend them to inter-firm agreements in section 4.. Conclusions follow in section 5.

2. WHAT GOVERNANCE STRUCTURE FOR NON-CONTRACTIBLE SERVICES? AN INCOMPLETE CONTRACT ANALYSIS.

The Incomplete Contract Theory's framework

Several reasons can be put forth to explain contractual incompleteness. They are mostly concerned with the bounded rationality of economic actors and the verifiability of relevant variables with regard to contract realization (Shavell, 1998; Masten, 1999).

Incomplete contract theory does not require bounded rationality to construct an organization theory and a theory of contractual relationships (Hart, 1990; Hart, 1991, pp. 151-152; Hart, 1995, pp. 80-82). Still, due to the difficulty of formalizing bounded rationality, it is easier to consider contractual incompleteness as the result of the non-verifiability of many variables. [2] Indeed, economic agents are able to foresee all contingencies that might affect the contract *and* decide what they should do. Nevertheless, they are unable to write a clear and enforceable contract because of the *non-verifiability* of some relevant variables. Incompleteness is therefore supposed to be the result of information asymmetries between contracting parties on the one side, and third parties on the other. [3]

The incomplete contract theory attempts to formalize the hold-up problem as pointed out by the transaction cost theory (Williamson, 1985) by considering the notion of residual rights of control involved in the allocation of property rights. Indeed, the owner of the assets is the one that has the power to decide *ex post* on all the contingencies not written in the contract. Such a situation induces inefficiency concerning *ex ante* investment levels. But the central argument is no longer the level of asset specificity needed to realize the transaction as in the transaction cost theory. Moreover, propositions are not the same (Fares and Saussier, 1998; Williamson, 1998). According to Grossman and Hart (1986), which way the ownership goes is important. Each stage makes its own investment decision and appropriates its own net receipts. According to transaction cost economics, the ownership of all stages is unified within the firm. Investments and strategic decisions are coordinated by hierarchy and disputes reach agreement through fiat. Although these two approaches are often opposed (Saussier, 2000b; Masten, 1999), but not always (Brousseau and Fares, 2000), we would like to consider the possibility that the two theoretical frameworks are complimentary.

Emphasized in the incomplete contract theory are the dimensions of the transaction that are non-verifiable and that might permit opportunistic behaviors concerning investments. It is particularly the case when minimum quality is required that is non-contractible and inconsistent with cost objectives. Indeed, if the contract cannot specify the exact quality level that is needed, a supplier may decide to reduce production costs, affecting quality while still following the contract terms. We can then talk about an adverse effect to quality. To illustrate this situation, we go back to one interesting model (Hart et al., 1997) before showing how a transaction cost economics approach could complete the picture. This model relates to the "proper scope of government". Nevertheless, we extended it without any cost to the case of private relationships.

Figure 2.1. Timing of incomplete contract models

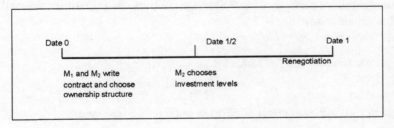

An Incomplete Contract Approach of Cooperation.

Basics

The classical timing of incomplete contract models is now well known (see figure 2.1). At date 0, the contracting parties sign a contract, in which several dimensions of the transaction (and especially investments) are non-specified because they are non-contractible. The contract is therefore incomplete. At date ½, investment or effort levels are chosen. At date 1, once investments are observed, the contract is renegotiated.

Following Hart et al. (1997), we assume that the supplier can make two types of effort. On the one hand, he may invest to reduce his production costs. On the other hand, he may invest to increase the quality of the product. We note e as efforts to reduce production costs and i as efforts to increase the quality of the product. Cost reductions resulting from e are appreciated through function $c(e)$. Adverse effects on quality are appreciated through $b(e)$. Quality improvements resulting from i are appreciated through $B(i)$. Adverse effect on production costs is appreciated through $C(i)$. [4]

If we noted M_1 as the buyer and M_2 as the supplier, B_0 as the utility level of M_1 if the original contract is not renegotiated and P_0 as the price of the transaction, we can analyze the different contracting solutions offered to the contracting parties.

Solutions

Several situations must be examined. The first-one is the first-best solution, where investment levels i and e are contractible. Contracting parties may then sign a complete contract. This situation is developed only as a benchmark, to be compared with other more realistic situations.

The first-best solution

If investments are perfectly contractible, the contract must maximize the total surplus, that is to say:

$$\max_{e,i}\{-b(e)+c(e)+B(i)-C(i)-e-i\} \quad (2.1)$$

The unique solution is (e^*, i^*) such as:

$$-b'(e^*)+c'(e^*)=1 \qquad\qquad (2.2)$$

$$B'(i^*)-C'(i^*)=\beta'(i^*)=1 \qquad\qquad (2.3)$$

Where $\beta'(i^*)$ is the net effect of effort in order to increase quality.

The market solution

The market solution is one where the contracting parties remain autonomous. The supplier may decide to make efforts to reduce production costs or in order to improve product quality. In the case where he decides to reduce production costs, he does not have to advise the buyer as long as the dimensions of production costs he wants to influence are non-contractible as well as the quality of the dimensions affected. He simply keeps the total surplus generated by his efforts.[5] On the other hand, in the case where the supplier decides to increase the quality of the product, the situation is more complicated. The supplier has no incentive to implement a new method to improve product quality without renegotiating the contract with the buyer. He would have no part of the generated surplus. In incomplete contract models, such a renegotiation is not modeled. It is simply assumed that it leads to a Nash solution where the two parties just divide the generated surplus.

The parties' payoffs are therefore:

$$U_{M1} = B_0 - P_0 + 1/2\beta(i) - b(e) \qquad (2.4)$$

$$U_{M2} = P_0 - C_0 + 1/2\beta(i) + c(e) - e - i \qquad (2.5)$$

M_2, the buyer, will choose e and i so as to maximize his payoffs:

$$\max_{i,e}\{1/2\beta(i) + c(e) - e - i\} \qquad (2.6)$$

The unique solution $(\overline{e_{M2}}, \overline{i_{M2}})$ is:

$$c'(\overline{e_{M2}}) = 1 \quad \Leftrightarrow \quad \overline{e_{M2}} > e* \qquad (2.7)$$

$$1/2\beta'(\overline{i_{M2}}) = 1 \quad \Leftrightarrow \quad \overline{i_{M2}} < i* \qquad (2.8)$$

The contracting parties renegotiate efficiently *ex post*[6], but there is an *ex ante* investment distortion. Since the contract is incomplete, the supplier does not assume the costs he inflicts on the buyer when he decides to make efforts to reduce his production costs. He is then over-incited (compare to the first best[7]: $\overline{e_{M2}} > e*$) to do so because he keeps the entire generated surplus. However, regarding quality improvements, the situation is different. Because of the incompleteness of the contract the supplier must negotiate with the buyer and may expect only half of the generated surplus. He is then under-incited (compare to the first best: $\overline{i_{M2}} < i*$) to make efforts in that direction.

The integration solution

To avoid such a problem, the buyer may decide to integrate the transaction. The situation may then become a case where the supplier is an employee that cannot implement any changes that may affect quality or production costs without a renegotiation with his boss. In any case, he cannot expect the entire surplus generated by his efforts to increase quality and/or reduce production costs. Furthermore, he is no longer autonomous as was the case in the market relationship. He can be replaced as soon as his efforts are recognized. Indeed, the possibility for the boss to replace his employee once efforts have been made depends on his capacity for acquiring his employee's competencies and his own or another of his employee's for implementing the changes. That will improve quality or reduce production costs. The more specific his competencies, the harder the employee can be replaced and the more substantial part of the generated surplus he can negotiate. We note λ, with $0 \leq \lambda \leq 1$, as the easiness for the boss to replace his employee. When he is irreplaceable, $\lambda = 1$.

The parties' payoffs are therefore:

$$U_{M1} = B_0 - P_0 + (1 - \lambda/2)[-b(e) + c(e) + \beta(i)] \tag{2.9}$$

$$U_{M2} = P_0 - C_0 + \lambda/2[-b(e) + c(e) + \beta(i)] - e - i \tag{2.10}$$

The employee will choose e and i such as:

$$\max_{e,i}\{\lambda/2[-b(e) + c(e) + \beta(i)] - e - i\} \tag{2.11}$$

The unique solution (e_G, i_G) is:

$$\lambda/2(-b'(e_G) + c'(e_G)) = 1 \quad \Leftrightarrow \quad \overline{e_{M2}} > e^* > e_G \tag{2.12}$$

$$\lambda/2\beta'(i_G) = 1 \quad \Leftrightarrow \quad i_G \leq \overline{i_{M2}} < i^* \tag{2.13}$$

Propositions

This model supports the reasons why we should observe the decision to integrate transactions. A strong adverse effect on quality, resulting from the possibility of the supplier to consider reducing his production costs is the main concern stressed by the incomplete contract theory. Since not all the dimensions of quality are contractible, the best way for the buyer to be protected against the adverse effect on quality might be the integration decision. However, such a decision reduces incentives to make efforts to reduce production costs as well as incentives to make efforts to improve quality. [8] The integration is therefore a trade-off that leads to the following proposition:

Proposition 1. The integration decision should be more likely observed when the adverse effect has a great impact on the buyer surplus and when potential improvements concerning quality are low.

One could say that such an adverse effect is not a problem as long as it remains possible to put several suppliers in competition. As long as a bilateral dependency does not exist, it is a possible answer. Nevertheless, in incomplete contract models, this dependency is postulated. It is given as an exogenous parameter. On the contrary, in the transaction cost economics framework, such a dependency is analyzed and explained by the presence of specific investments. Combining those two theoretical frameworks could thus put forward the two following propositions:

Proposition 2. Asset specificity is a necessary condition but not a sufficient condition to explain integration. The surplus must be furthermore appropriable by the supplier: that is the case if several dimensions of the transaction are not contractible and that is the main point of the incomplete contract theory's story; [9]

Proposition 3. Non-contractibility is a necessary condition but not a sufficient condition to explain integration. Contracting parties must be in a bilateral dependency relationship: that is the case if the transaction needs specific investments to be realized and that is the main point of the transaction cost theory.

3. WHAT GOVERNANCE STRUCTURE FOR NON-CONTRACTIBLE SERVICES? A TEST

Data

In order to test such propositions, we collected data regarding airway ground services. Such services are characterized by few potential improvements in terms of quality and few specific investments. But possible efforts to reduce production costs may have an adverse effect on quality. We are talking about services such as customer reception, luggage check, luggage transport, cleaning, catering, guidance, information to travelers, defrosting of airplanes, check-in desks and so on. They are perfect candidates when appreciating the effect of non-contractibility on the decision to integrate a transaction.

Obviously, contracts can address many dimensions of transactions. Norms are established by professional institutions in order to assure minimum quality, especially regarding the security of customers. The joint aviation authorities (JAA), the European equivalent for the federal aviation authorities (FAA) construct rules (JARS OPS Joint Aviation Regulation Operators) pertaining to minimum investments in physical assets as well as human assets in order to assure security. Nevertheless, such rules do not concern the quality level of the service provided to customers. Furthermore, these rules are a necessity for airway companies as long as transactions are organized internally. As soon as transactions are externalized, companies are required to assure themselves a control of their suppliers in order for those rules to be respected. In fact, such control is prohibitively costly and is not effective. That is why, although contracts can address some quality issues incompleteness is evident in several important areas. Such incompleteness could, in principle, compromise the quality of services delivered by a private contractor.

We used questionnaires to collect data, using the Likert scale (answers between 1 to 5). Our survey covered more than thirty ground services, concerning four European airway companies. They were chosen so as to represent different types of company. We retained one large national company, two companies of medium and small size and one company specialized in low-cost tickets. Sixty-seven questionnaires were collected.

The persons in charge of contracts in these companies were asked several questions regarding:

(i) Specific investments necessary to realize the transaction in order to appreciate bilateral dependency. Several questions were asked pertaining to each type of specific investment[10]. But it appeared that only one kind of specific investment was present in those transactions: dedicated assets (ASSETS). This point is interesting because, according to transaction cost economics, this kind of specific investments is the one that generates the fewer contractual problems. They usually do not explain the decision to integrate a transaction (Williamson, 1985). Thus, if we observe the internal organization for several of those transactions, it should not be explained only in reference to specific investments and transaction cost economics.

(ii) The effect of a quality variation to appreciate the impact of an adverse effect on quality. To appreciate the significance for the airway company of a possible quality variation, we ask for the impact of such a variation on the customers'satisfaction (WEIGHT). Since a variation is problematic only to the extent that the potential supplier cannot be easily controlled (because several dimensions of the transaction are not contractible), we appreciated the feasibility of such a control (CONTROL).

(iii) Frequency and uncertainty around the transactions; complexity and time constraints of the transaction. Such characteristics are important in a transaction cost economics perspective (FREQUENCY; UNCERTAINTY; COMPLEXITY; TIME).

Variables are presented in Table 2.1.

Table 2.1. Presentation of the used variables

Variable	Definition of the variables	Obs	Mean	Std. Dev.	Min	Max
WEIGHT	Impact of a variation of quality on customers' satisfaction, ranked between 1 to 5.	67	3.50	1.34	1	5
ASSETS	Non redeployability of dedicated assets, ranked between 1 to 5.	67	3.23	2.08	0	5
FREQUENCY	Frequency of the transaction, ranked between 1 to 5	67	4.49	1.04	1	5
UNCERTAINTY	Uncertainty around the transaction, ranked between 1 to 5.	67	2.19	1.18	1	5
CONTROL	Complexity of the control, ranked between 1 to 5.	67	2.52	1.01	1	4
CONT-WEIGHT	CONTROL*WEIGHT	67	9.40	6.25	2	20
COMPLEXITY	Complexity of the transaction, ranked between 1 to 5.	67	4.13	0.73	2	5
TIME	Significance of the deadlines for the transaction, ranked between 1 to 5.	67	4.31	1.15	1	5
AIR-ONE	Dichotomic variable equal to unity if transaction concerns the big size company.	67	0.15	0.36	0	1
AIR-TWO	Dichotomic variable equal to unity if transaction concerns the medium size company	67	0.44	0.50	0	1
AIR-THREE	Dichotomic variable equal to unity if transaction concerns the small size company	67	0.24	0.42	0	1
AIR-FOUR	Dichotomic variable equal to unity if transaction concerns the low cost company	67	0.16	0.37	0	1
INTERNAL	Dichotomic variable equal to unity if transaction is internalized.	67	0.58	0.49	0	1

Results

The model we wish to estimate in order to test our propositions is the following: Let GS_i be the governance structure chosen by the airway company for a service i. Let GS_i^I represents internal organization and GS_i^X represents market procurement. Then the outcome of the company's make or buy decision can be summarized as:

$$GS_i = \begin{vmatrix} GS_i^I \ \text{if} \ C_i^I < C_i^X \\ \\ GS_i^X \ \text{if} \ C_i^I \geq C_i^X \end{vmatrix}$$

C_i^I and C_i^X are respectively the cost of maintaining production internally and externally. If our propositions are correct, those costs are a function of the impact of a quality variation on customers' satisfaction and traditional transaction cost determinants.

For estimation purposes, we retained a linear specification of the model, with a constant term for cost of maintaining production internally as a measure of the "administrative burden" or costs of bureaucracy. We have then:

$$C_i = \begin{vmatrix} C_i^I = C + \alpha UNC_i + \beta ASSET_i + \chi COMPLEX_i + \delta FREQUENCY_i + \varepsilon WEIGHT_i + u_i \\ \\ C_i^X = \phi UNC_i + \varphi ASSET_i + \varphi COMPLEX_i + \gamma FREQUENCY_i + \eta WEIGHT_i + v_i \end{vmatrix}$$

We expect the differential effect of each transaction's characteristics to be to the advantage of the internal organization, that is to say: $C>0$; $\phi - \beta > 0$; $\varphi - \chi > 0$; $\gamma - \delta > 0$; $\eta - \varepsilon > 0$.

We used a probit model for our estimates, assuming a normal distribution of the error term. Such estimation is in the "spirit" of previous transaction cost empirical works on the subject.

We just added to the model the fact that some transactions are more important than others regarding customer satisfaction. This point might affect the decision of the companies to make or buy services. It is the message of the incomplete contract theory. The results are presented in Table 2.2.

Table 2.2. Econometric results (Probit estimates)

Variables	INTERNAL (1)	INTERNAL (2)	INTERNAL (3)	INTERNAL (4)
ASSETS	0,15	0,18	0,25	0,21
	(1,88)*	(2,09)**	(2,54)**	(1,69)*
FREQUENCY	0,52	0,58	0,64	0,53
	(2,65)***	(3,20)***	(3,31)***	(2,61)***
COMPLEXITY	0,09	0,25	0,14	0,18
	(0,36)	(0,95)	(0,52)	(0,65)
UNCERTAINTY	0,11	0,06	-0,1	-0,13
	(0,64)	-0,34	(-0,49)	(-0,58)
TIME	-0,12	-0,08	-0,13	-0,09
	(-0,80)	(-0,55)	(-0,81)	(-0,57)
CONT-WEIGHT	-	0,08	-	-
		(2,52)**		
WEIGHT	-	-	0,64	0,61
			(3,80)***	(3,40)***
AIR-ONE	-	-	-	0,85
				(1,09)
AIR-TWO	-	-	-	0,9
				(1,05)
AIR-THREE	-	-	-	0,79
				(1,11)
CONSTANT	-2,68	-4,34	-5,35	-5,63
	(-1,55)	(-2,36)**	(-2,74)***	(-2,86)***
Observations	67	67	67	67
Log Likelihood	-38,01	-34,63	-28,88	-28,07
Pseudo-R^2	0,16	0,24	0,37	0,39

Notes
* *denotes significance at 10% level;*
** *denotes significance at 5 % level;*
*** *denotes significance at 1% level.*

The results partially confirm our propositions. Regarding traditional variables used to test transaction cost propositions, we observe that asset specificity (dedicated assets in our case) plays a significant role in the decision to integrate services[11] as well as the frequency of the transaction (INTERNAL(1)). The complexity of the transaction as well as the time constraint regarding transactions (TIME), that may reflect what has qualified recently by the transaction cost theory as temporal specificity (Masten et al. 1991), do not play a significant role in the decision to integrate services.

The fact that the presence of asset specificity influences the decision to integrate transactions is not a surprise since many empirical studies already confirm this point (Masten and Saussier, 2000, for a survey). Nevertheless, as we have indicated, we are dealing with dedicated assets. Those assets are not crucial in the decision to integrate if we follow transaction cost economics reasoning. That may explain the fact that the variable ASSET is not very significant.

The effect of the frequency of the transaction is a very interesting one as empirical analysis have been largely unsuccessful in confirming the hypothesized effect of frequency. Indeed, several studies have failed to find any positive association between transaction frequency and hierarchical governance. We found such an association.

However, what appears to be eminent regarding the decision to integrate ground services is the consequences of a quality deviation (INTERNAL(2) and INTERNAL(3)). The more a quality deviation could be harmful to the buyer, the more probable the transaction would be integrated. Integration can then be viewed as a way for the buyer to be protected against opportunistic behavior that would affect the quality of the product. This result remains even if we consider the ability of the buyer to control his supplier activity (INTERNAL(2) vs INTERNAL(3)). This result confirm our proposition 1.

Note also that the constant term has a large effect on the probability of internalization. The negative coefficient reflects the predisposition of management toward external procurement. It can be interpreted as an indirect measure of the costs of bureaucracy incurred by internalizing a transaction.

Furthermore, we observed no fixed effect regarding every airway companies compared to AIR-FOUR, that is a low-cost company (INTERNAL(4)). Such a company is characterized by a high propensity to externalize transactions and to take the risk of a bad quality product that would affect her less than traditional companies. But this propensity is captured by variable WEIGHT and does not generate a fixed effect.

4. WHAT CONTRACTUAL CHOICES TO GOVERN NON-CONTRACTIBLE SERVICES? EXTENSIONS.

Hybrids and Incomplete Contract Models

Very few articles concern intermediate contractual solutions, between markets and hierarchies using an incomplete contract framework. Nevertheless, between the two solutions we studied, market or hierarchy, there exists a wide range of contractual arrangements, that we will call "Hybrids", after Williamson's terminology. Even if several contractual dimensions are non-contractible (that is contracts are necessarily incomplete), parties, while still protecting their autonomy, may shape mechanisms driving their contractual relationships. Those mechanisms or contractual safeguards (Ménard, 1997), permit to nuance obtained results. Indeed, (1) they permit the creation of incentives more significant than markets that allow the supplier to improve quality and (2) reduce the supplier's incentives to reduce production costs when an adverse effect on quality exists. The bargaining power is no longer split as shown in a Nash solution. [12]

If we go back to the model developed in section 2.2., such a situation can be represented in the following manner:

$$U_{M1} = B_0 - P_0 + (1-\alpha)\beta(i) + (1-\gamma)c(e) - b(e) \quad (2.14)$$
$$U_{M2} = P_0 - C_0 + \alpha\beta(i) + \gamma c(e) - e - i \quad (2.15)$$

With $0 < \alpha < 1$ and $0 < \gamma < 1$, where α and γ appreciate the level of contractual safeguards that contractual parties may implement even though quality and other contractual dimensions are non contractible.

(i) If $\alpha = \frac{1}{2}$, then contractual and extra-contractual safeguards the seller may implement to obtain more than half of the generated surplus by his efforts, are inefficient.

(ii) If $\gamma = 1$, then the contractual and extra-contractual safeguards the buyer may implement to avoid supporting the entire adverse effect on the quality of cost reduction from the seller, are inefficient. In either case, when contractual safeguards are inefficient, we fall back to market solutions.

M_2, the seller, will choose investment levels i and e so as to maximize his payoffs:

$$\max_{i,e}\{\alpha\beta(i) + \gamma c(e) - e - i\} \quad (2.16)$$

The only solution (e_{M2}, i_{M2}) is:

$$\gamma c'(e_{M2}) = 1 \quad (2.17)$$
$$\alpha\beta'(i_{M2}) = 1 \quad (2.18)$$

Contractual and extra-contractual safeguards will influence the value of α and γ. The higher α becomes, the greater the incentives for the seller to improve product quality. The closer γ is to zero, the greater the buyer's power to constrain the seller not to reduce his production costs.

Recent developments of the incomplete contract theory showed that first-best may be attainable in most specific situations. Recent models on this issue focus on very particular cases where there exist contractual solutions to the incompleteness problem pointed out by Hart (see, Aghion, Dewatripont and Rey 1994; Noeldeke and Schmidt, 1995). In other words, such models show that even when contracts are incomplete, first best is attainable. This calls the foundations of incomplete contract theory into question (Tirole, 1994; Hart and Moore, 1999; Maskin and Tirole, 1999). It is holds especially true whenever investments are "egoist" and affect only payoffs of the party that develops investments (Che and Hausch, 1998). Yet in our case, investments are "cooperative" in the sense that i and e influence not only the seller's payoffs but the buyer's payoffs as well. In such a case, contractual solutions cannot be implemented (Fares, 2000). Extra-contractual or organizational solutions must be found. Such solutions are connected to what is called governance structures by transaction cost economics. Transactions can no longer be governed exclusively by contract but also by extra-contractual means.

Comparison of the possible solutions

Incentives to reduce production costs
Compared to other governance structures, hybrid forms are characterized by an incentive level concerning production costs. This will depend on γ, which can be seen as the intensity of safeguards that contractual parties may implement in their relationships.

Figure 2.2. Incentives to reduce production costs: solutions according to the chosen governance structure

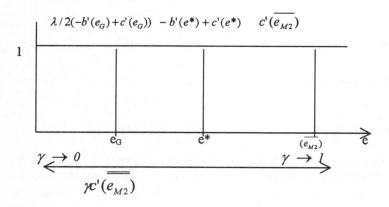

If γ equals one, then the seller will receive the entire surplus generated by reductions in production costs. The adverse effect on quality will then not concern him. It is the case on the market. However, the buyer can generally implement safeguards in order to be at least partially protected against this adverse effect. The better protected, the less incentive for the seller to take advantage of such comportment (that is, $\gamma \rightarrow 0$).

Incentives to improve quality
Hybrid forms, compared to other governance structures are characterized by an incentive level towards quality improvements. It will depend on α which can be seen as the intensity of safeguards against quality improvements that contractual parties may implement in their relationships. The more $\alpha \rightarrow 1$, the seller's greater part of the surplus generated by his efforts to improve quality.

Figure 2.3. Incentives to improve quality: solutions according to the chosen governance structure

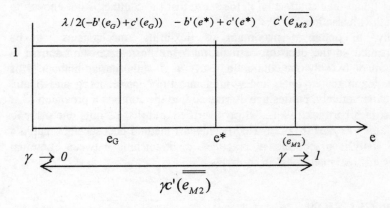

This leads us to a refinement of our first proposition: even when opportunistic behaviors are possible, with great effect for the buyer, contracting parties can, in a wide range of situations, implement safeguards which stabilize their cooperation. This solution will be especially sought after by the parties if the transaction is characterized by a high potential for quality improvements. The advantage of integration (reduction of the adverse effect on quality) is counterbalanced by its drawback (low incentives to improve quality for the seller).

This situation cannot be observed for ground services because they are not characterized by high potentiality for quality improvements. Nevertheless, such a proposition may explain the fact that several uncertain transactions, with a high level of specific assets and a high potential for quality improvements, are nevertheless very often organized through contractual arrangements, such as software contracts for example.

Safeguards
What types of safeguard may be implemented by contracting parties? Safeguards can be defined as mechanisms to secure contracting parties. They generate trust and permit adaptations to unforeseen contingencies. They can take several forms.

To stabilize relationships, contracting parties may implement mechanical contractual safeguards to realign incentives, including penalties and rewards.

To obtain more flexibility allowing easier adaptation to unforeseen contingencies, specialized mechanisms can be implemented by contracting parties in order to govern the transaction and settle potential conflicts. Parties construct their own contractual rules. The contract no longer specifies the transaction only but the way to accomplish it. Such mechanisms are more organizational than contractual in the sense that the contract is not enough to govern the transaction.

Finally, to obtain a maximum of flexibility, mechanisms can be implemented so the decisions can be made *ex post*, once the contract is signed, made by only one contracting party in an authoritarian manner. This can be negotiated *ex ante*, and written into the contract (Ang and Beath, 1993). Alternatively, parties may introduce into the contract a provision (that is sometimes harmless) that is always verified and that permits one party to decide alone *ex post* (Masten, 1998). This last method puts special emphasis on the analysis of contractual practices, distinguishing between "nominal terms" and "real intentions" in contracts.

5. CONCLUSION

Starting from an incomplete contract framework, we stressed the role of non-contractible dimensions of transactions in order to understand why transactions that do not involve specific assets may be realized internally. We used data concerning ground services gathered from four European airway companies. Results confirmed that non-contractibility is a necessary and sufficient condition for integration when potential opportunistic behavior has a great effect on a party's surplus. A transaction cost approach may be viewed as a complement. Yet, asset specificity does not seem a necessary condition for making the decision of integration to be taken. However, this is consistent with the probity hazard recently stressed by Williamson (1999).

However, incomplete contract theory does not permit an analysis of inter-firm agreements when internal organization is not retained. Again, transaction cost economics may be viewed as a complement. An analysis of contractual safeguards and hybrid governance as developed by transaction cost economics seems necessary to go a step further in that direction and to provide indications concerning the relative efficiency of contractual and hierarchical organizational forms.

NOTES

1. We would like to thank M'hand Fares, Eric Brousseau, Scott Masten and Oliver Williamson as well as participants at the third ISNIE Conference where a preliminary draft of this chapter was presented.
2. These assumptions are often called into question. It has been written that the logic out of which this set-up works is implausible (Kreps, 1996) and/or mistaken (Tirole, 1999; Maskin and Tirole, 1999). See Hart and Moore (1999) for an answer.
3. See Hart and Moore (1999) and Maskin and Tirole (1999) on this issue. The observable but not verifiable assumption is sufficient to justify a high degree of contractual incompleteness provided that the parties cannot commit themselves to renegotiating.
4. Several assumptions are made concerning functions $B(\ )$, $b(\ )$, $C(\ )$, $c(\ )$. $b(0)=0$; $b' \geq 0$; $b'' \geq 0$; $c(0)=0$; $c'(0)=\infty$; $c' \succ 0$; $c'' \prec 0$; $c'(\infty)=0$; $B(0)=0$; $B'(0)=\infty$; $B' \succ 0$; $B'' \prec 0$, $B'(\infty)=0$; $C(0)=0$; $C' \geq 0$; $C'' \geq 0$. In the paper, we focus on cases where (1) $B'-C' \geq 0$, i.e., cases for which there exists a positive net effect of quality efforts and where (2) $c'-b' \geq 0$, that is to say cases for which there exists a positive net effect of production cost efforts. We limit our analysis to cases where quality increases generate production cost increases and where production cost reduction generate quality reduction. Nevertheless, the model can be easily extended to cases of "standardization" of the production, for which the introduction of production norms usually reduce production costs without any decrease in the quality level.
5. Generally, incomplete contracting models make the assumptions that the transaction is entirely non-contractible (See Hart and Moore, 1999 for an attempt to develop a theory of "partial" incompleteness and Saussier, 2000a for a test in a transaction cost economics perspective).
6. This is one important difference between the incomplete contract theory and transaction cost economics. The former gives a crucial importance to ex post transaction costs that appear after the contract signature.
7. This result is obtained due to assumptions of note 3.
8. Indeed, the model points out that the market solution gives more incentives to the supplier regarding efforts to reduce production costs as well as efforts to improve quality.
9. In the transaction cost economics framework, it is implicitly supposed that the more specific investments are, the more important is the appropriable surplus. Nevertheless, and this issue has been already noted by Alchian-Woodward (1988), the degree to which resources are appropriable depends on what they called their "plasticity" and on monitoring costs. In our opinion, plasticity of investments directly refers to the non contractibility issues, and differences in plasticity levels as a possible determinant of vertical integration should be studied with more scrutiny.
10. The non-redeployability of assets may have several sources thus defining different types of asset specificity (Williamson, 1996). It can be explained by geographic localization (site specificity), physical characteristics (physical specificity), market size (dedicated assets),

specialized knowledge (human assets), identification to a brand name (brand-name capital) or synchronization needs (temporal specificity).
11. We tried to consider uncertainty, taking into account the fact that uncertainty is problematic only as long as specific investments are present to a significant degree by generating a variable equal to UNCERTAINTY*ASSETS. Such a variable is non-significant.
12. Results from incomplete contract models are very much dependent on the assumption of a Nash bargain. Crucial results have been called into question in recent articles where this assumption is relaxed (De Meza and Lockwood, 1998; Che and Chung, 1999).

REFERENCES

Aghion, P., Dewatripont, M. and R. Rey (1994), "Renegotiation design with unverifiable information", *Econometrica*, **62**, 257-282.

Alchian, A. and Woodward, S. (1988), "The firm is dead; long live the firm", *Journal of Economic Litterature*, **VI**, 65-79.

Ang, S. and Beath, C.M. (1993), "Hierarchical elements in software contracts", *Journal of Organizational Computing*, **3**, 329-361.

Brousseau, E. and Fares, M. (2000), "The Incomplete contract theory and the New-institutional economics approaches to contracts: substitutes or complements?", in D. Ménard (ed.), *Institutions, Contracts, Organizations, Perspectives from New-Institutional Economics*, Edward Elgar Pub.

Che, Y-K. and Chung, T.Y. (1999), "Contract damages and cooperative investments", *Rand Journal of Economics*, **30**, 84-105.

Che, Y-K. and Hausch, D.B. (1998), "Cooperative investments and the value of contracting", *American Economic review*, .

De Meza, D. and Lockwood, B. (1998), "Does asset ownership always motivate managers? Outside options and the property rights theory of the firm", *Quarterly Journal of Economics*, **CXIII**, 361-386.

Fares, M. and Saussier, S. (1998), "Théorie des contrats incomplets et théorie des coûts de transaction : où en sommes-nous ?", mimeo, ATOM.

Fares, M. (2000), "Contrats incomplets, cadre de renégociation et engagement de long terme", PhD., Université de Paris I Sorbonne.

Grossman, S.J. and Hart, O.D. (1986), "The costs and benefits of ownership: a theory of vertical integration", *Journal of Political Economy*, **94**, 691-719.

Hart, O.D. (1990), "Is bounded rationality an important element of a theory of institutions?", *Journal of Institutional and Theoretical Economics*, **146**, 696-702.

Hart, O.D. (1991), "Incomplete contracts and the theory of the firm", in The Nature of the Firm, O.E Williamson. and S.G. Winter (eds), Oxford University Press, 138-159.

Hart, O.D. (1995), *Firms, Contracts and Financial Structure*, Clarendon Lectures in Economics, Oxford University Press.

Hart, O.D. and Moore, J.M. (1999), "Foundations of incomplete contracts", *Review of Economic Studies*, **66**, 115-139.

Hart, O.D., Shleifer, A. and Vishny R.W. (1997), "The proper scope of government: theory and application to prisons", *Quarterly Journal of Economics, CXII*, 1127-1162.

Kreps, D.M. (1996), "Markets and hierarchies and (mathematical) economic theory", *Industrial and Corporate Change*, **5**, 561-597.

Macleod, B. (1999), "Comment on "public and private bureaucracies: A transaction cost economics perspective", *Journal of Law, Economics and Organization*, **15**, 343-347.

Maskin, E. and Tirole, J. (1999), "Unforeseen contingencies, property rights and incomplete contracts", *Review of Economic Studies*, **66**, 83-115.

Masten, S.E (1984), "The organization of production: evidence from the aerospace industry", *Journal of Law Economics and Organization*, **XXVII**, 403-417, reprinted in S.E. Masten, (1996) (ed), *Case Studies in Contracting and Organization*, Oxford University Press.

Masten, S.E. (1998), "Nominal terms, real intentions, and contract interpretation", IInd Annual *Conference of The International Society for New Institutional Economics* (ISNIE), Paris, September 19-21.

Masten, S.E. (1999), "Contractual Choices", *Encyclopedia of Law & Economics*, B. Boukaert and G. De Geest (eds), Edward Elgar Publishing and the University of Ghent.

Masten, S.E., Meehan, J.W. and Snyder, E.A. (1991), "Costs of organization", *Journal of Law, Economics and Organization*, (7), 1-27.

Masten, S.E. and Saussier, S. (2000), «Econometrics of contracts : an assessment of developments in the empirical literature of contracting», *Revue d'Economie Industrielle*, **92**, 215-236

Ménard, C. (2000), "The enforcement of contractual arrangements", in C. Ménard (ed.), *Institutions, Contracts and Organizations: Perspectives from New Institutional Economics*, Edward Elgar.

Nöldeke, G., and Schmidt, K.M (1995), "Option contracts and renegotiation: a solution to the hold-up problem", *Rand Journal Of Economics*, **26**, 163-179.

Saussier, S. (1999), "Transaction cost economics and contract duration", *Louvain Economic Research*, **65**, 3-21.

Saussier, S. (2000a), "Contractual completeness and transaction costs", *Journal of Economic Behavior and Organization*, **42**, 189-206.

Saussier S. (2000b), "When incomplete contract theory meets transaction cost economics: a test", in C. Ménard (ed.), *Institutions, Contracts and Organizations: Perspectives from New Institutional Economics*, Edward Elgar, 376-399.

Shavell, S. (1998), "Contracts", in *The New Palgrave Dictionary of Economics and The Law*, McMillan Publishers, London.

Tirole, J. (1999) "Incomplete contracts: where do we stand", *Econometrica*, **67**, 741-781.

Williamson, O.E. (1985), *The Economic Institutions of Capitalism*, New York, Free Press.

Williamson, O.E. (1996), *The Mechanisms of Governance*, Oxford University Press.

Williamson, O.E. (1998), "Transaction cost economics: how it works, where it is headed", *The Economist*, **146** (1), 23-58.

Williamson, O.E. (1999), "Public and private bureaucracies: a transaction cost economics perspective", *Journal of Law, Economics and Organization*, **15** (1), 306-342.

3. Internet Economics: a New Form of Cooperation?

Godefroy Dang-Nguyen and Thierry Pénard

1. INTRODUCTION

When the media talk about the Internet, they tend to focus on electronic commerce and the *dot com* companies. Who has not heard of Amazon.com or Yahoo? Even those who have never used the Internet, have at least heard of these two companies. The share price of the *dot com* has also been over-mediatized. The Yahoo share price has multiplied by 26 in three years.[1] E-bay, an auction site, increased by 792% from the first quotation in September 1998 to December 1999. All this commotion tends to hide what the Internet really is. Indeed, the commercial activities constitute only a small part of the services provided on the Internet. Most information and services on the Internet are not supplied by profit-making companies, but by benevolent individuals and institutions.

This can no doubt be explained by the origins of the Internet. For a long time, *the Internet* was a public-funded network of communications for research and education.[2] Access to this network was restricted and defined by the Acceptable Use Policy (AUP): only those institutions having research, educational or cultural activities could be connected to one of the regional access points or exchange nodes. The arrival of business firms since 1990 and the development of commercial on-line services have significantly modified the Internet. Even if the scientific community no longer makes up the majority of Internet users, its influence currently remains prominent in the organization of the Internet and interaction among its users. The modes of coordination and exchange are still largely founded on cooperation and gifts. Countless users spend time leading newsgroups, creating free information web sites or developing software for the Internet without claiming any copyright.

In this chapter, we put forward the idea that the institutional context in which the Internet has emerged cannot entirely explain the importance of *services*[3] and the vitality of cooperative behavior on this network. This phenomenon is consubstantial with Internet Economics. In fact, the Internet is a universal network of *co-production, co-consumption* and *exchanges* of electronic services, promoting efficient and stable cooperation, distinct from traditional forms of cooperation.

Two classic forms of cooperation are generally distinguished: voluntary cooperation and necessary cooperation. This distinction is established according to whether the end product of collective action is separable or not. In voluntary cooperation, the product is separable. Consequently, the partners must first agree *ex ante* to share the rules of the outcome.[4] These agreements may be unstable since one might be tempted to appropriate one's partners' share. This opportunist or hold-up behavior is made possible by the separability of the final product. The enforcement of a sharing agreement requires detecting cheats without delay and punishing them severely at any re-occurrence. Voluntary cooperation will be stable if, and only if, the net gain from cheating is lower than the cost of being punished. Factors that hinder or promote such cooperation are well known: for example, imperfect information, asymmetry or heterogeneity between partners or a weak preference for the future weaken a cooperative agreement by increasing the cheating gain or reducing the harshness of the punishments. The multiplicity of sharing solutions may also hinder any agreement. The proper theoretical framework for studying this form of cooperation is that of repeated games and a classic application deals with collusive agreements between firms. Other examples of voluntary cooperation have been analyzed by Axelrod (1984), whether in the Senate or in the trenches during the First World War.

With the second form of cooperation, each partner contributes to a joint or non-separable product. The effort of a contributor cannot be isolated from the efforts by others and cannot be self-appropriated. Consequently, cooperation is necessary in order to obtain an outcome. In this type of relation, opportunism does not concern sharing the final product but the efforts provided by the partners. Indeed, the outcome will depend on the sum of efforts supplied, these efforts depending on the initial incentives. The efficiency of incentive rules may be questionable, because each partner has an interest in hiding their real competence or overestimating the cost of their efforts in order to be better remunerated for their efforts or to contribute less. Such opportunistic behavior generally stems from incomplete information about the characteristics of each partner and requires implementing revelation mechanisms on hidden information. The theoretical frameworks dealing with these problems are cooperative game theory and the incentive theory. A classical example of necessary cooperation is the supply of a public good. By definition, a public good is not separable or privately appropriable: it benefits indifferently those who contribute and those who do not. It may result in free-riding and the under-supplying of public goods. This phenomenon has largely been studied by Olson (1965). The latter underlined that the perception of a common interest is not enough to run a collective action. A possible remedy is either to provide private incentives to those who agree to contribute to the public good or to make participation and contribution compulsory. Olson gave some examples of incentive mechanisms used by American trade unions[5] or lobbying professional groups.

In sum, with voluntary cooperation, the main problem is not participation in the collective action, but opportunist behavior when sharing the end product. Conversely, in necessary cooperation, sharing opportunism disappears, but it is replaced by the problem of free-riding. Voluntary cooperation rather involves decentralized and informal relations, the characteristic of market relations, whereas necessary cooperation is more in line with formal and hierarchical relations.

In this chapter, we contend that the Internet has favored a new form of cooperation, distinct from *voluntary or market cooperation* and from *necessary or hierarchical cooperation*. The specificity of *Internet cooperation* lies not only in the absence of centralization on the Internet and the importance of institutions, but in the technical features of the Internet, which combine the network effects of the telecommunication industry and the dynamic innovation process of the computer industry. These different elements contribute to transforming necessary interaction into voluntary cooperation. Conversely, the Internet allows voluntary interaction to be converted into necessary cooperation. Internet cooperation, with its necessary and its voluntary dimensions, guarantees agreements more efficient and stable than with either market or hierarchical cooperation and explains why gifts and cooperative behavior play such a major role in the supplying of many Internet services.

A clear understanding of Internet cooperation must start by a classification of different Internet services. First, the Internet can be defined as a mesh of numerous heterogeneous networks (Kavassalis and Solomon, 1997). All the networks can exchange data and services through a common language defined by the TCP-IP protocols. These protocols establish a net separation between the services of data carrying (the lower tier of the Internet) and the user applications or services (the upper tier), the latter being independent from the former (Kavassalis and Lehr, 1998). User services can fulfill three objectives: communication (e-mail, newsgroups), information (websites) and transaction (e-commerce). All services activate many software applications or modules from the lower and upper tiers of the Internet. The Internet, through its universal protocols, allows these modules to become compatible.

The following section explains how Internet cooperation is voluntary and stable. We stress the symmetry of Internet participants and their dual status of both Internet service provider and consumer. It can be exemplified by the organization of newsgroups and the interconnection agreements between Internet carriers.

Section 3 deals with the efficiency of Internet cooperation. Our arguments focus on the strong modularity of Internet services and the ease of diffusion and reproduction, which limits or hinders the self-appropriation of these services. The development of "open source software" and free information web sites illustrates these arguments.

2. THE INTERNET: A VOLUNTARY COOPERATIVE NETWORK

The Symmetry Principle

The Internet is based on a symmetry principle in two ways. On the one hand, the Internet guarantees identical treatment to each user whatever the services. On the other hand, all the users are both providers and consumers to a certain extent.

On the first point, we have already mentioned that the Internet is a network of heterogeneous networks, made compatible through the TCP/IP protocols. These protocols manage to make the heterogeneity totally invisible or transparent for users. They convert the Internet into a universal network where everyone is in a symmetric position in relation to the others. For example, at the lower tier, each Internet carrier is identified by its Autonomous System (AS) number, which allows it to interconnect directly or indirectly with every other network, whatever its geographic coverage or its capacities, and to exchange data without any problem of compatibility. At the upper tier, we find the same principle in action. Each user has an electronic address, which gives him the same right, or the same ability to receive messages from and send messages to every other user, whatever her nationality or her social status. Similarly, the Web and its domain name system establish an equal proximity between all the web sites. With a browser any site can be reached virtually in one click. This virtual symmetry and proximity is a factor that may facilitate the implementation of stable and efficient cooperation.

The second noticeable Internet characteristic is that it is a network of both co-production and co-consumption. Indeed, each user directly participates in the production of her present and future services. Above all, there is no clear separation between those who are suppliers and those who are customers. For example, each Internet carrier supplies connectivity services to other carriers, but is also a buyer of connectivity if it wants to attain universal coverage. Similarly, on newsgroup or web sites, everyone both seeks and provides information. This reversibility of roles hinders the emergence of a classic marketplace. It creates a double bind: each user depends on the other as a service supplier but also as a service consumer. This double bind allows the transformation of necessary relations into voluntary cooperation by deterring free-riding behavior. Indeed, if a user does not provide the required level of effort or investment for a given service, he will be punished directly by consuming a low-quality or low-capacity service. Moreover the other suppliers may also punish him. If he consumes the services provided by his partners, without providing fair reciprocity, he may be excluded as a service supplier. Since the majority of Internet services cannot be provided without the assistance of other suppliers this punishment has a real deterrent effect and guarantees the efficiency of Internet cooperation. Above all, this threat of reprisal is credible because excluding a user does not require too much effort and does not destroy the cooperation between the remaining partners.

These ideas are illustrated by the examples of news groups and of peering agreements between Internet carriers.

Peering Agreements

Carrying services are the most invisible for the user, although un-dissociable from other user services. Above all, these services require a minimum of coordination among Internet network operators, if the latter are keen to guarantee universal connectivity to their customers (Huston, 1999). One of the most interesting forms of cooperation among operators called ISP (Internet Service Providers) concerns peering agreements. These are exchange agreements without financial compensation: each ISP takes care of conveying all the traffic addressed to its network for free and gets revenues only from the fees paid by its own subscribers.[6] This form of bartering is very different from the interconnection practices developed for international voice traffic by telephone companies. They have in fact set up clearing agreements where incoming and outgoing traffic between a pair of carriers is metered, and payments are made to the company for excess incoming traffic.

On the Internet, peering may be justified from both a technical and an economic point of view. Given its operating principles, the Internet cannot in fact guarantee a quality of service provision, which makes it difficult to pay for the conveyance, despite the opinion of some economists.[7] In particular, a system counting the in and outgoing packets would be costly to set up, and would slow down the transmission rate.

The near symmetry between the networks involved in the peering process may also explain the stability of these flexible and largely informal cooperation agreements.[8] Stability relies on threats of retaliation or exclusion of any ISP partner adopting an opportunistic behavior. This is a tit for tat strategy (Axelrod, 1984). Here opportunistic behavior would involve under-investing in one's network and using the partner's network to carry part of one's own traffic, with substantial savings. Such behavior is quickly detected and "punished", through the breakdown of the peering agreement.

Nevertheless, peering might be threatened by the current concentration among data carriers.[9] Thus Worldcom, owner of one of the largest Internet networks after its merger with Uunet and MCI, has, since May 1997, refused to peer with small ISPs. If the latter want to exchange traffic they have to pay access fees like any customer, through a transit agreement. The attitude of Uunet has been imitated by the largest ISPs. The growing asymmetry between networks with, on the one hand, a few transcontinental carriers, most of them American and, on the other hand, numerous small regional ISPs, is likely to restrict the room for cooperation. Large ISPs are increasingly refusing to peer with small networks that do not abide by the implicit reciprocity rule and consequently have to pay an access charge. A second limit to peering agreements between ISPs of even equal size could come from competition among themselves on access and usage services. The sources of conflict are numerous and the struggle to get new customers is often harsh. Occasionally some ISPs canvass the customers of other ISPs or sell off their access tariffs. This rivalry can lead two ISPs to refuse a direct interconnection with each other. Consequently, traffic exchanges are transiting through third party networks, with lesser quality of service (Baake and Wichmann, 1998; Dang-Nguyen and Pénard, 1999).

In short, the weakening of the symmetry principle questions peering practices. The rivalry between ISPs is driven by the desire to attain a large size and reinforces asymmetry. Each of the ISPs actually has a strong incentive to hold a large customer base in order to build up a "club". Thus peering may weaken the benefits of an exclusive club, in particular the quality of transmission. To preserve this source of competitive advantage, ISPs are led to refuse peering with their closest rivals. Yet beyond these specific cases, peering still continues to shape relations between many ISPs.

Communications Services

Communications services are the keystone of all cooperation instances on the Internet. How can one actually imagine a cooperative relationship without communication? The Internet was in fact designed to enable researchers scattered around the world to collaborate on scientific projects, and to facilitate remote working and document interchange.[10] The scientific community was very quickly attracted by the speed of this communications tool and the absence of payment. The propensity of researchers to share ideas and join collective projects accelerated its diffusion, through a classical network effect: The higher the number of subscribers, the greater the incentive to subscribe, with a subsequent "avalanche effect".

With the worldwide takeoff of the Internet, communications services have achieved a new dimension. One of the most remarkable outcomes has been the creation of numerous virtual communities and discussion forums upon diverse topics, between people who do not know each other *a priori*. All these communities work on a cooperative principle of information sharing and mutual support (Kollock and Smith, 1999). All services provided inside the community are free. For example, a users' community of some given software allows the submission of queries, which the most knowledgeable members of the community will try to answer. In other communities, personal experiences are shared or practical advice is given. Within groups, it is often the rule to practice self-discipline. Each new member has first to consult and accept Netiquette, namely the rules of behavior and the objectives specified at the groups' creation. The new member also has to be aware of the frequently asked questions (FAQ) before taking part in discussions. If he or she does not comply with Netiquette, they can be simply excluded or punished through a flame war, namely a flow of aggressive messages addressed to his or her mailbox. One can imagine the consequences when the group consists of several thousand members. Therefore a principle of coordination with rules has been established on the Net, with an obvious feature of self-organization.[11] The subsequent appearance of commercial activities on the Internet has not weakened these principles. On the contrary, business players have been paying court to these communities in order to receive the approval and attention of these Internet users.

However, the cooperative mind pervading the communications services may be threatened by the exponential growth of Internet users. The massive connection of new participants ignoring the rules of behavior could really disturb the working of these virtual communities. Their most active members could leave these places of free exchange and cooperation, if too many free riders drop in. Moreover, the possibility of easily changing one's identity on the Internet could limit the reputation mechanisms that are essential in any cooperation.[13] In fact, it does not always happen like this. Whether the participants in a discussion group are anonymous or not, social categories quickly emerge like the "novice" or the "old timer", the latter performing the task of educating the former, who in turn will sometimes contest his "totalitarianism". Therefore true social conventions are set up which stabilize relationships, reinforce the feeling of community membership and reduce the probability of free riding. Voluntary cooperation is thus strengthened by this socialization process.

To sum up, for both peering and virtual communities, necessary cooperation has become voluntarily accepted, provided two features were present: symmetry of size among the players involved and symmetry of roles; each being a producer and a consumer. When this does not hold, or when there is rivalry among players, voluntary cooperation is endangered, as shown by the peering case.

3. THE INTERNET: A NETWORK OF NECESSARY COOPERATION

The Modularity Principle

An Internet service is seldom the outcome of one single player's effort, but rather a combination of multiple modules elaborated by different authors. These modules may be data or software programs. The modularity principle is explained both by the easy diffusion and reproduction of the modules. The diffusion or reproduction of digital information have an almost zero cost and can be implemented on a large scale and very quickly.[13] Also, the cost of production of Internet services is highly reduced through the easy reusability of certain existing service modules. Indeed, a service does not disappear nor is it altered when consumed. Conversely, each user may improve it through the modification of modules or through the addition of new ones. This production dynamics, to which everybody can contribute at a low cost, enables steady quality and adaptability of services.

These features nonetheless hinder the establishment of restrictive copyrights. Attempts at protection may be costly and useless regarding the technical opportunities of diffusion and reusability brought about by Internet. Since it is not possible to acquire exclusive ownership of the final product, cooperation becomes necessary. The quality of the services thus depends on the collective efforts on the part of the relevant parties. Truly enough, some may be deterred from providing services because of piracy and the misappropriation of their work. However the low cost of participation and production compared with the significant gains provided by high quality services suited to one's needs, always enables the critical mass to be reached for many Internet services.

Open source software and information sites on the Web exemplify this efficient cooperation very well. In the first case, simple voluntary cooperation is transformed into necessary cooperation thanks to a licensing system that prevents any private appropriation of the software. In the second case, hypertext links between sites impose cooperation on the authors of these sites.

The "Open Source Software" Model

Software development has undoubtedly provided the most interesting instance of cooperation. Without the Internet, "open source software" would not have been so successful as to have shaken Microsoft. Linux, a free operating system competing with Windows NT, held more than 17% of the server market for operating systems in February 2000, and more than half of all Web sites are managed with the Apache open source software. Before analyzing this phenomenon, it is important to define it.

Open source software is characterized above all by the availability of the source program (namely the code) and thus the possibility for each user to transform and improve it. Conversely, it is wrong to link the term "open source" with free of charge because, first, some free software is not open source (the user cannot access the program code) and, second, open source software may be charged for or traded.[14] Open source software is protected by different licenses (Berkeley, BSD, GNU Public License, and so on). The GNU Public License (GPL) even extends this free availability to any derived modified or adapted version. These licenses are in fact collective contracts governing the relationships between programmers, distributors and users.

Beyond the issue of licenses, open source software is first the outcome of collective work by many developers, who know each other only virtually most of the time. Projects are largely decentralized, but generally have coordinators who manage the development and diffusion of the software. For Linux, the coordinator is Linus Thorvald. In "The Cathedral and the Bazaar", Raymond (1998) analyzes the success of open source projects on the Internet, which rely mainly on the *bazaar* model as opposed to the *cathedral* model of much proprietary software. According to the *bazaar* principle, preliminary and imperfect versions of the software are distributed very quickly in order to benefit from the opinion of users, who are themselves generally developers. When a bug is detected and reported, several solutions or patches are proposed and implemented by the developers in the community. Each is evaluated and commented on by other developers. Finally the best solution is retained through consensus. This pattern of software development is not time and resource saving, since dozens of programs representing hundreds of hours programming may be proposed to solve a minor problem, but it gives high quality, reliable software. Each developer who contributes to open source software abandons his or her copyright, but is ensured of having his or her name on the software license. According to Linus Thorval, what pushes so many developers to work on cooperative projects is less the search for glory than the pleasure of writing programs and above all the concern to obtain the high performance software suited to their needs.

Technical reasons can also be explained by the success of this approach. Computer software is in essence coded information (binary code), much easier to transmit and share than tacit information (Winter, 1987). Collective programming and code sharing have always existed. Nevertheless the Internet has given a new impetus to the phenomenon, by enabling thousands of programmers scattered around the world to be organized and work together on ambitious projects. Stallmann, the founder of FSF (Open source software Foundation) whose aim is to promote open source software, underlines that the philosophy of open source software is not so much the systematic copying of software packages as the collective appropriation of the creativity elements embedded in those packages, that is, the source code.

Giving up intellectual property rights, however much surprising compared to the traditional system of patents and copyrights, may be economically sensible. Regarding information technology, patents are not the only forms of protection. Hence, software producers compile programs, which makes the contents impossible to understand. Protection through encryption and very restrictive user licenses contracts, give rise to strong penalties supposed to discipline the behavior of the users.[15] Supporters of open source software claim that these methods are inefficient in the context of rapid technological progress and that they are undertaken at the expense of the consumer. They thus propose collective production without any specific property right on the source program. A pragmatic view might suggest that their approach is not pure utopia and can be reconciled with an economic rationale: some property rights can be assigned on some more specific applications and services, complementary to the open source programs.[16]

The real threat may actually come from internal dissension inside the open source software community. There exists a disagreement between supporters grouped around FSF, who plead for a more centralized organization in charge of collecting funds and monitoring the projects on the one hand, and supporters of the bazaar model of self-organization on the other (Browne, 1998). Tensions also exist concerning the choice of license regime (GPL or BSD license) and the role of business players in the development of this software. The risk may be the fragmentation of projects, which may damage the credibility and the visibility of open source software, in particular *vis-à-vis* business users.

Information Sharing

For a long time, scientific and academic information has represented the bulk of Internet contents. Such information is by nature free and freely accessible, because it is in everyone's interest to diffuse their work in order to receive comments and acknowledgement from their peers. This free nature is inherent in the academic world competition model of *publish or perish*.[17]

With the development of the Internet, the supply of information has become abundant and more diversified than ever before. Information of a commercial or leisure-time nature (personal pages, entertainment sites and so on) have a significant place on the Net. However, information is mostly free of charge, even on business sites. As in the case of open source software, it seems that people voluntarily agree to provide their effort for free.

Several reasons may be put forward. The desire for fame and acknowledgement is not limited to the scientific community and can be found in most individuals and companies. The Internet is a showroom and a promotional tool.[18] However information on the Internet has all the features of a public good: its consumption by one individual does not alter or diminish the amount available to others. Moreover, in most cases it is also a non-excludable good,[19] with free access. Paradoxically, it does not seem to create a free rider issue.[20] Most users find it to their advantage to provide public information and to endure some of the effort made in producing it, even if they know that others will benefit freely from it. Moreover, technological progress in digitization and information formatting makes the production of digitized information more and more easy. The Internet thus contributes to abolishing the frontier between those who produce and those who consume and it enables private interest (obtaining acknowledgement) to coincide with collective interest (contributing to the production of publicly available information).

The free nature of information and free access to it nonetheless raise the issue of quality and reliability.[21] Even if some intermediaries and search engines like Yahoo or Altavista can select and authenticate information, some extreme forms of low quality may exist (revisionism, unfounded rumors about questioning the reputation of people or institutions and so on). Beyond these extreme cases, the quality regulation is in fact undertaken by the users themselves. On information sites, as long as reputation and quality are the objectives, a self-selection mechanism is set up. Firms or individuals try to give the best image of themselves, in the fear that the acceleration effect of diffusion on the Internet may lead to a result contrary to the objective, if quality is not provided.

Finally, it is always in the interest of an information site to produce quality information if its author wants to survive on the Web. Indeed, if it only consumes information from other sites without producing any itself or without any concern for quality, it will receive no hypertext links from other sites. As these links are taken into account by browsers and search engines when assessing the interest and the quality of a site, a site with few links will never appear in the search engines. Conversely, a site to which many others point will be better referenced. The risk of isolation for those who do not contribute to information provision is thus a strong incentive to cooperate. For sites with neighboring interests or themes, hypertext links create solidarity and a necessity to cooperate if they want to be visible and recognized by search engines and Web users.

In short, free information on the Internet does not suffer from too much opportunism. The effects of reputation and the tradition of cooperation without financial compensation are sufficient to stabilize the production of this "public" good.

The two examples of open source software and information provision show how voluntary relations are transformed into a necessary cooperation by the Internet. Thanks to the modularity of Internet services, cooperation does not require strong individual efforts and is rather a piecemeal process. Moreover, since Internet services are generally public goods, it is more efficient to leave them free of charges than to try and protect them. The symmetry principles and the mechanisms of mutual recognition (through peering agreements, hypertext links or the membership of a community) give sufficient incentives to provide the necessary effort.

4. CONCLUSION

Initially the Internet was a network of non-profit-making institutions ruled by cooperative relationships. With the entry of business firms in the 1990s, many thought that the Internet would tip into a business network built on strong contractual relations, mostly exemplified by e-commerce. However, we have shown that the Internet growth has gone hand in hand with a diversity of relationships in which giving and cooperating play a key role: this is the case of peering or the development of open source software which commits business and non-business players linked together through the contractual relationships of licenses. [22] We have seen that these forms of cooperation stem from the features of the Internet. The latter is characterized by network and club effects as in the telecommunication industry. The Internet also shares the same dynamics of innovation as the computer industry. Yet, the Internet imposes a way of creating standards and communications protocols more cooperative than in the telecommunication and computer industries. The community of users plays a central role in stimulating cooperation and the free exchange of services.

ACKNOWLEDGEMENT

The authors thank the anonymous referees and the participants at the ADIS congress for their comments

NOTES

1. The share price increased from $12.69 to $333.81 between April 13 1996 and December 12 1999.
2. On the history of the Internet: [http://www.internetvalley.com/intval.html].
3. Non-profit-making services are not necessarily free. Some can carry a charge to cover costs. Conversely, profit-making organisations can provide free services with indirect financing.
4. The "Tragedy of Commons" described by Hardin (1968) comes under this category. When a common limited resource exists, everyone is tempted to appropriate as much as possible at the expense of the others, until the resource is exhausted. To escape this tragedy, the user must enter into voluntary cooperation and agree on sharing or using rules of the common resource.
5. For example, a trade union whose collective actions of defending worker conditions and improving their wages is a public good (it benefits both unionists and non-unionists) can force the applicants to join a union if they want to be hired.
6. It is a "sender keeps all" scheme. The network originating the traffic keeps all the money paid by its customers to access other networks (see Bailey, 1997)
7. See the book by Bailey and McKnight (1997), which presents the different tarification methods for Internet usage.
8. Data on the Internet are transported in packet form; each packet may follow a different route. They go through routers that direct them to other routers until they reach their final destination, using a best effort principle. In case of congestion, packets can be destroyed by one of the routers and must be sent again.
9. The supply of transport services, as well as access services, involves fixed costs or at least strong indivisibilities. Thus access and transport services compete with increasing returns, and this favors the survival of a few Internet service providers, vertically integrated in access and transport services, and geographically differentiated (Srinagesh, 1997).

10. On the initial researchers' community, see, for example, Hauben and Hauben (1998).
11. There are more formal control mechanisms. Some groups may have a moderator who screens messages and discussions. They are nominated by cooptation: as volunteers, they spend many hours on this task. Another example is the voting procedure for the creation of a new discussion group in the Usenet community. First the creator of the new group presents the motivation behind the project, its positioning *vis-à-vis* existing groups and the topics likely to be discussed. Then Usenet community members express their opinion by e-mail (approval or refusal). If the creation gets 80 more yes's than no's and if their proportion is greater than three quarters of the opinions expressed, the creation of the group is endorsed after a one-week period to allow for protest.
12. In a real community (a firm, village and so on) the concern for reputation deters the individuals from adopting opportunistic behavior or breaching the rules of the group. In a virtual community an individual can escape punishment by using another identity as noticed by Friedman (1998). Moreover Kollock and Smith (1996) underline that the absence of well defined borderlines in those communities can weaken cooperation by enabling individuals to get in and out easily.
13. One can realise this when viruses are put on the Internet. They spread all over the world within several days, most often using the victims' address book.
14. This is the case of Linux that is sold by companies like RedHat. The Java programming language is an extreme case of open source software: the license is sold by its creator Sun Microsystems company and the source code is provided.
15. It is possible, however, to patent software in the US, and this does create some problems, since large software companies take advantage of this to patent anything patentable, even if the programs form part of the developers' common knowledge. It risks wrecking creativity, innovation and the growth of small companies, since practically any new software in the US is likely to breach at least one or two patents.
16. See Barlow «Economy of Ideas: Selling Wine Without Bottles on the Global Net», [http://www.eff.org/EconomyOfIdeas.html].
17. In the case of publication, it is also in the authors' interest to make available on the Internet information and sources related to their research (annexes, details of a demonstration, the program used for simulations) so that the reader can verify the validity of the results.
18. Public administrations also see in the Internet a way to enhance their institutional action, often at a small marginal cost. With numerous public information sources (reports, studies, statistics) the Internet has become a real fountain of knowledge.
19. It is the case when exclusion is not feasible or too costly.
20. Here a free rider is someone who consumes information without providing any.
21. Normally prices are a good indicator of quality when markets are operating well.
22. Even if there are firms in the open source software activity, non-profit-making players are dominant.

REFERENCES

Axelrod, R. (1984), *The Evolution of Cooperation,* New York, Basic Books.

Baake, P. and Wichmann, T. (1998) "On the economics of internet peering" *Netnomics* 1, 89-105. [http://www.berlecon.de/tw/peering.pdf].

Bailey, J.P. and McKnight, L. (1997) *Internet Economics,* Cambridge, MIT Press, 155-168.

Bailey, J.P. (1997) "The economics of internet interconnection agreements", in L. McKnight and J.P. Bailey (eds) *Internet Economics,* MIT Press, Cambridge, 155-168.

Browne, C. (1998) "Linux and decentralized development", *FirstMonday Journal of Internet*, **3** (3), [http://www.fisrtmonday.dk/issues/issue 3_3/].

Dang-Nguyen, G. and Pénard, T. (1999), "Interconnection between ISPs, vertical differentiation and capacity constraints", ENST Bretagne, Working Paper.

Friedman, E. (1998) "The social cost of cheap pseudonyms: fostering cooperation on the internet", [http//:econ.rutgers.edu/home/friedman/ research.htm].

Hauben, M. and Hauben, R. (1998). "Netizens: on the history and impact of usenet and the internet" *Firstmonday Journal of Internet*, **3** (7), [http://www.firstmonday.dk/issues/issue3_7/].

Hardin, G. (1968), "The tragedy of commons", *Science* **162**, 1243-1248.

Huston, G. (1999) "Internet, peering and settlements" [http//:www.telstra.net/peerdics/peer.html]

Kavassalis, P. and Solomon, R.J. (1997), "Mr Schumpeter on the telephone" *Communications et Stratégies* **26**, 371-408.

Kavassalis, P. and Lehr, W. (1998), "Forces for integration and disintegration on the internet", *Communications et Stratégies* **31**, 135-154.

Kollock, P. and Smith, M. (1996), "Managing the virtual commons: cooperation and conflict in computer communities", http://www.sscnet.ucla.edu/soc/faculty/kollock/papers/vcommons.html

Kollock, P. and Smith, M. (1999), *Communities in Cyberspace*, Routledge, London.

Olson, M. (1965), *The Logic of Collective Action, Cambridge*, MA, Harvard University Press.

Raymond, E. (1998), "The Cathedral and Bazaar", *FirstMonday Journal of Internet*, 3 (3), [http://www.fisrtmonday.dk/issues/issue3_3/].

Srinagesh, P. (1997), "Internet cost structures and interconnection agreements", in L. McKnight and J.P. Bailey (eds) *Internet Economics*, MIT Press, Cambridge, 121-154.

Winter, S. (1987), "Knowledge and competence as strategic assets" in D. Teece (ed) *The Competitive Challenge*, Ballinger.

4. Copyright Management in the Digital Age: the Evolving Forms of Cooperation

Joëlle Farchy and Fabrice Rochelandet

1. INTRODUCTION: THE COLLECTIVE LICENSING OF COPYRIGHT.

Copyright corresponds to the moral and patrimonial prerogatives recognised by law to authors of works (author's right) and to their economic partners (neighboring rights of performers and producers). Copyright protection thus allows rightsholders to prevent others to use their works without their authorisation, for example, by making illicit copies from records or unauthorised broadcast. Individual copyright owners (COs) are thereby granted the commercial utilisation of their works during a limited period. Copyright law is supposed to provide them with incentives to produce new works. They can administrate their rights themselves like artists on the art market or film producers. However, the costs of copyright enforcement may be prohibitive for individual agents. Collective administration offers another means of enforcing copyright. Arrangements vary according to the country of origin.[1]

Beyond these various forms of copyright administration, two main models of copyright administration exist. On the one hand, the Walrasian view defends a totally decentralised coordination between autonomous entities. Advocates of this theory consider that only individual rights management permits a higher social welfare through more intense competition between COs. On the other hand, the institutional view emphasises the crucial role of intermediaries. The history of copyright shows that COs are inclined to cooperate, particularly when major technological change occurs.

In essence, collective management of copyright implies cooperation. COs coordinate their efforts in order to share negotiation costs, enforcement and collection of rights. Collecting societies (CSs) correspond to the pooling or the mutualisation of copyrights in a repertoire and act as intermediaries between COs and users, while realising the common interests of the former. The first authors' society was set up in France at the instigation of Beaumarchais in 1777 before the institution of *droits d'auteur* during the French Revolution. Historically, the CSs were both unions and pressure groups: by regrouping isolated artists, they permitted the lobbying of lawmakers and the reinforcement of the authors' bargaining power over their partners. Each society specialised in a category of rights: for instance, the SACEM[2] in France managed members' copyright in the field of music.

The collective administration of copyright is characterised by two successive transactions: first, the collection of rights between CSs and users and second, the allocation of the receipts to their members. Such an arrangement offers some advantages. The centralisation of management by a single organisation makes economies of transaction costs possible. It represents a simplification both for users and COs and a significant reduction in identification, negotiation and enforcement costs. Moreover, the subadditivity of the cost function creates considerable economies of scale and scope: the monopoly status of most of the CSs appears to be one of the main conditions for an efficient collective administration. Learning effects also occur with the repetition of the same activity of contractualisation, enforcement and management of rights. Lastly, contrary to individual COs, it internalises deterrent effects on potential infringers[3] whenever a CS wins a case.

However, the drawbacks of collective management are important too. The classic criticism made against monopoly applies to the CSs. On the one hand, they can benefit from their monopolistic positions by imposing excessive tariffs on users and therefore restricting the production and diffusion of works. It hence causes a potential social welfare loss due to underutilization of cultural goods. On the other hand, a CS is generally in a situation of monopoly towards its members. So a CS can dictate some contractual restrictions on its members as the European Commission's GEMA[4] decision showed in 1971. In particular, this organisation was reproached with discriminating against foreign music publishers.

Nowadays these observations are called into question by digital technologies and the emergence of multimedia markets. As Demsetz noted in 1967, every technological change represents a fundamental factor of evolution for the property rights system. Copyright law had to be adapted to technological change: photography, phonograph, the cinema, radio and television. Most of the questions raised by the multiplication of immaterial production are brought to a climax by the emergence of multimedia and digital networks. More precisely, the question is whether the traditional collective devices of copyright administration are adapted to new cultural products and exploitation. So there remains to determine which mode of coordination is preferable to face the multimedia industry: on the one hand, some advocate a "Walrasian" solution, that is, the generalisation of individual copyright management without intermediaries by using new technologies. On the other hand, some call for a reinforcement of collective administration and a closer cooperation between agents. In this chapter, we show that digital technologies and multimedia do not mean desintermediation, but new forms of cooperation, both horizontal and vertical, between the agents. The set up of new institutions, in particular, focuses on the importance of the capabilities and complementarities of CSs.

2. TRADITIONAL COOPERATION BETWEEN COLLECTING SOCIETIES.

If collective administration means cooperation between individual COs, technological and institutional changes imply another level of cooperation, that is between CSs themselves. As a matter of fact, they often cooperate through their function of unions and at the level of copyright administration.

Nature and Purpose of Cooperation between Collective Rights Organisations

The cooperation between CSs mainly assumes the form of new structures. In France, there are several historical examples related to the authors' union and to technical coordination. SDRM is one of the most important organisations: it was established in 1935 to administrate the mechanical reproduction rights corresponding to the repertoires of its members, that is the major French authors' societies in the fields of music, fiction, theatre, documentary, etc. SDRM does not manage its own repertoire, but it signs blanket licences with IFPI (International Federation of Phonographic Industry) record producers' association and with video publishers from the GICA. It both facilitates the management of audio and video copyright and increases the market power of its members when negotiating with users' associations, administration or international institutions. CFC is another joint venture, which operates on behalf of authors' societies and publishers' associations in the field of reprography rights. It controls, negotiates with, and grants contractual licences directly to the firms and the public administrations, which make use of photocopies. It is linked with other national reproduction rights organisations through an international association.

More recently, as a result of the French copyright law in 1985 instituting neighbouring rights for artists-performers and phonogram producers as well as a private copying tax system, several forms of coordination between CSs were established. These joint ventures facilitate copyright management in the maze of the newly created rights. SPRE, one of the new societies, administrates the performers' and producers' copyright and acts on behalf of their own societies in the field of broadcasting rights. Two others oversee the receipts of the private copying fee charged by the French state on sales of blank tapes. These societies then distribute the collected sums to their respective members, that is CSs of authors, performers and producers. The cooperation is therefore primarily technical and allows both to avoid duplication of costs and to economise significantly on transaction costs. Each CSs no longer has to allocate some of its technical or labour resources to this type of operation while the state is in charge of negotiating overall licensing fees.

At the international level, two main forms of cooperation exist. First, national CSs have implemented *ex nihilo* joint organisations in order to lobby and negotiate with international authorities like WTO, WIPO and the European Commission. Other organisations also deserve a mention: CISAC (International Confederation of Societies of authors and composers), a well-known body, which currently coordinates most of the initiatives of the authors' societies in the field of digital technologies[5]; GESAC (CISAC's European counterpart) and BIEM (mechanical reproduction right organisations).

Moreover, various national CSs are linked together through reciprocal contracts of representation. These arrangements concern the national CSs that manage the same repertoire. It consists in giving a CS the right to another national CS to license its own repertoire to users. For instance, SACEM, (the French composers' society) administrates and enforces the rights of the members of the German society GEMA for the uses of German protected musical works in France. This contract is reciprocal because GEMA administrates the SACEM repertoire in Germany. The benefits of these contracts are obvious since the creation of subsidiaries in every country could dramatically increase the costs of international collective administration. Moreover, the collected sums will often be small in comparison of the costs of institutional adaptations. So cooperation through reciprocal contracts is caused by prohibitive costs of geographical distances and institutional differences. The emergence of online commerce of works and the harmonisation of copyright laws could challenge this form of cooperation by abolishing these two obstacles in the future (see section 4).

Why don't Collective Rights Organisations Merge?

One can wonder why the CSs of a given country do not merge their repertoires. Indeed, their integration could allow them to benefit fully from scale and scope economies, all the more since their contents are increasingly composite. In comparison to cooperation, integration allows better control of information and tasks within the organisation and to less uncertainty. Using transaction cost terminology, hierarchy allows a significant reduction in lead-time and information delays along with a more intense, efficient use of resources and competencies. Moreover, integration eliminates opportunist behaviour from partners who try to get discretionary power and so seize some part of the exchange surplus.

However, integration between CSs is unfeasible because of the difficulty in transferring specific assets. Of the five limits highlighted by Monetari and Ruffieux (1996), only two are suited to collective administration.

The first one is the legal appropriability associated to the protection of assets. As a matter of fact, each CS administrates exclusive copyrights which are specific assets and thereby very difficult to transfer. Historically, SACEM has conflicted with SACD, another CS, in order to manage some of its repertoire in the field of theatre. The former won and subsequently became France's first CS. Yet, the transfer of rights was not complete and a great deal of time and resources was spent in judicial procedures.

The second limit to the transfer of specific assets stems from the complexity of knowledge and to the heterogeneous experiences and experience among organisations. Each repertoire corresponds to one or several well-delimited markets. Joint use of these heterogeneous repertoires – for example, valorising them into audiovisual or multimedia markets – offers some advantages. However merging them could generate organisational costs due to the mix of incompatible human and technical competencies. These costs could significantly overshoot those generated by the sale and scope economies. Indeed, a repertoire is also a specific method to distribute collected sums – according to specific distribution keys – and specific legal practices: competencies in the fields of films are not the same as those in musical rights. Finally, every method is the result of longstanding experience and so is not easily transferable. Thus cooperation is a better, more flexible solution that creates new resources and permits CSs to maintain their monopoly over their respective repertoires while they coordinate their operations in various forms. The multimedia markets are a case in point.

3. COOPERATION IN OFFLINE MULTIMEDIA.

Multimedia brings the debate between proponents and detractors of collective administration to a climax. Multimedia is not a market, but rather an aggregate of various, interconnected activities that share the use of digital technologies. They allow digitalisation and compression of heterogeneous data: writing, sound and picture. So they both facilitate immediate, costless and perfect reproduction of copyright contents and have contributed the emergence of digital networks. Two main markets are to be distinguished: offline multimedia (for example, the CD-Rom market) and multimedia online (e.g., the electronic commerce of works).

In the first case, cooperation is horizontal and includes only the CSs. The institutions set up in this case are based on pre-existing structure and experiences. In this respect, offline multimedia markets do not pose any specific problem because of their similarities with traditional cultural industries. As a matter of fact, these cultural goods are reproduced on physical supports and generally commercialised in the same ways. This is not the case with online multimedia (see section 4).

Europe's Current Arrangements: Information Office and Joint Collective Organisation

One essential feature of CD-Rom products lies in the mix of text, sound and pictures, thus making CSs' repertoires complementary. Several European one-stop-shopping experiments are currently carried out to make the most of these complementarities. The system consists in regrouping the acquisition of several rights at the same time and place. This way, digital technologies facilitate the management of analogical rights with the creation of easily identifiable Internet websites like "ccc.com". Two main models of one-stop-shopping exist in Europe: on the one hand, the German and Dutch models in the form of an information office, and on the other, the France's SESAM that achieves quasi-integration between authors' societies.

The first model comprises an information office created by some CSs and whose function is to provide users with information about the copyright features of a given work. Is it currently protected or out of copyright? Which are its COs? Are they currently the actual assignee or do they transfer their copyright to a publisher? What are the length and the geographical scope of their rights? and so on. Germany's CMMV[6] is a relevant case of such an information office. It was created in November 1996 and a pay runs database delivering online information on copyrighted works. The purpose of this type of organisation is to offer an easily identifiable intermediate, which turns potential users towards COs. It is a non-profit multimedia rights clearing house. However, it does not take the place of its members in negotiating and managing copyright. So CMMV does not fully exploit scale economies.

On the other hand, France's SESAM presents a more sophisticated form of cooperation between authors' societies. It was established in 1996 by the main authors' societies. In addition to giving information to potential users, its main purpose is to take charge of copyright administration on behalf of its members in the fields of offline and online multimedia. It administrates the granting of rights and the distribution of collected sums according to conditions and tariffs determined by its members. This organisation does not hold its own repertoire. Rather, it joins together the multimedia capabilities of the authors' societies and thus represents a specific form of technical coordination seeking to adapt to the digital environment.

SESAM is also open to any COs, like publishers, for more efficient collective management. On the one hand, it facilitates COs' identification and right acquisition by users. Therefore reduced transaction costs and more complete contracts are obtained. On the other hand, it benefits from higher economies of scale and scope. However, acquiring copyright in order to produce derived works or exploit commercially existing works is one aspect, while electronic commerce of cultural goods is of a different nature: it requires even more enlarged cooperation that includes some users of works (see section 4).

SESAM benefits from the technical resources of SACEM and the competencies of its various members. Its first task was to finalise a pricing system adapted to each type of multimedia products (ludotainment, video games, and so on). The prices schedule and the online calculation of amounts to be paid are freely available on the SESAM site. Then, this joint organisation relies on learning and competencies of the SDRM (mechanical rights CS) in the field of the drawing-up of general contracts, the management of heterogeneous repertoires and the fight against piracy as well as the monitoring of blank CD factories and retail stores. Finally, SESAM can be described as a horizontal quasi-integration. There, CSs organise and valorise their resources and competencies and then negotiate the distribution of the rent created within this joint organisation. This way, they adapt to the growth of the CD-Rom market by coordinating and operating complementarities between their specific and intangible assets. They benefit therein from the fact that offline multimedia is similar to traditional cultural industries: both activities have the same distribution and sales networks, which are easily supervised. No new competencies need to be developed.

Toward more Competition between CSs on Membership?

Currently, CSs compete for the new membership of multimedia creators, which are also potential COs. Infographists, multimedia scriptwriters and designers are difficult to locate in the tangled map of copyright. Accurate classification of multimedia products is often impossible, except for video games for which the publisher is presumed to take charge of rights on behalf of creators (*work-made-for-hire*). So interference zones between criss-crossing repertoires expand and constitute areas for intense competition. Three French CSs – SACD (theatre, audiovisual fiction), SGDL (writers), SCAM (audiovisual documentary) – currently compete for the control of interactive scripts management. Finally, as a first mover – obtaining a dominant position on key assets – CSs can now lock in this new field and secure further expansion.

However, the regrouping of new COs could be hampered by incumbent membership and so generate insiders/outsiders effects. Insiders' opposition can be explained by the fear of less individual distribution, increasing charges due to diversification, refusal to share organisational benefits, previous conflicts, and so on. This situation shows that the cooperation between members is tightly linked with the historical compromises between them. In the case of the cinema, Jeancolas et al. (1996) underline the opposition between SACD insiders (theatre) and outsiders (film directors). The arguments of the former rest on the superiority of the dramatic art on popular entertainment, but above all they were afraid of competition from the movie theatres. The same situation currently occurs with the French composers' opposition to the membership of techno DJs.

4. NEW PRACTICES IN COPYRIGHT ADMINISTRATION OF ONLINE MULTIMEDIA.

Multimedia online represents new potential sources of remuneration for creators and producers of existing contents and digital works. It leads to more enlarged cooperation than offline multimedia. The original forms of coordination must be extended to all the agents involved in these activities.

Current Practices Called into Question.

The e-commerce of protected works gives arguments both to those who anticipate the break-up of copyright legislation and those in favour of more protection thanks to new technical potential. The arguments of the latter are twofold: on the one hand, the dematerialization of cultural goods and their distribution on networks make any illicit reproduction and use easier and cheaper. On the other hand, COs may enforce their prerogatives more efficiently by benefiting from the new technologies. The Electronic Copyright Management System (ECMS) designates all these new technical devices.

First, one can notice the inefficiency of traditional methods of copyright enforcement on the networks. Lawsuits as a warning or the simple monitoring by sworn agents have little or no deterrent effect on network users faced with quasi-public goods. Moreover, analogical supervisions generate high costs because of the great number of websites and hacking practices. So digital technologies make free riding and opportunistic behaviours like software online piracy possible. However, digital technologies do not only allow online copyright management. They also offer better protection against illicit practices. To achieve these purposes, many new technologies already exist: watermarking, overprinting, digital encryption and registration, electronic payment and surveillance, and so on.. They generally consist in visible or invisible insertion of writings and graphics in a digital work. Watermarking in the case of overprinting is visible, contrary to steganography that qualifies a technique of marking (hidden marking) designed to concealing copyright information within the digital copy.

Further, some conclude that direct and competitive negotiations are made possible between users and COs thanks to these new possibilities. According to this opinion – shared by both lawyers and economists –, the new networks are synonymous with a total desintermediation between agents and so increase social welfare, in contrast with the current situation, which implies intermediaries. As Hugenholtz noted (1995, pp. 4),

"The emerging digital networked environment is creating exciting new possibilities of solving the complexities of licensing a multitude of rights. Perhaps, the built-in intelligence of the superhighway will enable individual right holders to grant and administer licenses to users directly, without any intervening mechanism. Works disseminated over the superhighway might carry identifying "tags", inviting prospective users to automatically contact right owners, or "permission headers", with pre-determined licensing conditions (...). Such a system of "self-administration of rights" might eventually replace collective or cooperative licensing. If so, the digital network would bring back to right holders what they (nearly) lost in the age of mass copying: the power to transact directly with information users."

According to this scheme, prices decrease, competitive negotiations between COs and users occur and thus no cooperation is required. Our point of view is somewhat different.

The emergence of digital networks not only strengthens the tendencies toward cooperation but also toward more competition between CSs. Indeed, the harmonisation of national legislations and the cutting out of the costs of geographical distances represent the conditions of increasing competition. For instance, the reciprocal contract of representation could be challenged. The German CS would be therefore able to compete with the French one on the European markets without any additional costs of infrastructure. GEMA's managers have already touched on this prospect: "In the multimedia age, the European authors will still be able to choose which of the existing collecting societies in the member states of the EU they would like to join. In this way they can benefit from the differences that certainly exist in the services and costs charged (…)" (Kreile and Becker, 1996, pp. 17). Indeed, GEMA can offer lower tariffs to the SACEM members. Besides, CSs must cooperate if they are to manage their complementarities and this cooperation takes a vertical dimension.

Organisations will have to set up new management systems using very expensive digital technologies, to make up for their lack of competencies. Alliances then are required with other agents located downstream of multimedia industries in order to appropriate these lacking competencies as well as to obtain a dominant position in the membership field. The nature of cooperation is essentially pre-competitive and so takes place before the markets are formed. The partners currently seeking to exploit at best complementary resources and capabilities they control individually and collectively. Studying existing ECMS illustrates this point while questioning the desintermediation approach. More precisely, we show that cooperation is present and required through these new systems.

First, an ECMS is a technical system of copyright management in multimedia online activities including various technologies (overprinting, watermarking, encryption, digital monitoring and enforcement, e-payment, etc.) that allows for e-commerce of works and transfer of rights. According to ACN (1998), such a system would be ideal if it fulfils the following objectives:

provide copyright-protected material to users upon request; provide a means for remuneration (or a facility to grant or refuse licence) to flow to the owner; track usage of material (…) without interfering with the privacy of the user; prevent unlawful appropriation of the copyright material by people who are outside the system; prevent unlawful use of the copyright material by users who obtain the material legitimately in the first instance; ensure the integrity of the intellectual property; allow for a reasonable flow of information between owners to users (…) in the public interest (…); and allow for the effective operation of fair dealing within the ECMS.

So an ECMS fulfils two main functions. It requires close cooperation between the protagonists (CSs, owners of rights portfolios (majors), producers of contents and multimedia firms). On the one hand, ECMS and the Internet allow the setting up of *one-stop shopping*, namely a centralising system for the identification and negotiation of copyright and to which users turn in order to acquire rights for traditional or multimedia uses. "It would function as an intermediary between the commercial parties, users and rightsholders (…)." (Hulsink, 1996, pp. 5) Contrary to CSs, clearing houses do not hold any exclusive rights but they just facilitate the acquisition of rights. On the other hand, ECMS permit the emergence of e-commerce in works through the institution of norms. This implies that protagonists agree on the features and prerogatives of their joint organisation. The study of one ECMS experiment – the IMPRIMATUR demonstrator – illustrates these different points by pointing out how e-commerce in works requires the establishment of intermediaries. In particular, it shows what role CSs are likely to assume.

The IMPRIMATUR Demonstrator: A Concrete Application

Automated copyright management on digital networks and e-commerce use the same technologies, resulting in a large number of experiments being carried out in the USA and European countries. Recently, France's SESAM and other major European CSs have cooperated in a common project – Verdi (Very Extensive Rights Data Information) – within the Info 2000 European framework. Verdi consists in setting up a European information and granting online system designed to facilitate the acquisition of rights by multimedia producers. These various projects are the fruit of cooperation between CSs, publishers and collective users like libraries and online operators, all of which generally require the appropriation and the development of costly electronic devices. Individual COs thus would not be able to bear the costs of and control these tools on their own.

IMPRIMATUR (Intellectual Multimedia Property Rights Model and Terminology for Universal Reference) is currently one of the most operational, polyvalent ECMSs. It was part of ESPRIT, a European project that handles some experiments on new technologies applied to the copyright management. ALCS[7] coordinated the project from 1995 to 1998. It was established in order to estimate the impacts of methods of online buying and selling protected works as well as the online management of copyright. It is based on the cooperation of aforementioned agents that are indispensable for the project to become operational. A strict consensus is a *sine qua non* condition for the digital exploitation of works.

The basic scenario is the following: a supplier (publisher, producer, and so on) makes its catalogue of digitised works available to an online distribution company. This company stores the contents in a database and offers a promotional list to potential online consumers. They can consult the list freely, even listen to some extracts and then choose whether to buy online copies through electronic payment. The online distributor allows any COs of the stored contents to monitor its sales figures after receipt of its negotiated share. From this basic model, agents must add the ECMS functions, that is first to insert an authentication system and security of the transactions, and then to identify, monitor and grant licences.

As regards transaction security and authentication, partners must be able to identify each other before any exchange. This measure must be coupled with confidentiality about agents and contents. The SSL technical device fulfils these objectives: its features both cover data encryption and authentication of users and sellers through public key certificates. The implementation of an identity cards reader will improve the protocol. Besides, licences are granted, identified and policed by a single organisation, which assigns an ISW (International Standard Work Code) to each work. Furthermore, the codes supplier manages a database that lists and indexes copyright and COs. If the IMPRIMATUR project cannot prevent copyright infringements, it still facilitates their detection through digital encryption and watermarks of transmitted works. An ISWC is therefore incorporated when the work is digitised and before its supplier makes it available to online distributors. This one in his turn integrates specific codes to each copy it sells. This system thus allows traceability of works through the use of specific decoders.

The task of monitoring the actual uses of works ought to be carried out by an independent agent. As Koblin and Kockelkorn (1997, pp. 4) noted, "[i]n a fully fledged system, an independent Monitoring Service will mainly be concerned with large-scale supervision of financial and licensing transactions". To us, CSs could take charge of this function. As a matter of fact, they benefit from organisational capabilities and a large experience of monitoring, certification, price negotiation and both judicial and private settlements between COs and users.

Lastly, the granting of licences *in fine* must fulfil two main purposes. First, it must be able to provide suppliers and online distributors with copyright for the transmitted works from each individual CO. Secondly, it must grant licences to COs and suppliers whenever they produce multimedia works using original woks. For instance, an online designer can obtain rights via this system when he needs to incorporate protected contents such as musical samples or drawings into his website. Currently, licensing is temporarily based on blanket contracts, whereby which online distributors are authorised to sell an unlimited number of copies.

The IMPRIMATUR project is thus one of the first operational ECMSs. The resulting demonstrator articulates various components that combine both copyright management and e-commerce: identification number, encryption, electronic licensing and payment, copyright databases, and certification procedures. This prototype is all the more dynamic since its structure is based on independent modules and then is adjustable to technological innovations. Each component is replaceable by more effective or additional ones are transplantable like monitoring and metering systems. These various results imply close cooperation as shown by Liquid Audio, a Californian online music distributor and other British CSs (see appendix). This example also emphasises the persisting role of CSs in a digital world.

The Persisting Role of Collective Right Organisations.

Another lesson to be drawn by the study of the principles of demonstrators like IMPRIMATUR is that emerging e-commerce in cultural goods does not necessarily lead to total desintermediation between agents. Among the new online institutions, CSs could play a major role in shaping the copyright system: "[i]n the multimedia environment, the collecting societies expect to play a leading role because of their familiarity and expertise in the field of copyright, the information on rightsholders, and their exclusive position vis-à-vis granting access to the repertoire of a CS, and their authority in authorising licences to users and producers". (Hulsink, 1996, pp. 7) Nevertheless, various alternative organisational forms can complete the different roles allotted to cooperation: authors' societies are better run in France whereas union action is often preferred in Anglo-American countries. So should cooperation take the sole form of trade unions or the complex form of CSs (including the former)?

CSs first historical and institutional function is to act as unions, which lobby national and international institutions (cultural administrations, WIPO, European Commission) on behalf of their members. In addition, as unions they have to negotiate remuneration and take legal action against copyright infringes. So CSs employ competent lawyers in the fields of copyright and contractual laws. However what distinguishes these societies from others unions is their second function, that is the collective management of copyright. However, some maintain that new technologies challenge this additional function. According to them, it is henceforth possible to conceive an efficient arrangement in the form of labour division between CSs and their members. The former would enforce their members' rights whereas the latter would set their licence fees and conditions of use individually to form an electronic control and payment system monitoring the effective uses of their works. In other words, CSs should keep administrative copyright enforcement and maintenance of databases providing information on COs, their works and the various rights flows.

Such a system was first envisaged by the Besen et al. (1992) model. The *competitive licensing* system attempts to reconcile the advantages of competition with those of cooperation. Its main purpose is then to promote competitive negotiation between COs and users while keeping the advantages of collective administration in terms of economies of scale and scope. Indeed, the subadditivity of collective management costs leads individual agents to cooperate. Yet, the competitive licensing model aims to substitute individual licences and competition between COs for blanket licensing currently issued by CSs and monopolistic tariffs while maintaining collective administration. As a matter of fact, these organisations are supposed to be efficient in their enforcement tasks and so have to focus on them. Although blanket licensing results in monopoly pricing and therefore extracts all the users' surplus, competitive licensing would allow to be curtailed the royalties per work because of more competition between COs and direct negotiations with users. "Each user would be free to determine the number of songs for which he or she obtained licences, and the aggregate fee paid by a licensee would depend both on the number of works used and the fees set by copyright holders". (pp. 408). Moreover, this model assumes the existence of a single organisation in order to minimise transaction costs. Finally, all member share the equal costs of their organisation and then negotiated prices include their share plus marginal production cost of their works. As for direct competition between CSs, the monopolistic rent is partly transferred to users: competition between COs brings their price down to the level of administrative costs and marginal production costs.

However, if allocative efficiency can be reached, the same does not hold true for productive efficiency because of the largely higher management costs due to competitive licensing. Indeed, the number of transactions to be checked is higher in this case than in a blanket (once-for-all) contract. So the higher the administration costs, the larger the individual contribution and the lower the remuneration of each member. Beyond the break-even point, there is no incentive for membership and there are too few producers for competition to be practicable. It thereby mitigates the output restrictions prevailing under the blanket licence system. However, according to Besen et al. (pp. 409), "(...) these potential benefits must be balanced against the predictably higher administrative costs under competitive licensing".

In our view, this drawback in terms of prohibitive costs could be eliminated in the digital context. Indeed, ECMS projects like IMPRIMATUR can significantly bring down negotiation and enforcement costs. Once a CO has set his conditions and tariffs for a general database, the user can either pay or try to negotiate with him. However, there is no need for systematic negotiation nor for any recourse to compulsory licences or the uniform tariffs of blanket licences. CSs both focus on administration tasks and on their functions of certification and monitoring. They can exploit size economies and as unions they benefit from their members' confidence. Lastly, they can play additional roles, for example, in valuation and settlements between COs. They could become specific intermediaries.

5. CONCLUSION

New information and communications technologies finally allow more competition in the negotiations between COs and works' users. However they either eliminate cooperation, nor the need for it between the different stakeholders, or reduce the importance of copyright collectives. Antitrust authorities should take these observations into account every time they pass judgement on agreements between the various COs.

APPENDIX: A CONCRETE IMPRIMATUR APPLICATION: THE COOPERATION BETWEEN PRS/MCPS AND LIQUID AUDIO

The IMPRIMATUR prototype aims to facilitate the emergence in e-commerce of works. Setting up this system thus implies horizontal and vertical cooperation. This is undertaken in order to share resources and capabilities and test the operationality of the project. A concrete application is the alliance between MCPS and PRS (Performing right society), British CSs and Liquid Audio, a US online music distributor. This firm has finalised an integrated system of promoting/marketing/selling music on the Internet.

More specifically, the cooperation takes place upstream from an emergent activity: online distribution of digital music. It consists in grafting an ECMS on the product conceived by Liquid Audio, so it is brought into compliance with copyright law. As Hill (1998, pp. 1) notes, "[s]pecifically, the trial will involve the development of a prototype Web interface to provide users of Liquid Audios' systems, and other online music distribution companies, an integrated solution for managing copyright clearance for musical works (...) It will identify current rights ownership from its extensive database of sound recordings and musical works to process licence applications and, later, calculate the royalties due following the submission of associated usage data collected by companies such as Liquid Audio."

Carrying out such an automated system facilitates the emergence of e-commerce by accelerating licences from COs to users. After the system has confirmed whether COs allow their representative to grant rights, licences are automatically granted (or refused) to consumers by e-mail.

Thanks to the modularity of the IMPRIMATUR prototype, CSs can take advantage of any innovation by Liquid Audio in the fields of anti-piracy or digital encryption. These forms of cooperation represent learning opportunities for contributing parties in the digital markets. As a matter of fact, "[i]t is a prototype development from which it is anticipated that the contributing parties will learn more about the infrastructure requirements for licensing in the online environment, such as the scalability of systems required to match the volume of transactions" (Hill, pp. 2). Finally, this experiment allows PRS and MCPS to prove concomitant reproduction and distribution rights can be exercised on line, and that Liquid Audio can offer a law-abiding commercial system.

NOTES

1. Compulsory licensing is the third solution when neither individual nor collective exercise of copyright is possible. However COs are only entitled to perceive an institutional fee corresponding to the effective uses of their works. All these alternatives finally consist in collecting the social value of the works.
2. Société des auteurs, compositeurs et éditeurs de musique.
3. See Hollander (1984), Besen and Kirby (1992).
4. Gesellschaft für musikalische Aufführungs- und mechanische Vervielfältigungsrechte.
5. In 1999, under the aegis of CISAC, major CSs set up a coordinating system of their online databases: the Common Information System (CIS).
6. Clearingstelle Multimedia der Verwertungsgesellschaften für Urheber- und Leistungsschutzrechte.
7. Authors' licensing and collecting society, UK

REFERENCES

ACN (1998), "ECMS: what are they?", [acn.net.au/resources/ip]

Besen, S.M., Kirby, S.N. and Salop, S.C. (1992), "An economic analysis of copyright collectives.", *Virginia Law Review*, **78** (1), 387-413

Bessy, C. and Brousseau, E. (1997), "The governance of IPRs: patents and copyrights in France and in the US", WP ATOM, Université de Paris 1

Brousseau, E. (1996) "What institutions to organize electronic commerce.", *OECD Tokyo Workshop on the economics of the IS*, March 4-5.

European Commission (1997), *Proposal for a European Parliament and Council Directive on the harmonization of certain aspects of copyright and related rights in the Information Society.*

Dam, Kenneth W. (1999), "Self-help in the digital jungle", *Journal of Legal Studies*, **28** (2), pp.393-412.

Demsetz, H. (1967), "Towards a theory of property right", *American economic review, Papers and Proceedings*, **57** (2), May, 347-359.

Hill, K. (1998), "MCPS/PRS alliance to develop prototype systems to support online music licensing transactions", [www.imprimatur.alcs.co.uk]

Hoeren, T. (1995), "Long term solutions for copyright and multimedia products", in *The Information Society: copyright and multimedia*, LAB/EC, [www2.echo.lu].

Hollander, A. (1984), "Market structure and performance in intellectual property. The case of copyright collectives", *International journal of industrial organization*, **2**: 199-216.

Hugenholtz, P.B. (1995), "Licensing rights in a digital multimedia environment", in *The Information Society...* LAB/EC, [www2.echo.lu].

Hulsink, W. (1996), "Intellectual property rights in Europe's digital era. The coordination problems of creative and collective societies", SPRU, University of Sussex, [www.databank.it/ dbc/fair/wpseries.hmt].

Jeancolas, J.P, Meusy, J.-J. and Pinel, V. (1996), "*L'auteur du film - Description d'un combat*", Actes Sud - Institut Lumière - SACD, Arles.

Kaufmann, T. (1995), "Competition issues relevant to copyright and the information society", in *The Information Society: copyright and multimedia*, LAB/EC, [www2.echo.lu].

Koblin, J. and Kockelkorn, M. (1997), "The IMPRIMATUR multimedia IPR management system", [www.imprimatur.alcs.co.uk].

Kreile, R. and Becker, J. (1997), "Collecting societies in the information society. Economic and legal aspects", [www.gema.de/eng/public/jahr97]

Merges, R.P. (1996), "Contracting into liability rules: IPRs and collective rights organizations", *California Law Review*, **84** (5): 1293-1393.

Monateri, J.-C. and Ruffieux, B. (1996) "Le temps de la quasi-intégration : une approche dynamique.", *in* RAVIX, J-L. (eds), *Coopération entre les entreprises et organisation industrielle*, CNRS éditions, Paris.

Ravix, J.L. et al. (1996), *Coopération entre les entreprises et organisation industrielle*, CNRS éditions.

Smith, D.A. (1986), "Collective administration of copyright: an economic analysis", *Research in Law and Economics*, **8**, 137-151.

5.Strategic Technology Alliances: Trends and Patterns Since the Early Eighties

John Hagedoorn and Sarianna Lundan

1. INTRODUCTION

This chapter analyses some basic trends and patterns in inter-firm strategic technology partnering over the past two decades. The growth patterns in strategic technology partnering reveal that this phenomenon has become increasingly relevant during the period under investigation. Joint ventures, once the dominant form of partnering, have to a large extent been replaced by a wider variety of contractual agreements. International patterns in partnering are also discussed for the Triad (USA, Europe, Japan) in terms of changes in the distribution of domestic and cross-border alliances. Finally, the extent to which growth in contractual alliances complements foreign investment as a strategy for gaining access to competitive assets abroad is discussed.

2. A BACKGROUND TO R&D PARTNERSHIPS: MOTIVES, ORGANIZATIONAL SETTINGS AND SOME DEFINITIONS

Inter-firm R&D partnerships are part of a relatively large and diverse group of inter-firm relationships that lie between 'arm's length' market transactions and integration by means of mergers and acquisitions. When inter-firm relationships began to attract attention in both the economics and the business and management literature, a number of taxonomies of different modes of inter-firm relationships were introduced. Contributions such as those by Auster (1987); (Chesnais 1988) Contractor and Lorange (1988); Dussauge and Garrette (1999); Hagedoorn (1990, 1993); Narula (1999); Osborn and Baughn (1990) and Yoshino and Rangan (1995) have gradually become integrated in the literature to the extent that it now seems sufficient to outline the main forms of inter-firm relationships. Since the focus in this chapter is particularly on R&D partnerships, we will briefly discuss the antecedents to those partnerships, one can expect to have an impact on R&D, innovation and technological development.

If the degree of organizational interdependency is used as the criterion to distinguish between different types of co-operative arrangements (see for example, Hagedoorn (1990, 1993)), one arrives at the following classification:

- Licensing refers to agreements that provide unilateral technology access, frequently through patents, to a licensee in return for a fee. Cross licensing is a bilateral form of licensing whereby companies usually swap packages of patents to avoid patent infringements or exchange existing, codified technological knowledge.
- Second-sourcing agreements regulate the transfer of technology through technical product specifications in order to produce exact copies of products. In the case of mutual second sourcing this transfer takes place between two or more companies that transfer the technical specifications of different products.
- Customer-supplier relationships are co-production contracts and co-makership relations that basically regulate long-term contracts between vertically related, but independent companies that collaborate in production and supply. A specific case of customer-supplier relationships is R&D contracts where one company is sub-contracted by another company to perform particular R&D projects.
- Joint R&D pacts and joint development agreements are contractual relationships through which companies perform jointly-funded R&D projects or, in the case of joint development agreements, jointly work on the development of new products or processes.
- Joint ventures combine the economic interests of at least two separate companies in a distinct organizational entity. Profits and losses are usually shared in accordance with the equity investments by the parent companies. Joint ventures act as separate organisations that have regular company objectives such as production, marketing and sales, but also R&D if relevant, as a specific objective of the partnership.

In this context we will refer to R&D partnerships as the specific set of inter-firm collaborations where two or more firms, which remain independent economic agents and organisations, share some of their R&D activities. Such R&D partnerships are primarily related to two of the above-mentioned categories, that is, equity-based joint ventures and contractual partnerships, such as joint R&D pacts and joint development agreements. Since both of these modes of cooperation feature prominently in the following analysis, and since they are also the (empirically) most important forms of bilateral

R&D exchanges and joint R&D undertakings, we will discuss the joint venture and contractual modalities in somewhat more detail.

Joint ventures are certainly one of the oldest modes of inter-firm partnering. Joint ventures, including those involving a specific R&D program, have become well-known during the past decades (see, Berg et al. (1982); Hagedoorn (1996); Hladik (1985)). Joint ventures are organizational units created and controlled by two or more parent companies, and as such, they increase the organizational interdependence of the parent companies. Although joint ventures can be seen as 'hybrids' that fall between markets and hierarchies, they do come close to hierarchical organizational structures as parent companies share control over the joint venture (Williamson, 1996). However, joint ventures can also act as semi-independent units that perform standard company functions such as R&D, manufacturing, sales, marketing, and so on. It is this semi-independent status that enables companies to apply joint ventures in a broader strategic setting where companies enter new markets, reposition themselves in existing markets or use exit strategies in declining markets (Harrigan, 1988).

According to Hagedoorn (1996) and Narula and Hagedoorn (1999), the empirical evidence points to a decline in the popularity of joint ventures when compared to other forms of partnering. It can be hypothesized that the decreasing popularity is probably due to the organizational costs of joint ventures together with their high observed failure rate (Kogut (1988); Porter (1987)). More specifically, problems with the continuation of joint ventures, as discussed in the literature, are related to the risk of sharing proprietary knowledge, the 'appetite for control' by one partner and a divergence of strategic objectives (Harrigan (1985, 1988); Hladik (1985)).

Recent studies have established that non-equity, contractual forms of R&D partnerships, such as joint R&D pacts and joint development agreements, have become most important modes of inter-firm collaboration as their numbers and share in the total of partnerships has far exceeded that of joint ventures (Hagedoorn (1996); Narula and Hagedoorn (1999); Osborn and Baughn (1990)). These contractual agreements cover technology and R&D sharing between two or more companies in combination with joint research or joint development projects. Such undertakings imply the sharing of resources, usually through project-based groups of engineers and scientists from each parent company. Capital investment costs, such as laboratories, office space, equipment, and so on, are shared between the partners. Although these contractual R&D partnerships have a limited time-horizon due to their project-based organization, each partnership nonetheless appears to require a relatively strong commitment from the companies involved and a corresponding level of inter-organizational interdependence during the joint project. However, compared to joint ventures, the degree of organizational dependence between companies in an R&D partnership is still smaller, and the time-horizon of the project-based partnerships is, by definition, almost shorter (Hagedoorn, 1993).

The practical difference between the two main sub-categories of contractual R&D partnerships, that is, R&D pacts and joint development agreements, is quite small, and largely depends on the industry-specific importance of R&D. Thus in high-technology industries such as biotechnology, pharmaceuticals and information technology, these contractual arrangements are frequently focused on in-depth research activities, while in many other industries such partnerships will focus more on the development and engineering of new products or new processes rather than research.

Given the somewhat more informal nature of this form of collaboration, the R&D pacts and joint development agreements cover a wide variety of legal and organizational arrangements. Also, even more than in the case of joint ventures, these contractual R&D partnerships are to be seen as incomplete contracts,[1] since it is *a priori* impossible to specify the concrete results of the joint effort. Consequently, the causes for the popularity of contractual arrangements are to be found in the flexibility that companies achieve through entering into such relatively small-scale projects. Specifically, the costs of both intended and unintended terminations are much lower when compared to the costs of the termination of a joint venture, which involves the dissolution of a separate organization.

An interesting issue in this context is the overall motivation of companies to enter into different R&D partnerships. In general, it would appear that both a cost-economizing and a strategic rationale play a role. Cost-economizing motivation applies when at least one company enters the partnership, mainly to lower the cost of some of its R&D activities by sharing the costs with one or more other companies. The cost-economizing rationale can be expected to play a role, particularly in capital and R&D-intensive industries, such as the telecommunications equipment (capital goods) industry, where the costs of a single, large R&D project are beyond the reach of most individual companies (Hagedoorn, 1993). However, the strategic rationale becomes important when, for instance, companies decide to selectively enter into R&D partnerships that are not related to their core activities, while keeping their primary R&D activities within their own domain (Teece, 1986). The strategic intent of R&D partnerships is also apparent in those cases where companies jointly perform R&D in new, high-risk areas of R&D, whose future importance for the partners' technological capabilities remains uncertain for a considerable period of time.

From the results of several studies on the motives for inter-firm partnerships, It becomes apparent that in many cases the cost-economizing and strategic motivations are intertwined. Most studies on R&D partnerships or similar forms of alliances stress a variety of motivations for these relationships (see, Das et al. (1998); Eisenhardt and Schoonhoven (1996); Hagedoorn (1993); Hagedoorn et al. (2000); Lorenzoni and Liarini (1999); Mowery et al. (1996)). The most often discussed motivations (in no particular order) are:

- the need to monitor and engage in the cross-fertilization of technological disciplines,
- the need to achieve economies of scale and scope in R&D,
- the need to share the costs of R&D projects,
- the need to shorten the innovation cycle,
- the desire to incorporate complementary technologies,
- the desire to search for technological synergies,
- the desire to capture a partner's tacit knowledge,
- the desire to jointly manage R&D uncertainty.

Although partnerships are a crucial element in the overall strategy of many companies, for others they are irrelevant, and play only a complementary part in their strategic activities. There is some evidence to indicate that leading companies (market leaders and technology leaders) seek partnerships outside their core activities, searching for new activities and new technological oortunities beyond their current domain (Hagedoorn (1995); Hamel (1991); Hamel and Prahalad (1994). However, in general one can expect that many companies' motives for entering into R&D partnerships frequently have both a cost-economizing background and a strategic intent. Furthermore, it is important to comprehend the dynamic aspect behind this, as the motives of a company with multiple research programs can change over time due to both developments in the company itself, as well as within its environment and the partnership (Harrigan, 1988).

3. GENERAL PATTERNS IN R&D PARTNERSHIPS

Previous empirical research has established that inter-firm partnerships involving all types of cooperative agreements seemed to have flourished during the eighties (Chesnais (1988); Hergert and Morris (1988); Hladik (1985); OECD (1986; 1992)). This general growth pattern also alies to the particular group of partnerships studied in this chapter, that is, R&D partnerships, as shown in Figure 5.1, where the development of strategic alliances over time is charted by plotting the number of strategic alliances formed in a given year. In addition to the total number of new alliances entered into each year, the other two series represent the number of equity-based joint ventures and contractual alliances.

In fact, the 1980s mark a steep increase from about two hundred partnerships created annually to over five hundred new R&D partnerships each year at the turn of the decade. The first couple of years of the 1990s show a drop in new partnerships, to about three hundred and fifty annually. Yet, another peak is reached in 1995, with a record of nearly seven hundred new R&D partnerships. At the end of the twenty years or so for which data is available in the MERIT-CATI database,[2] the number of new R&D partnerships decreased again, to about five hundred new partnerships per annum. However, this number remains considerably higher than in most years since the early 1980s. One can thus conclude there has been a clear growth pattern in the new R&D partnerships since 1980.

Figure 5.1. Modes of alliances

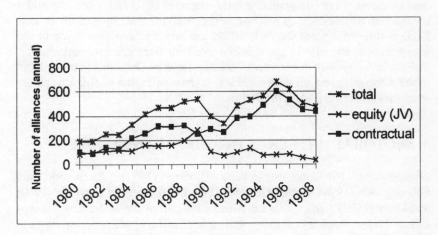

Possible explanations offered in the literature for this overall growth pattern of new R&D partnerships were discussed in the previous section. They were found to relate to the economic factors forcing companies to collaborate on R&D. Major factors mentioned in this context are linked to industrial and technological changes in the 1980s and 1990s, which led to the increased complexity of scientific and technological development, higher uncertainty surrounding R&D, increasing costs of R&D projects, and shortened innovation cycles that favor collaboration (see Contractor and Lorange

(1988); Hagedoorn (1993; 1996); Mowery (1988); Mytelka (1991); OECD (1992)).

In our discussion of the record to date, we also indicated that previous contributions had already established that during the 1980s the relative share of joint ventures in the total number of partnerships dropped considerably. It appears that contractual forms of partnering, in particular, have become an important instrument of inter-firm collaboration. When looking at the specific trend for R&D partnerships over the past two decades, one arrives at a similar conclusion.

If some small oscillations around an overall trend in Figure 5.1 are ignored, the most striking development is the explosion in contractual forms of alliances over the past 20 years. While in 1980 joint ventures and contractual alliances accounted for roughly half of all annual alliance formation, by 1998 contractual alliances accounted for about 90% of annual alliances. The trend has remained constant since the mid 1990s.

Thus the overall trends in inter-firm R&D partnering indicate two major developments. First, companies, in large measure, increasingly seem to prefer contractual partnerships to joint ventures. Second, that the growth in new R&D partnerships since the early 1980s has broadly been an outcrop of the overwhelming increase in the absolute numbers of contractual partnerships. The explosive growth in contractual alliances will be examined in more detail in the subsequent section with reference to the distribution of alliances across industries and other underlying factors.

4. SECTORAL PATTERNS IN R&D PARTNERSHIPS

Contributions by, amongst others, Ciborra (1991), Eisenhardt and Schoonhoven (1996), Gomes-Casseres (1996), Harrigan and Newman (1990) and Oster (1992) suggest that inter-firm partnerships are associated with so-called high-technology sectors and other sectors where learning and flexibility are important features of the competitive landscape. In such industries, partnerships enable companies to learn from a variety of partners in a flexible setting of (temporary) alliances across the value chain. Hagedoorn (1993), Link and Bauer (1989) and Mytelka (1991) also indicate that many of these partnerships are concentrated in a limited number of mainly R&D intensive industries.

Since this chapter is concerned with the patterns of R&D partnerships, we would expect that, given the asymmetrical distribution of R&D efforts across industries, the R&D partnerships would also be concentrated in specific industries. In particular, increased partnering in R&D-intensive industries should naturally ensue. For the purposes of this analysis we follow the OECD (1997) classification of sectoral R&D intensities, as measured by the share of total R&D expenses in total turnover. Accordingly, pharmaceuticals (including biotechnology), information technology and aerospace and defense are classified as high-technology sectors with R&D intensities between 10% and 15%. Instrumentation and medical equipment, automotive, consumer electronics and chemicals are classified as medium-technology industries with R&D intensities ranging between 3% and about 5%, while industries such as food and beverages, metals, oil and gas are classified as low-technology with an R&D intensity of below 1%.

Figure 5.2. Sectoral distribution of alliances

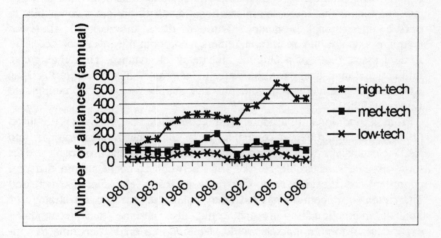

The 1980s and 1990s mark a period where the growth in R&D intensive industries, influenced by biotechnology and a range of information technologies, is reflected in the rising importance of these industries in R&D partnering. In Figure 5.2, the annual number of new alliances is divided into high, medium, and low-technology sectors. It can be observed that from 1980 to 1998 the share of high-technology industries in all newly established R&D partnerships grew from about 50% to over 80%. During the same period the share of medium-technology industries in these new R&D partnerships decreased sharply from about 40% to less than 20%. Thus, in addition to contributing to the explosive growth of contractual forms of alliances, high-technology alliances account for the vast majority of newly formed alliances over the past ten years.

5. INTERNATIONAL PATTERNS IN R&D PARTNERSHIPS

In many contributions to management literature (de Woot (1990); Ohmae (1990); Osborn and Baughn (1990); Yoshino and Rangan (1995)) and international business literature (Auster (1987); Contractor and Lorange (1988); Dunning (1993); Duysters and Hagedoorn (1996); Hagedoorn and Narula (1996); Mowery (1988); Mytelka (1991)) international partnerships or alliances are considered an important element in the international strategies of a growing number of companies. The basic argument in most of these contributions is that increased international competition forces companies to pursue international strategies. Through these international strategies companies do not only seek foreign market entry but they also seek access to foreign assets (both of a tangible and intangible nature). They thus create international inter-firm partnerships for the international sourcing of R&D, as well as for international production and supply (see e.g., Dunning and Lundan (1998)) .

From a traditional transaction cost economics perspective (Williamson (1996)), one would expect companies to be somewhat hesitant to enter into R&D partnerships with foreign companies due to the lack of control over long distances, a possible lack of trust between companies from different countries, and the high asset specificity of R&D. However, as increased international competition has led many companies to follow a strategy of gradual internationalisation, one could also assume that accumulated experience in foreign markets would also tend to a gradual opening to non-domestic R&D partnerships (Hagedoorn and Narula, 1996). Consequently, one would expect that, in the context of the overall importance of internationalisation to companies, the share of international R&D partnerships in the total number of R&D partnerships should have increased as well in the last two decades.

In Figure 5.3, the top line represents the total number of annually alliances, while the other two series included in the figure represent the number of domestic and international alliances respectively. Somewhat contrary to expectation, the internationalisation trend seems to demonstrate a gradual downturn from about 70% in the early 1980s to about 60% of all alliances in the early 1990's. In fact, the late 1990s end with a below 50% share of international partnerships in all new R&D partnerships. Remarkably this share in the total number of new alliances is more than twice as high as in 1980.[3]

Figure 5.3. International alliances

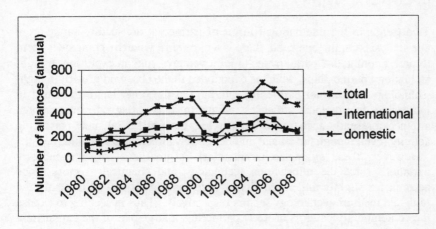

Table 5.1. Total counts and proportional share of different alliance types 1980-1998

	international	domestic	Total	equity (JV)	contractual	Total
high-tech	3336	2728	6064	1158	4908	6066
	55%	*45%*	*100%*	*19%*	*81%*	*100%*
med-tech	1290	643	1933	930	1003	1933
	67%	*33%*	*100%*	*48%*	*52%*	*100%*
low-tech	357	296	653	250	404	654
	55%	*45%*	*100%*	*38%*	*62%*	*100%*
Total	4983	3667	8650	2338	6315	8653

Source: MERIT-CATI database

Out of all the alliances entered into from 1980 to 1998 (in a total count of 8650), 70% are high-technology alliances, and out of the high-technology alliances, 81% are contractual alliances. By examining the proportional share shown in Table 5.1., one finds that, while in absolute terms high-technology alliances are much more prevalent than medium or low-technology alliances, the share of international alliances is highest for medium technology, and to a lesser extent, high technology categories, while the share of contractual agreements is overwhelmingly dominant in high-technology alliances.

6. CONCLUSIONS

Two trends in the international forms of partnering are readily aarent from our analysis. On the one hand, there is a clear shift whereby companies seem to prefer contractual partnerships to joint ventures, and an explosion in high-technology partnerships, which is expounded in the observed growth in high-technology contractual partnering activity. On the other hand, the trend in increasing international alliances seems to have changed. International alliances presently account for slightly less than half of all new partnering activity (even though the annual number of new alliances has doubled).

However, these aggregate trends mask a great deal of inter-industry variation, since the information technology and chemicals sectors alone account for slightly under and slightly over half of all new alliances in the high and medium-technology sectors respectively. Thus in seeking to expose the contemporary patterns of R&D partnering, a large part of the explanation arises from the behavior of the 'representative firm', which at end of the 1990s is an American information technology company that forms a contractual alliance with a domestic (or international) competitor.

Any industry-specific developments aside, the overall growth in partnering activity is related to the internationalisation process of firms within the Triad, and 'second generation' thinking concerning the value of knowledge-intensive assets outside the firm, whether located domestically or abroad. While in the earlier stages of internationalisation, firms tend to keep their R&D-related activities closer to home, the increased partnering activity is an outgrowth of the internationalisation of the R&D function, which has also resulted in the establishment of corporate R&D centres abroad. While equity-based forms of collaboration will still be preferred in some instances, the extent of foreign sourcing of knowledge-based assets in highly competitive industries is such that only contractual modes can often be considered cost-effective.

NOTES

1. It is recognised that to an extent, all contracts are incomplete, and achieve their completeness from the institutions that are involved in their enforcement, including the social capital existing between the parties.

2. The composition of the MERIT-CATI database has been discussed extensively, see for example, Hagedoorn and Narula (1996).
3. While our investigation is not strictly limited to the Triad countries, in practice 95% of all R&D partnerships within the database occur within the Triad of the United States, Europe and Japan (Narula and Hagedoorn (1999)).

REFERENCES

Auster, E.R. (1987), " International corporate linkages: Dynamic forms in changing environments", *Columbia Journal of World Business,* **22,** 3-13.

Berg, S. V., Duncan, J., and Friedman, P. (1982), *Joint Venture Strategies and Corporate Innovation,* Oelgeschlager, Gunn & Hain, Cambridge, MA,.

Chesnais, F. (1988), "Technical cooperation agreements between firms", *STI Review,* **4,** 51-120.

Ciborra, C. (1991), "Alliances as learning experiments: cooperation, competition and change in high-tech industries", In L. K. Mytelka, (ed) *Strategic Partnerships and the World Economy*, London, Pinter.

Contractor, F. J., and Lorange, P. (1988), "Cooperative strategies in international business", Lexington, MA, Lexington Books.

Das, S., Sen, P. K., and Sengupta, S. (1998), "Impact of strategic alliances on firm valuation", *Academy of Management Journal,* **41,** 27-41.

DE WOOT, P., 1990, *High Technology Europe: Strategic Issues for Global Competitiveness*, Blackwell, Oxford.

Dunning, J. H. (1993), *Multinational enterprises and the global economy,* Wokingham, Berkshire, Addison Wesley.

Dunning, J. H., and Lundan, S. M. (1998) "The geographical sources of competitiveness of firms: An econometric analysis", *International Business Review,* **7** (2), 115-133.

Dussauge, P., and Garrette, B. (1999), *Cooperative Strategy - Competing Successfully through Strategic Alliances,* Wiley, Chichester.

Duysters, G., and Hagedoorn, J. (1996), "Internationalization of corporate technology through strategic partnering: an empirical investigation", *Research Policy,* **25,** 1-12.

Eisenhardt, K. M., and Schoonhoven, C. B. (1996), "Resource-based view of strategic alliance formation: Strategic and social effects in entrepreneurial firms", *Organization Science,* **7,** 136-150.

Gomes-Casseres, B. (1996), *The Alliance Revolution : the New Shape of Business Rivalry,* Harvard University Press, Cambridge, MA.

Hagedoorn, J. (1990), "Organisational modes of inter-firm cooperation and technology transfer", *Technovation,* **10,** 17-30.

Hagedoorn, J. (1993), "Understanding the rationale of strategic technology partnering: inter-organizational modes of cooperation and sectoral differences", *Strategic Management Journal*, **14**, 371-385.

Hagedoorn, J. (1995), "A note on international market leaders and networks of strategic technology partnering", *Strategic Management Journal*, **16**, 241-250.

Hagedoorn, J. (1996), "Trends and patterns in strategic technology partnering since the early seventies", *Review of Industrial Organization*, **11**(5), 601-616.

Hagedoorn, J., Link, A. L., and Vonortas, N. (2000), "Research partnerships", *Research Policy*, **29**, 567-586.

Hagedoorn, J., and Narula, R. (1996), "Choosing organizational modes of strategic technology partnering: International and sectoral differences", *Journal of International Business Studies*, **27** (2), 265-284.

Hamel, G. (1991), "Competition for competence and inter-partner learning with international strategic alliances", *Strategic Management Journal*, **12**, 83-103.

Hamel, G., and Prahalad, C. K. (1994), *Competing for the Future*, Harvard Business School Press, MA, Boston.

Harrigan, K. R. (1985), *Strategies for joint ventures*, Lexington, MA, Lexington Books.

Harrigan, K. R. (1988), "Joint ventures and competitive strategy", *Strategic Management Journal*, **9**, 141-158.

Harrigan, K. R., and Newman, W. H. (1990), "Bases of interorganization co-operation: Propensity, power, persistence", *Journal of Management Studies*, **27**, 417-.

Hergert, M., and Morris, D. (1988), "Trends in international collaborative agreements", In Contractor, F. J., and Lorange, P. (eds.) *Cooperative strategies in international business*, Lexington Books, Lexington, MA.

Hladik, K. J. (1985), *International joint ventures*, Lexington Books, Lexington, Mass.

Kogut, B. (1988), "Joint ventures: Theoretical and empirical perspectives", *Strategic Management Journal*, **9**, 319-332.

Link, A. N., and Bauer, L. L. (1989), *Cooperative research in U.S. manufacturing: Assessing policy initiatives and corporate strategies*, Lexington Books, Lexington, MA.

Lorenzoni, G., and Liarini, A. (1999), "The leveraging of interfirm relationships as a distinctive organizational capability: A longitudinal study", *Strategic Management Journal*, **20**, 317-338.

Mowery, D., Oxley, J. E., and Silverman, B. S. (1996), "Strategic alliances and interfirm knowledge transfer", *Strategic Management Journal*, **17**, 77-91.

Mowery, D. C., (1988), *International Collaborative Ventures in U.S. Manufacturing*, Ballinger, Cambridge.

Mytelka, L. K. (1991), *Strategic Partnerships and the World Economy*, Pinter, London.

Narula, R. (1999), "Explaining the growth of strategic R&D alliances by European firms", *Journal of Common Market Studies,* **37** (4), 711-23.

Narula, R., and Hagedoorn, J. (1999), "Innovating through strategic alliances: moving towards international partnerships and contractual agreements", *Technovation,* **19**, 283-294.

OECD (1986), *Technical Cooperation Agreements between Firms: Some Initial Data and Analysis,* Paris, OECD.

OECD (1992), *Technology and the Economy,* Paris, OECD.

OECD (1997), *Revision of the High Technology Sector and Product Classification,* Paris, OECD.

Ohmae, K. (1990), *The Borderless World,* HarperCollins.

Osborn, R. N., and Baughn, C. C. (1990), "Forms of interorganizational governance for multinational alliances", *Academy of Management Journal,* **33** (3), 503-519.

Oster, S. M. (1992), *Modern Competitive Analysis,* New York, Oxford University Press.

Porter, M. E. (1987) "From competitive advantage to corporate strategy", *Harvard Business Review,* May-June, 3-59.

Teece, D. J. (1986), "Profiting from technological innovation: Implications for integration, collaboration, licensing and public policy", *Research Policy,* **15**, 285-305.

Williamson, O. E. (1996), *The Mechanisms of Governance,* Oxford University Press, Oxford.

Yoshino, M. Y., and Rangan, U. S. (1995), *Strategic Alliances,* Boston, MA, Harvard Business School Press.

PART II

Process and Evolution of Cooperation

6. Important Collaboration Partners in Product Development

Preben Sander Kristensen and Anker Lund Vinding

1. INTRODUCTION

The benefits of external collaboration for a firm's product development were already pointed out in the 1972 SAPPHO studies (Rothwell et al., 1974), and although the benefits of collaboration are overshadowed by stronger intra-firm factors in studies of product development success (Cooper and Kleinschmidt, 1987; Hartley et al., 1997), they have since been central to many publications on product development focusing on collaboration within dyads (von Hippel, 1998), networks (Håkansson, 1987) and systems (Lundvall, 1992). In empirical studies, the unit of analysis has accordingly varied from studies of dyads (Senker and Sharp, 1997) over studies of multi-party collaboration (Håkansson, 1987, ch. 3) to studies of systems (Fagerberg, 1992). The methods vary from studies of single (Wood et al., 1996) and comparable (Senker and Sharp, 1997) cases to surveys of collaboration, of which the Community Innovation Survey (CIS) (Smith, 1997) is the most comprehensive. Finally, the theoretical background for the studies vary from transaction cost economics (De Jong, 1999) to the manifold traditions found in management science literature (Harabi, 1998, n.8). In these terms, the present study of partner importance is a survey of dyadic collaboration based on propositions from management science.

Whereas the benefits and the extent of collaboration are often described, the costs associated with realising product development collaboration are less frequently examined. Nevertheless, as discussed by Leonard-Barton and Sinha (1993); Leverick and Littler (1994); Bruce et al., (1995a); Bruce, et al., (1995b) and Littler et al., (1995) they are quite considerable and are not always matched by the importance of the collaboration for the overall outcome of the product development process.

In short, no empirical evidence exists to support a claim that in general product development involving collaboration is, as a whole, more advantageous to individual firms than intra-firm product development, given the capability firms have for mastering collaboration activities. Or, as expressed by Day (1994): "Despite recent emphasis on the establishment, maintenance, and enhancement of collaborative relationships, few firms have mastered this capability and made it a competitive advantage". On this basis, it can be concluded that a need exists for advice on better management of collaboration.

Here, a single management problem is addressed: the initial screening of potential partners.

At one end of the spectrum, the frequent assertions concerning the benefits of collaboration can result in the involvement of too many partners, and this may in turn prove to be counterproductive. The task for such projects is to identify and eliminate those partners whose importance to the project will most probably only be small.

At the other end of the spectrum, the often considerable concerns firms have with respect to the inconvenience and costs associated with establishing a collaborative relationship, compared with carrying out the project in-house, can prevent the establishment of the collaborative relationships which may have been productive and profitable. In such projects, the task is to screen for partners who could be profitably approached and invited to take part in collaboration because of the high probability they could be important to the project.

On this basis, the objective of this study is to identify the characteristics, which can be observed before a collaborative relationship is established. This correlates to the subsequent evaluation of the importance of the partner's contribution to the project.

Scaling of Dependent Variables

The simplest expression of the importance of different types of partners for a firm's product development, is a count of how often the types of partner concerned feature as collaboration partners in the respective firms and projects studied. One type of partner can in this respect have one of two values:
- taking part in one or more of the firm's projects
- not taking part in any of the firm's projects.

The quantitative observation that customers, for example, feature as partners in firms' development projects more often than universities could be said to illustrate the extent to which collaboration with customers is of greater importance to the sum of firms' product development in a national economy than to collaboration with universities. But the observation says nothing about the extent to which the individual firm had established a better collaborative relationship with customers than with universities. It could well be the case that customers' contributions to product development are more likely to be small and trivial, whereas universities' contributions – in the few instances in which they are partners – are more likely to be large and innovative.

For this reason, the scaling of the importance of individual collaboration partners for product development projects has been expanded. This takes place in two dimensions.

First, it is assumed that, compared to a partner who simply takes part in a random project in the firm, a partner who takes part in precisely the project which the firm itself considers to be its most important development project is of greater importance. In this respect, one type of partner can have one of two values:

- taking part in the most important of the firm's projects
- taking part in one or more of the firm's other projects.

Next, it is assumed that scaling can be continued for the partners in the most important project by asking the firm about the importance the partner had in the completion of the project.

In CIS studies, the answers to the importance of different sources of information were Likert scaled from insignificant to crucial. In a study of the importance of different customer- and supplier-cooperative modes for the innovative activities Harabi (1998) uses a similar 5-point scale from "not important at all" to "very important".

In the present survey the scale used when the informant was asked about the importance of each partner for the completion of the firm's most important project was: "don't know", "little importance", "some importance", "great importance" or "crucial importance". A few linguistic subtleties aside, the scale can be seen as parallel to that used in the CIS surveys.

For scaling, it is crucial that partners who had subsequently proven to be of no importance to the completion of the project be included. Therefore, in the first part of the interview, the informant was asked which partners the firm had collaborated with at all, that is, avoiding any lower limit for the importance of the collaboration.

The questions concerning the importance of each of these partners were not asked until the second the part of the interview was conducted several months later.

Independent Variables

The objective was to examine the extent to which there was a relationship between the importance the partner ultimately had for the project and variables, which could be observed before establishing collaboration. The survey examined characteristics in the partner, in the project and in the firm itself.

2. THE STUDY

The focus of the survey was on the extent and patterns of collaboration with domestic and foreign partners in the development of products in Denmark's manufacturing industry. The interviews were computer-administered telephone interviews conducted in 1997/98. They consisted of two parts for each firm.

The part of the questionnaire that is of interest here had three levels of analysis: initially, the focus was on the total number of collaboration partners involved in all product development in the firm within the past two years. Next, the focus moved to the partners involved in the most important collaboration project, and finally, the focus moved to the importance of each individual partner.

"KO", a Danish database, was used to identify firms. This database comprised 5923 firms with 10 or more employees listed under the heading Manufacturing (NACE codes 15 to 36). Among these, 1500 were randomly selected and contacted by telephone.

The first part of the interview was conducted on 1022 manufacturing firms. Analysis of the incidence of non-contact and non-response showed (Kristensen et al., 1998, tab. 1, 2) that the bias between the firms in the entire population and the interviewed firms distributed according to firms' size and industry is so small that we consider it to have no importance.

In the interview, a common understanding of the concept of "product development" was established by reading the following statement to the informant:

> In this survey "product development" means the development of a tangible product which in its design, its construction, its productive capacity or in any other way is new to the company. We are not thinking of small modifications which only affect the appearance of the product. Nor are we thinking about cases where the company's products are adapted to each individual customer as a matter of routine. Nor does the survey cover development of new processes in the company's

production, such as introducing machinery with new technology or a new organisation of the production process.

If the informant expressed doubt, it was further clarified (Kristensen et al., 1998, "help screen 6").

Out of the 1022 firms, 548 had developed one or more products over the last two years. These firms were then asked whether they had collaborated with different types of domestic and foreign partners during the development processes. If the informant expressed any doubt, the following explanation was provided: "It is collaboration if, for example, the collaboration partner has specially designed a component or provided knowledge about something which is important for product development. On the other hand, it is not collaboration if in connection with the development of a product a supplier has made a bid to supply a certain number of standard components".

A total of 531 firms had developed one or more of the products in collaboration. Among them, the second part of the interview was completed with 294 firms. In this case too, analysis showed (Kristensen et al., 1998, tab. 1, 2) that there was no significant bias between the firms where continuation of the interview was relevant and the interviewed firms.

If we assume that the proportion of all firms in the original population where collaborative development took place is just as high as the known proportion among the firms who answered the first part, it is possible to estimate the response rate for the second part of the interview: (68% of 76%)= 52%, with no significant bias.

3. RESULTS AND DISCUSSION

Importance of Partners

Collaboration on most important projects
In the first part of the interview, the informants were asked which of the product development projects on which the firm collaborated was of greatest importance to the firm. In the second part of the interview, the firms were asked what it was about the project which had made the informant consider the project of greatest importance. Responses were recorded and transcribed.
The results show that 15 projects were the most important for the trivial reason that they were the only ones, and 37 could either not be placed under one category or no response was obtained.

Process and Evolution of Cooperation

Figure 6.1. Number of collaboration partners by type

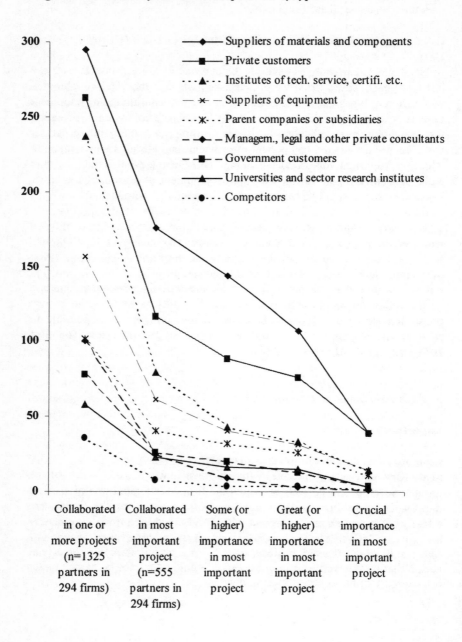

In the remaining 241 responses, the largest group concerned 87 projects which were chosen as the most important because of their market potential.

The second largest group concerned 49 projects of importance to the firms' product portfolio, and the remaining 105 projects were coded in minor categories, for example, 12 were important because the development involved new technology for the firm.

When market potential is cited as the reason, it could be rationalisation after the fact, in instances where the project had since proven to be a market success. Conversely, other reasons could be given for those projects, which have since failed on the market.For each project, the informant was asked: "Has the project led to a successful market introduction of a new product?". The projects which were singled out as being important because of their market potential do not distinguish themselves to any significant degree from the others in terms of whether they exceeded or met expectations.

Importance to the completion of the project.
The following question was asked to each partner: "How do you rate the importance of this partner as a collaboration partner for the completion of the project?". For 60 among the 555 partners who took part in the 294 projects, the answer was "don't know". The following tables are based on the 495 partners where importance was rated.

Figure 6.1 shows the responses of the 294 firms, which answered both the first and second parts of the interview. It first shows the 1325 partners in all projects in the firms. Then follow the 555 partners who took part in the most important project in each firm. The number of partners who were of "little or no importance" or where the answer was "don't know" is then subtracted to give the next value to the right. From this value, the number of partners of "some importance", and finally, the number of partners of "great importance" is subtracted.

In this case, too, an endeavour has been made to validate the responses. In the survey, the following open question was asked about each partner: "What expertise from this partner was exploited in this project?". If it is true that a partner was of little importance, it will accordingly be very difficult to describe the expertise involved, whereas, at the other end of the scale, it is unlikely to be difficult to describe the expertise possessed by a partner of crucial importance. This also proved to be the case. For the partners who were cited as being of little importance to the project, 46% of informants could not describe the expertise involved. For the partners who had been of crucial importance, the corresponding figure was 4%.

Importance as a Function of More than One Variable

The "importance of partner" variable was determined on the basis of the informant's subjective assessments. The variable is of course correlated with a range of other subjective assessments of the same partner in the survey, for example, trust in the partner and the reputation of the partner. In addition to these tautological correlations, the variable may be correlated with a number of observable variables:
- in the partner:
    (a) the location of the partner (domestic; foreign),
    (b) whether the partner concerned had previously been involved in collaboration on product development (old; new),
    (c) the type of partner in relation to the value chain for the eventual product.
    Analysis of the results for each of the types of partner in Figure 6.1 showed that there are only minor intra-group variations if they are pooled in the following three groups: suppliers; partners outside the value chain; customers.
- in the project:
    (d) man-months invested in the project (0-12; 13-),
    (e) duration of the project, months (0-12; 13-24; 25-),
    (f) the reason for the importance of the project (market; other),
- in the firm itself:
    (d) number of employees (10-49; 50-),
    (e) industrial sector (supplier-dominated; scale-intensive; specialised suppliers; science-based).
A logit-linear estimation of importance as a function of these variables using CATMOD procedure (SAS, 1989, ch. 17) shows significant ($p < 0.01$) correlation with the type of partner and with previous collaborative relationship. In the following tables, the material is classified in accordance with one or both of these two variables.

Characteristics in the Partner

Type of partner
From Table 6.1A it can be seen that both the absolute frequency and its importance are highest for the types of partner who over and above their role in the firms' product development process also play a role – and are designated accordingly as customers and suppliers – in the value chain for the products which the firm manufactures and develops.

Previously collaborated with partner

For each of the 495 partners, the survey asked: "Had you previously developed products in collaboration with this partner?" Overall results in table 6.1B show that firms most often collaborate with new partners. However, it is interesting that for both suppliers and partners outside the value chain, there is a significant correlation showing that old partners were attributed with being of greater importance to the completion of the firm's most important project than new partners involved in the project.

Compared to a previous study where respondents freely listed factors affecting the outcomes of collaborative development (Bruce et al., 1995) and where past collaboration experience was only given by 2% of respondents, results in table 6.1B are surprising. It may accordingly be seen as an overall expression of the correlation with a range of other partners' characteristics, which had been experienced and developed through previous collaboration. Nor is there any doubt that the figures reflect a screening on the basis of the firm's experience, inasmuch as some of the previous partners proven to be unimportant in earlier projects are disregarded when a firm sets about initiating a new collaborative relationship.

Table 6.1. Importance by characteristics in the partner

| | Importance of partner: | | | | |
	Little	Some	Great	Crucial	N
(A) type of collaboration partners **					
Suppliers	15%	21%	39%	24%	217
Outside value chain	29%	17%	33%	21%	146
Customers	18%	14%	35%	33%	132
					495
(B) previous partners (old) and first-time partners					
Suppliers **					
Old	9%	16%	45%	31%	94
New	20%	25%	35%	20%	123
Outside value chain **					
Old	20%	14%	38%	28%	76
New	39%	20%	27%	14%	70
Customers [ns]					
Old	13%	16%	39%	32%	56
New	22%	13%	32%	33%	76
					495

(C) old and new domestic and foreign collaboration

Old suppliers ***

Domestic	8%	15%	56%	21%	62
Foreign	9%	19%	22%	50%	32

New suppliers [ns]

Domestic	22%	27%	30%	22%	74
Foreign	18%	22%	43%	16%	49

Old outside value chain [ns]

Domestic	24%	14%	42%	20%	50
Foreign	12%	15%	31%	42%	26

New outside value chain [ns]

Domestic	43%	21%	23%	13%	53
Foreign	24%	18%	41%	18%	17

Old customers *

Domestic	10%	10%	46%	34%	41
Foreign	20%	33%	20%	27%	15

New customers [ns]

Domestic	22%	12%	39%	27%	41
Foreign	23%	14%	23%	40%	35

* chi-square tests of independence   495
* $p < .10$; ** $p < .05$; *** $p < .01$; ns = not significant

Characteristics in the Firm

Size

It is often assumed (Rothwell et al., 1982) that product development processes proceed differently in small firms compared to larger firms. Table 6.2A shows that, apart from the customers attributed with greater importance by small, as opposed to larger firms, the results from the small firms deviate surprisingly little from those from the larger firms.

Industrial sector

Making use of the SPRU database, Pavitt (1984) developed a taxonomy of sectoral patterns of innovation: supplier-dominated; two types of production-intensive (scale-intensive and specialised suppliers) and science-based.

Suppliers can be expected to be attributed with greater importance by firms in the supplier-dominated sector than by other firms. According to Pavitt, technological progress is dependent on external actors, such as suppliers. In the survey, we found evidence of this pattern. As can be seen from Table 2B, suppliers are of greater importance to firms in the supplier-dominated sector than to other firms.

Table 6.2. Importance by characteristics in the firm

	Importance of partner:				
	Little	**Some**	**Great**	**Crucial**	**N**
A) partners collaborating with firms in each size					
Suppliers ns					
10-49 employees	17%	23%	38%	23%	133
50 or more employees	12%	19%	42%	27%	84
Outside value chain ns					
10-49 employees	27%	13%	34%	26%	92
50 or more employees	31%	24%	31%	13%	54
Customers *					
10-49 employees	17%	10%	39%	34%	92
50 or more employees	20%	25%	25%	30%	40
					495
B) partners collaborating with firms in					
Suppliers *					
Supplier dominated	12%	12%	51%	25%	59
Other sectors	16%	25%	35%	24%	158
Outside value chain ns					
Science-based	29%	18%	32%	21%	28
Other sectors	29%	17%	33%	21%	118
Customers ns					
Specialized suppliers	15%	15%	44%	27%	41
Other sectors	20%	14%	31%	35%	91
** chi-square tests of independence*					495

* $p < .10$; ns = not significant

Partners outside the value chain could be expected to be more important to firms in the science-based sector. As shown by Pavitt, the main source of technology in these firms is in-house development, together with the underlying science developed in universities. However, as illustrated in Table 6.2B, no significant correlation is evident.

Finally, customers could be expected to be of greatest importance to firms in the sector of specialised suppliers. For these firms the collaboration pattern is primarily based on user interaction, in accordance with Pavitt. Nor in this case is the expected correlation evident.

Characteristics in the Project

Projects important for market-related reasons.
As shown above, the survey revealed 87 projects for which the market was cited as being the reason for the project's importance.

As expected (Day, 1994), there are, among these projects, more customers who feature as collaboration partners (0.6 as opposed to 0.4 customers per project). Yet, as shown in Table 6.3, given that they participate, these customers are not attributed to a significantly greater degree with being of great or crucial importance to the completion of the project.

There are no noteworthy differences with respect to suppliers. However, there is an interesting significant correlation for partners outside the value chain. The correlation can be illustrated by using universities as an example. They were not involved in any of the projects which were singled out as being important for market-related reasons but were involved as partners in 11% of the other projects.

Table 6.3. Importance by characteristics in projects given as important for market and for other reasons

	Importance of partner:				
	Little	Some	Great	Crucial	N
Suppliers [ns]					
Market reasons	11%	30%	33%	26%	57
Non market reasons	17%	18%	41%	24%	160
Outside value chain **					
Market reasons	41%	26%	11%	22%	27
Non market reasons	26%	15%	38%	21%	119
Customers [ns]					
Market reasons	13%	12%	42%	33%	52
Non market reasons	21%	16%	30%	33%	80
* *chi-square tests of independence*					495

** $p < .05$; ns = not significant

Importance to the Firm's Product Development Capability in the Long Run

The final question in the interview extended beyond the project concerned: "I would like your assessment of the overall importance of the partner to your firm's possibilities for product development in the long run: How do you rate the importance of this partner as a collaboration partner for your firm's ability to develop new products?". The scale used was the same as for importance for the project. Among the 495, the answer was "don't know" for 12.

Table 6.4. *Old and new partners by importance in the long run and in the project*

	Greater in long run than in project	Same in long run and in project	Lesser in long run than in project	N
Suppliers [ns]				
Old	23%	53%	23%	94
New	34%	46%	20%	122
Outside value chain [ns]				
Old	19%	53%	27%	73
New	32%	45%	23%	65
Customers [ns]				
Old	38%	38%	24%	55
New	27%	49%	24%	74
* chi-square tests of independence				483

[ns] = not significant

When the responses to the questions on importance in the project and those in the long run are juxtaposed as in table 6.4, it can be seen that 38% of the old partners from amongst customers are attributed with being of greater importance in the long run than there are to the most important project, whereas this only applies to 27% of the new partners.

This contrasts with the situation for partners outside the value chain and suppliers. In this case, more often than previous partners, the new partners are being of greater importance in the long run than they are for the project concerned.

The figures are not significant but may reflect a more long-term dynamic in the choice of partners outside the value chain and amongst suppliers than amongst customers.

4. IMPLICATIONS

Management

The overall picture of collaboration with universities and other partners outside the value chain in projects of market-related importance could be said to support the notion that the market makes demands which often require producers to supplement their present proficiency levels to meet them. However, the fact that no university was a partner in a project of market-related importance, indicates that it cannot be ruled out that customers in the market screen which orders they feel their suppliers can manage within the collaboration framework of their traditional suppliers. This supports the advice for a firm to focus its market observations on demanding lead-users (von Hippel, 1986) and not to consider projects to be important solely because they are based on wants and needs expressed by customers as such.

Further advice can be formulated as heuristic for the initial screening of potential partners: if a firm wants to concentrate its collaborative relations on those partners who are most likely to be of great or crucial importance to the project, the best advice is to establish collaboration with a (lead) customer and a supplier. If several options are available, the firm should give preference to those with whom it has previously collaborated and to the untried collaboration partners which the firm expects could be important in the long run and which – when that time comes – can offer the further benefits of being experienced collaboration partners.

Research

The result above shows that a unilateral assessment of the benefits – expressed here as how important the partner was for the completion of the project – significantly reveals better values for established partners. It appears to support the rationale behind the recommendations (Dyer and Ouchi, 1993; Ford, 1998) that firms should maintain long-term relationships.

Finally, the fact that a number of new partners outside the value chain and new suppliers were attributed with having greater importance in the long run than for the project concerned, would seem to reflect motivation for preferring these new partners in the short run as well. The equivalent figures are not as apparent for new customers, and this may indicate that another dynamic exists for partner choice upstream in contrast to downstream. The difference probably demonstrates that firms often establish collaborative relationships with customers wherever possible, whereas collaboration with other types of partners reflects, to a greater degree, an active choice from amongst several potential partners. The figures strengthen the need for further research on the basis of the assumption (Ottesen, 1995) that initiatives toward establishing relationships do not just stem from the firms' pursuit of new customers but also from activities in the other direction from firms which exhibit buyer-initiative and seek relationships with new suppliers.

ACKNOWLEDGEMENTS

This research is part of a project on the Danish innovation system in a comparative perspective (DISKO). A project description can be found at "http://www.business.auc.dk/disko/". The project is coordinated by professor Bengt-Åke Lundvall, Aalborg University, and financed by the Danish Council for Industrial Development. The questions referred to from the survey questionnaire were formulated by the first author and assistant professor Poul Thøis Madsen. The authors thank professor Carsten Stig Poulsen and the anonymous referees on the present book for useful comments and are grateful to the firms who so willingly gave their time to this study.

REFERENCES

Bruce, M., Leverick, F. and Littler, D. A (1995a), "Management framework for collaborative product development" in M. Bruce and W. G. Biemans (eds), *Product Development: Meeting the Challenge of the Design-Marketing Interface*, John Wiley & Sons, Chichester , 161-180.

Bruce, M., Leverick, F., Littler, D and Wilson, D. (1995b), "Success factors for collaborative product development: a study of suppliers of information and communication technology", *R&D Management*, 25(1), 33-44.

Cooper, R. G., Kleinschmidt, E. J. (1987), "New products: what separates winners from losers?", *Journal of Product Innovation Management*, 4, 169-184.

Day, G. S. (1994), "The capabilities of market-driven organisations", *Journal of Marketing*, 58(Oct.), 37-52.

De Jong, G. (1999), *Causal Loops in Long-Term Supply Relationships*, Labyrint Publication, Ridderkerk, ISBN 90-72591-62-3.

Dyer, J. H. and Ouchi, W. G. (1993), "Japanese-style partnerships: giving companies a competitive edge", *Sloan Management Review*, 35(1), 51-63.

Fagerberg, J. (1992), "The home market hypothesis re-examined: the impact of domestic user-producer interaction on export specialisation", in B-Å Lundvall (ed), *National Systems of Innovation: Towards a theory of innovation and interactive learning*, Pinter Publishers, London, 226-241.

Ford, D. (ed.) (1998), *Managing Business Relationships*, John Wiley & Sons, Chichester.

Harabi, Najib. (1998), "Innovation through vertical relations between firms, suppliers and customers: a study of german firms", *Industry and Innovation*, 5(2), 157-179.

Hartley, J. L., Meredith, J. R., McCutcheon, D. and Kamath, R. R. (1997), "Suppliers' contributions to product development: an exploratory study", *IEEE Transactions on Engineering Management*, **44**(3), 258-267.

Håkansson, H. (ed) (1987), *Industrial Technological Development: A Network Approach*, Croom Helm, London.

Kristensen, P.S., Madsen, P.T. and Vinding, A.L. (1998), *Methodology and Data Collection in the DISKO survey on product development collaboration,* [http://www.business.auc.dk/disko/disko-attach/workplan2-.html]

Leonard-Barton, D. and Sinha, D. (1993), "Developer-user interaction and user satisfaction in internal technology transfer", *Academy of Management Journal*, **36**(5), 1125-1139

Leverick, F. and Littler, D. (1994), "Conjuring up rabbits out of hats: an absence of magic in collaboration", in W.G. Biemans and P.N. Ghauri (eds), *10th IMP Annual Conference Proceedings*, University of Groningen, Groningen, 846-871.

Littler, D., Leverick, F. and Bruce, M. (1995), "Factors affecting the process of collaborative product development: a study of UK manufacturers of information and communications technology products', *Journal of Product Innovation Management*, **12**(1), 16-32.

Lundvall, B. Å. (ed.) (1992), *National Systems of Innovation: Towards a theory of innovation and interactive learning*, Pinter Publishers, London.

Ottesen, Otto. (1995), *Buyer initiative: Ignored, but imperative for marketing management.* Occational papers, Högskolen i Stavanger, ISSN 0803-6888.

Pavitt, K. (1984), "Sectoral patterns of technical change: towards a taxonomy and a theory', *Research Policy*, **13**, 343-373.

Rothwell, R. and Zegveld, W. (1982*), Innovation and the Small and Medium Sized Firm*, Frances Pinter, London.

Rothwell, R., Freeman, C., Jervis, P., Robertson, A. and Townsend, J. (1974), "SAPPHO Updated – Project SAPPHO Phase 2", *Research Policy*, **3**(3), 258-291.

SAS Institute Inc., (1989), SAT/STAT, User's Guide; Version 6, Fourth Edition; Volume 1, Cary, NC: SAS Institute Inc., Ch. 17.

Senker, J. and Sharp, M. (1997), "Organizational learning in cooperative alliances: some case studies in biotechnology", *Technology Analysis and Strategic Management*, **9**(1), 35-51.

Smith, K. (1997), "Innovation measurement and the CIS approach", in: *Innovation measurement and policies.* Luxembourg 20 and 21 May 1996. Conference proceedings. Luxembourg: Office for Official Publications of the European Communities, ISBN 92-828-2043-2, 20-26.

von Hippel, E. (1986), "Lead users: a source of novel product concepts", *Management Science*, **32**(7), 791-805.

von Hippel, E. (1998), *The Sources of Innovation.* New York: Oxford University Press.

Wood, C. H., Kaufman, A. and Merenda, M. (1996), "How Hadco became a problem-solving supplier", *Sloan Management Review*, **37**(2), 77-88.

7. The Dynamics of Cooperation between Public Research and SME: what role for informal relations?

Corine Genet

---

1. INTRODUCTION: THE WEIGHT OF INFORMAL RELATIONS – A TOPIC THAT NEEDS EXPLORING

The main purpose of this chapter is to account for the weight of informal interaction in relations between public research and SMEs. The vast majority of studies on relations between the public and private sectors have focused on the analysis of forms of contractual relations. Various authors, drawing on case studies of collaboration formalized in a cooperative contract, licence or some other form of agreement, have developed different facets of the process of diffusion to industry. Some have tried to show the effectiveness of interactions through corporate and research strategies (Gonard, 1992), others the expectations, goals or motivations of firms (Feller and Roessner, 1995; Bozeman and Papadakis, 1995) or the cultural and institutional barriers to public-private collaboration (Van Dierdonck and Debackere, 1988). Yet Faulkner and Senker (1995) point out that these formalized relations account for only "the tip of the iceberg".

It therefore seems essential to go further than the study of contractual forms of interaction and focus on informal relations. That is the aim of this chapter, which sets out to measure the weight of relations, not mediated by formal mechanisms, in the genesis of collaboration between SMEs and public laboratories. It also analyses their role as coordination mechanisms and their effects on the laboratory's networks and partnerships. We first define what we mean by informal in the context of relations between public research laboratories and SMEs, and then present the model that serves as a framework of analysis for the study. Finally, we interpret empirical results.

2. THE INFORMAL IN RESEARCH – ENTERPRISE RELATIONS.

What is Meant by Informal?

Interest in this concept in organizations really started only in 1938, with Barnard's theory, which used the "formal-informal" duality to describe behaviours and relations between individuals in organizations. By "informal organization" Barnard referred to all contacts and interactions between people that were neither controlled nor administered by any formal organization. In his definition Barnard not only described the origin or form of these relations, he also noted their most real effect on individuals' experience, knowledge and attitudes. Barnard's interest in this concept was more than descriptive; he did not want to establish a dichotomy between the formal and the non-formal in an organization, but to understand how these two types of organization interact.

Dalton (1959) also focused part of his analysis on relations between formal and informal actions. To distinguish between the two concepts he compared spontaneous, flexible relations guided by the personal feelings and interests of members of an organization, to the relations that are planned and initiated or structured by organizations.

When Macdonald (1996) compared informal and formal information flows he emphasized that, unlike the latter, informal information passes through channels that are not structured by organizations.

Whereas these three authors referred primarily to informal phenomena that exist within an organisation, von Hippel (1987, 1996) and Schrader (1991) highlight the exchange of information or know-how between organizations. They use the concepts of "informal information trading" or "informal know-how trading". Based on the results of empirical research carried out on US firms in the steel industry, these authors show that firms prefer informal channels for transferring information to more formalized procedures such as contracts and licences. To characterize informal relations between members of different or even rival organizations, von Hippel and Schrader use concepts similar to those of Barnard, Dalton and Macdonald. The formal/informal distinction also concerns the contrast between the spontaneity of relations and the structuring/mediation of relations by organizations.

In light of the different points of view presented, we can define informal relations as flexible and fluid relations that are spontaneously built up between individuals without being structured or mediated by one or more organizations. This chapter is not concerned with the analysis of informal relations present within a single entity, but with that of informal interactions existing between two types of organization: public research laboratories and SMEs.

Public Research – Enterprise Relations and Informal Ties

Several authors have highlighted the presence of informal relations in the interaction between laboratories and firms. For Roessner (1993) the seminars, consultancy and visits to laboratories, which he describes as informal relations, account for a substantial part of interaction between researchers and firms. While most often authors (Freeman, 1991; Dickson, 1996; Roessner and Bean, 1994; Roessner, 1993) simply mention the presence of this type of relationship, Faulkner and Senker (1995) go further by actually focusing part of their study on the subject.

The results of their analysis empirically show the importance of informal relations in the transfer of knowledge between public research and firms. These forms of interaction can precede or succeed collaboration, as well as exist without any formal type of relationship between the partners. Advice given by a researcher to an industrialist during a conversation could serve as an example. As Kreiner and Schultz (1993) show in their study, research-industry cooperation often stems from informal contacts during congresses, conferences, professional shows, clubs or simply during interpersonal relations related to recreational activities or the same socio-professional trajectory. Several authors refer to this type of relation as "informal networks" (Johanisson, 1987; Szarka, 1989; Steward and Conway, 1996; Kreiner and Schultz, 1993). The information circulating in these informal networks provides the actors with considerable resources; in the case of SMEs these networks are the main source of information. Unlike large corporations, SMEs do not have an organized system of competitive intelligence enabling them to capture outside information: informal relations are their only alternative (Macdonald, 1995).

Two arguments can be put forward to explain the importance of these informal interactions between laboratories and firms. First, it is important to recall that in many cases the emergence of relations between researchers and firms depends largely on their ability to build relationships of trust, mutual respect and develop a common language. Trust, like respect, is an interpersonal phenomenon established over time on the basis of informal interaction incorporating the notion of reciprocity. Trust relates to a judgement based on past relations. Rather than being the result of a deductive calculation, it seems to be the product of inductive judgement that is revised as knowledge of the partner increases. Informal relations favour mutual learning and thus help to forge the trust needed for the emergence of collaboration between researchers and firms.

Secondly, this type of interaction allows firms to acquire knowledge that is tacit to a greater or lesser degree.[1] By nature, the transfer of tacit knowledge remains limited and generally requires face-to-face contact (Faulkner and Senker, 1995). When a firm, more especially an SME, collaborates with a public research laboratory it is usually looking for a solution to a problem and/or competencies and technical and scientific information for innovation purposes. The knowledge and/or information that it then needs rarely exists in a codified "ready to use" form; it is most often embodied in people. It is often owing to the ties it has already formed through informal relations that a firm will be able to identify the laboratory best equipped to provide it with the required knowledge. Then, to understand, transform and integrate that information or knowledge, especially if it is tacit, the firm will necessarily need to interact regularly and directly with the laboratory. It seems that this need for informal interaction during the transfer process is particularly important for SMEs, for their weak absorptive capacity[2] due to a lack of in-house R&D competencies makes it difficult for them to assimilate outside knowledge, even in a codified form.

We thus see that in the context of research-enterprise relations, informal interactions are as important in the initial phase of relationships as during the collaboration proper. The process of knowledge and/or information transfer from the public laboratory towards SMEs takes place progressively throughout the action, and involves a series of informal interactions between individuals. The model proposed by Kreiner and Schultz (1993) provides a relevant framework of analysis for an empirical account of this phenomenon.

3. A FRAMEWORK FOR ANALYSIS

Kreiner and Schultz's Model (1993)

Through an analysis of university-industry collaboration, Kreiner and Schultz (1993) showed how informal interpersonal relations between researchers and firms can lead to successful research cooperation. In order to analyse the mechanisms shaping this collaboration, the authors developed a model. This conceptual framework highlights the existence of three successive stages.

- The first, *discovering opportunities*, corresponds to the emergent phase, the discovery of one or several collaboration opportunities during chance encounters and interpersonal interaction at conferences, shows, dinners or even a game of golf. Apart from Kreiner and Schultz, other authors such as Steward and Conway (1996), Szarka (1989) or Johanisson (1987) have shown the valuable role of this first stage in the dynamics of inter-organization collaboration. It consists of informal relations built through social networks articulated around what they call recreation networks, profession networks, scientific networks, user networks and friendship networks.

- The second phase, *exploring possibilities,* accounts for the period of validation of ideas that usually implies new discussions and laboratory tests or trials, and ends in the formulation of the first lines of a common project. Like the first, this phase also involves numerous interactions before a contract is eventually signed.

Table 7.1. Formation of networks of collaboration

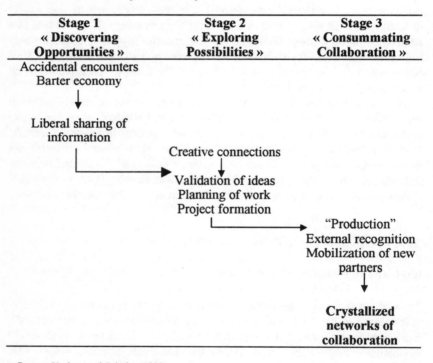

Stage 1 « Discovering Opportunities »	Stage 2 « Exploring Possibilities »	Stage 3 « Consummating Collaboration »
Accidental encounters Barter economy		
Liberal sharing of information	Creative connections	
	Validation of ideas Planning of work Project formation	
		"Production" External recognition Mobilization of new partners
		Crystallized networks of collaboration

Source: Kreiner and Schultz (1993)

- The third stage, *consummating collaboration*, characterizes the realization of the bilateral project and its transformation into multilateral collaboration. During this phase informal interaction continues (telephone conversations, face-to-face encounters, an so on.), as it will after the conclusion of the project, when partners may consider future collaboration.

An Original Framework for Analysis

Adopting this type of model for our study seems relevant in two respects.

First, it allows us to adopt an approach close to the economic theory of action.[3] It shows that technological opportunities and opportunities for transfer do not exist *ex ante*, but appear during the action. It is thanks to interaction that collaboration projects between laboratories and SMEs gradually take shape. When an SME enters into a relationship with a laboratory, actors on both sides progressively grasp the stakes and constraints involved, as well as the other party's requirements. This learning, acquired as contacts develop, enables the actors to modify and improve their perception and hence their actions. In this respect Lane et al. (1995) said: "interactions amongst the participants in a generative relationship can induce changes in the way the participants conceive of their world and act in it" (p. 15).

Secondly, it highlights the dynamics of informal mechanisms that favour the emergence and consolidation of cooperation. Owing to the pre-existence of personal relations, actors will be capable of identifying the most appropriate interlocutor. Similarly, it is thanks to frequent informal interaction that they will be able to adjust to a common project. Informal relations are perceived as a framework for learning that enables actors to construct new problems and solutions.

Following Kreiner and Schultz's model, our empirical analysis is articulated around three points: the role of informal interactions in the genesis of relations; their role in coordination and learning mechanisms; and, their action on the dynamics of cooperative contracts.

The genesis of relations: as in Kreiner and Schultz, analysing the origin of cooperation is the focal point of our empirical study. It is interesting to isolate the action of informal interactions in the emergent phase of relations between public research and SMEs. Addressing this subject on the basis of a sample composed entirely of SMEs is original because earlier empirical studies[4] never focused exclusively on relations between public research and small firms. It is therefore important to identify whether cooperation between laboratories and SMEs stems from direct contact between researchers and firms or whether it was mediated by institutional mechanisms.

Coordination mechanisms: In the framework of public-private relations, these mechanisms are based on the elaboration of incomplete contracts – which, through terms of reference, define the different tasks to be performed by the SME and the laboratory – and/or the trust binding the partners. Membership of the same interpersonal networks and frequent informal interaction between partners before and during the collaboration builds up trust between the actors. In this context, mutual adjustment based on trust becomes a preferred mode of coordination. In their model Kreiner and Schultz highlight the fact that informal interaction before formalising a contract enables the actors' gradual adjustment to the development of a common project. Little by little, through discussions and work sessions informal ties crystallize around a formalized cooperation project. In this context the trust that is built up step by step during successive interaction becomes an important coordination mechanism.

The consequences of relations: This point concerns the characterization of types of relations and their dynamics. It is interesting in this context to compare the type and effects of relations resulting from informal contacts and those of relations stemming from contacts mediated by formal mechanisms. Such a comparison highlights the effects of learning related to informal links or to the dynamics of relations. The analysis is also focused on the effects of relations on the laboratory's network of partners, which thus enables us to confirm Kreiner and Schultz's conclusions on the capacity of cooperation to mobilize new partners.

4. EMPIRICAL ANALYSIS

Methodological Approach and Identification of Key Variables

Unlike the empirical work done on the subject of public-private sector relations, the method of inquiry chosen for this analysis does not take industrial contracts as a starting point. Informal interactions cannot be identified on the basis of such a framework. Only a methodological approach based on the actors themselves makes it possible to grasp the informal dimension. Our data collection therefore started with laboratories and their staff.

The data used were taken from a survey performed between 1997 and 1998 on a panel of 20 laboratories. A sample consisting of ten CEA and ten INRA laboratories was selected after interviews with the DTA[5] and the DRIV[6]. It was based on one criterion: their degree of openness towards the industrial world. A typology of four groups was established: six technology resource centres (CRT)[7] or equivalents; six laboratories open to industrial collaboration; four laboratories closed to collaboration; and four laboratories in between. The number and form of these laboratories' industrial relations varied widely. While the variety of this sample sometimes tends to make the interpretation of empirical results more complex, it has the advantage of making allowances for a degree of representativeness concerning the type of relations that all the INRA and CEA laboratories have with SMEs.

For each laboratory studied, face-to-face interviews with the researchers, engineers or technicians concerned enabled us to record 48 cases of relations with SMEs. Interviewees were selected with the director of each unit, depending on the degree of involvement in projects concerning SMEs. The aim was to interview the person with the most knowledge about the origin, development and conclusion of the cooperation. Researches chose their own cases. Two priorities nonetheless guided this choice: the project had to be concluded and, preferably, had to involve new partners.

These case studies provide information on the way in which the laboratory made contact with the SME, the nature of relations (cooperation, service provision, licences), the type and frequency of interactions during the relationship, and the economic, academic or relational consequences of this cooperation. These data enable us to isolate different indicators concerning the three key variables of our analysis: the origin of the relations, modes of coordination, and consequences of the relations.

Main Results

Origin of relations
In the sample of 48 cases of relations between INRA or CEA laboratories and SMEs, only 13 (27%) were mediated by interface structures. More precisely, seven contacts were made through structures outside the two institutes and six through structures within them.

Table 7.2. Origin of relations between a laboratory and an SME

Mediated contacts		New partner	Direct contacts		New partner
External mechanisms	7	57% (4)	Prospection	11	73% (8)
Internal mechanisms	6	100% (6)	Shows	3	67% (2)
			Networks	21	57% (12)
Total	**13**	**77% (10)**	**Total**	**35**	**63% (22)**

The 35 relationships formed without a formal structure (that is, 73%) stemmed either from prospection by the laboratory or from encounters at exhibitions or networks. In the 11 relationships established as a result of prospection, the SMEs had identified the partner laboratory in articles. Use of the literature to transmit laboratories' scientific and technical information towards firms has already been highlighted by Faulkner and Senker (1995). These authors note that literature and interpersonal contacts as channels for transmitting information are often used in tandem. In the five cases where literature played a role, the articles were published not in academic journals but in the specialized press closer to SMEs' preoccupations, as it is, above all, more accessible.

According to the results presented in Table 7.2, we note that in 21 cases the relationship was started through the mobilization of various types of network. In the sample studied, five "typical" informal networks are characterized: networks related to the socio-professional trajectory of the actors; networks of suppliers or subcontractors; "scientific" networks; "partnership" networks; and networks formed around a club.

Networks related to the socio-professional trajectory: for example, the laboratory researcher and the SME member underwent the same training, or the laboratory researcher was previously employed by the SME. This type of network originated six relationships.

Supplier/subcontractor networks: Partner SMEs are the laboratory's suppliers or subcontractors. During a conversation between the firm's sales representative and a laboratory member, the possibility of cooperation emerges. It is how five partnerships were initiated.

Scientific networks: A researcher in another unit guides the SME towards the laboratory. This researcher is familiar with the laboratory because s/he is used to exchanging scientific and technical information with it. In the sample three relationships were thus established.

Partnership networks: A firm that was a laboratory's partner on a previous contract introduces it to a new partner. In three cases the relationship was initiated in this way.

A network articulated around a club: One of the laboratories in the sample formed a club of partner laboratories. The members of the club regularly attend briefings on the results of collective research. These briefings often present an opportunity for bilateral discussions that develop into cooperative projects. This club originated of four relationships.

The table also shows that in 67% of the cases studied the partner is new, that is to say, the laboratory has not had previous research relations, in the broad sense of the term (consultancy, service provision, cooperation contract, licence contract, and so on), with the SME. In this respect supplier or subcontractor SMEs are considered to be new partners because the relations they formerly had with the laboratory were limited to client-supplier or principal-subcontractor relations. If we compare mediated contacts and direct contacts in this respect, we see that the proportion of new partners is generally greater when the relationship is initiated by one of the two institutes' formal mechanism of. The proportion of new partnerships stemming from informal networks is relatively small (57%) when compared to the percentage initiated at exhibitions (67%) or by prospection (73%).

As Kreiner and Schultz showed for collaboration between universities and firms in Denmark, a substantial proportion of relations between public research laboratories and SMEs is initiated through informal networks. We can see, however, that although the share of contacts mediated by the CEA's or INRA's institutional mechanisms is relatively small (13%), these mechanisms enable laboratories to establish relationships with new partners and thus expand existing networks.

Coordination mechanisms
Drawing up detailed terms of reference is more systematic in relations mediated by a formal mechanism than relations stemming from direct contact between researchers and firms (Table 7.3).

Table 7.3. Detailed terms of reference

	Mediated contacts		Direct contacts	
Terms of reference	11	**85%**	27	**77%**
No terms of reference	2	**15%**	8	**33%**
Total	13	100%	35	100%

This result shows that forms of coordination are not independent from relations existing between the actors. When the actors belong to the same interpersonal networks, relations between them in the framework of partnerships, licence agreements or service provision are characterized by trust, mutual respect and a common language developed beforehand. This mutual trust then acts as a strong coordinating mechanism and the actors feel less of a need to commit themselves in formal terms of reference.

When researchers and members of a firm did not know each other before embarking on cooperation, a certain period of time is needed before a firm commitment is made, so that a common language and perception as well as mutual trust can be built up around a project. Thus, the time between the first meeting and the signing of the contract generally tends to be longer for relations mediated by a formal mechanism (22 months) than for relations formed directly (14 months).

Kreiner and Schultz also highlight the importance of the time period in which several informal interactions are needed to validate and support initial intuitions. Irrespective of the way in which the laboratory and the SME come together, meetings and tests carried out before any formal commitment seem to be useful steps in the crystallization of relations. In 96% of the cases studied, one or more meetings were held so that the SME could present its request and/or problem to members of the laboratory. These initial discussions allow partners to assess the motivation, state of knowledge and technical capacities of the other party. At the end of this first stage, the partners can still decide whether to continue the relationship or not. When they decide to proceed, tests are carried out in the laboratory or the firm so the technical and financial feasibility of the project can be assessed. In the sample studied such tests were carried out in 50% of the cases (Table 7.4). When the tests were conclusive, in 52% of the cases the laboratory formalized its technical and financial proposal to the SME. Further interaction is often necessary to adjust various details before drawing up the contract. These successive stages favour the emergence of a learning context. The partners test each other and mutual trust is established. The relationship progressively crystallizes until a contract is finally signed.[8]

Table 7.4. Steps before signing a contract

	Meetings	**Tests**	**Proposals/Quotations**
Presence	44 (96%)	23 (50%)	24[9] (52%)
Total	46	46	46

Apart from the informal interactions prior to signing the contract, many such relations are also present during the cooperation. They enable the actors to mutually adjust in order to periodically redefine the goals and the expected results. Flexible modes of interaction such as telephone conversations or face-to-face encounters are generally used, rather than rigid modes of interaction such as letters. This characteristic is even more marked for relations stemming from direct contact where the frequency of informal encounters is very high and the use of letters comparatively rare.

All these results show that the presence of informal interactions between actors before and during cooperation generates sufficient trust to play a decisive role in the coordination of researchers and firms during the relationship.

Consequences of relations

Table 7.5 compares the two types of relations: those resulting from direct contact and those mediated by formal mechanisms. We note that cooperative research is often rooted in interpersonal contact because in many cases this type of cooperative project can be set up only if the actors concerned know one another well. "Marriages" based on interface mechanisms result far more often in service contracts than in cooperation.

Table 7.5. Type of relations

	Mediated contacts	Direct contacts	Total
Collaboration	15% (2)	31% (11)	27% (13)
Licences	23% (3)	20% (7)	21% (10)
No contract	0	6% (2)	4% (2)
Services	62% (8)	43% (15)	48% (23)
Total	100% (13)	100% (35)	100% (48)

This result can partly be explained by the dynamic effect of relations, which seems stronger for cooperative research contracts than for service provision contracts. In 69% of cases the cooperative contract followed formal or informal relations between the researcher and the firm. By contrast, service provision contracts are more often an opportunity for the actors to build up a relationship. Yet this type of relationship does not remain isolated and is also part of a certain dynamic.

Table 6 shows that in 78% of all cases service provision led to other relations. In a sense, this type of relationship provides an ideal context for actors to test their partner's competencies and behaviour. When this initial experience is positive the partners can initiate other relations. It is therefore not surprising that the first relations, and particularly those mediated by formal mechanisms appear essentially in this form.

Table 7.6. Capitalising on relations

	Collaboration	Licences	No contract	Services
Follow-up	92% (12)	70% (7)	100% (2)	78% (18)
No follow-up	8% (1)	30% (3)	0	22% (5)
Total	100% (13)	100% (10)	100% (2)	100% (23)

As far as cooperative research contracts are concerned, results in Table 7.6 confirm the existence of a veritable cooperation dynamic. In 92% of the cases cooperative contracts led to other projects between the partners. For the laboratory this dynamic reveals real advantages because, more than others (services and licences), this form of relationship enables it to expand its network of industrial and academic partners (see, Table 7).

Table 7.7. Consequences of relationships

Expanding the network	Collaboration	No contract	Licences	Services
Industrial	54% (7)	50% (1)	50% (5)	43% (10)
Academic	54% (7)	0	40% (4)	17% (4)

As Kreiner and Schultz showed in their model, relationships make it possible to mobilize new partners, either through the results obtained or through the opportunities they provide for making new contacts. According to the results presented in Table 6.7, 50% of the relationships with SMEs, irrespective of their form, contributed to the opening of the laboratory's industrial network towards new partners. On the other hand, we see that when it comes to the network of academic partners, it is collaboration rather than services that plays a part in the expansion of the laboratory's network. This result is linked to the academic effects of the laboratory's relations with a SME. While cooperative contracts enable the laboratory to publish in 54% of all cases, service contracts enable it to do so in only 31% of the cases. It is therefore generally in the laboratory's interests to engage in collaboration, as it is more fruitful from an academic point of view.

From these findings, when informal interactions between researchers and SMEs lay at the origin of relations, they result in cooperation rather than service provision. By contrast, contacts resulting from interface mechanisms are more likely to lead to service contracts. To emerge, cooperative projects require learning by the participants. This learning is based on prior contracts or on informal relations between the parties. Cooperative contracts are therefore grounded in a real dynamic. Service contracts are not, however, simply isolated relations; they are often the starting point of a series of subsequent relationships. Like cooperative contracts, they enable laboratories to expand their industrial network, even though they contribute very little to the opening of their academic network.

5. CONCLUSION

Cooperation between public research and SMEs is profoundly marked by informal relations. It therefore seems necessary to broaden the analysis to take account of the influence of this type of interaction if the mechanisms favouring the genesis of the cooperation process are to be explained. Although hardly representative from a statistical point of view, the case study presented in this article makes it possible to identify the role of informal relations on three levels.

- In the emergent phase, the informal networks to which researchers and firms belong seem to play an important part in promoting contact. Therefore the existence of informal relations substantially increases the probability of cooperation between public research and SMEs.
- The presence of informal interactions before and during collaboration strengthens the participants' learning process. Work sessions, telephone conversations and tests carried out before the contract all tend to reduce the uncertainty and risks inherent in any cooperation. It is in this context that trust emerges and develops into a privileged mode of coordination.
- The effect of informal ties on the dynamics of relations is not neutral. The relations that partners continue to maintain after cooperation favour the elaboration of new contracts in which new problems will be addressed and new solutions found.

Despite the exploratory nature of this analysis, initial results provide enough elements to confirm the influence of informal mechanisms on the cooperation process. The demonstration of the critical role of these informal interactions in cooperation tends to question the specialization of the interface function as operated in recent years in public research institutes. Through their action, which consists primarily of promoting contact between laboratories and firms, these mechanisms separate the phases of emergence and crystallization of relations. The presence of an intermediary between the researcher and the firm becomes an obstacle hindering direct and informal interaction between actors which, as shown, helps to a large extent to stabilize relations and promote successful cooperation.

NOTES

1. Tacit knowledge is, by definition, incorporated in people and cannot initially be codified in any way.
2. For Cohen and Levinthal (1989) who introduced this notion into economics, absorptive capacity is a product of R&D activities. It implies that the use of outside knowledge, even codified, generally requires internal R&D competencies, which SMEs often lack.

3. Cf Lane, Malerba, Maxfield and Orsenigo, 1995.
4. Kreiner & Schultz (1993) and Faulkner & Senker (1995)
5. *Direction des Technologies Avancées*: Advanced Technology Division.
6. *Direction des Relations Industrielles et de Valorisation*: Industrial Relations and Technology Transfer Division.
7. *Centres de Ressources Technologiques*.
8. All the cases in the sample ended in cooperation, but the information provided by one of the laboratories questioned showed that at each step in the process several projects were abandoned. Thus, out of the 152 contacts made by the laboratory in 1997, only 70 resulted in a proposal and 45 in a contract.
9. Out of the 24 cases where a proposal was made before signing the contract, 20 cases concerned a CEA laboratory. This procedure is therefore closely linked to the laboratory's institutional culture.

REFERENCES

Barnard, C.I. (1938), *The Functions of the Executive*, Harvard University Press, Cambridge and London.

Bozeman, B. and Papadakis, M. (1995), "Company interactions with federal laboratories: What they do and why they do it?", *Technology Transfer*, December, 64-74.

Cohen, W.M. and Levinthal, D.A. (1989), "Innovation and learning: the two faces of R&D", *Economic Journal*, **99**, 569-596.

Dalton, M. (1959), "The interconnections of formal and informal action", in *Men who Manage*, John Wiley & Sons, New York, 222-232.

Dodgson, M. (1993), "Learning, trust, and technical collaboration", *Human Relations*, **46**, (1), 77-95.

Faulkner, W. and Senker, J. (1995), *Knowledge frontiers*. Clarendon Press, Oxford.

Faulkner, W. and Senker, J. (1995), "Policy and management issues in company links with academic and government laboratories: a cross-technology study", *The Journal of High Technology Management Research*, **6** (1), 95-112.

Feller, I. and Roessner, D. (1995), "What does industry expect form university partnerships?", *Issues in Science and Technology*, **12** (1), 80-84.

Foray, D. and Mowery, D. (1990), "L'intégration de la recherche industrielle: nouvellles perspectives ", *Revue Economique*, 501-530.

Freeman, C. (1991), "A synthesis of research issues", *Research Policy*, **20**, 499-514.

Gonard, T. (1992), *L'efficacité des relations recherche publique/industrie : les situations et les stratégies de la recherche publique*, PhD thesis, Ecole Centrale Paris.

Granovetter M. (1973), "The strengths of weak ties", *American Journal of Sociology*, **78**(6), 1360-1380.

Guillaume H. (1998), *Rapport de mission sur la technologie et l'innovation*, Ministère de l'Education Nationale de la Recherche et de la Technologie, Ministère de l'Economie des Finances et de l'Industrie, Secrétariat d'Etat à l'Industrie.

Johanisson, B. (1987), "Beyond process and structure: social exchange networks", *International Studies of Management and Organisation*, **17** (1), 3-23.

Joly, P-B, Lemarié, S. and Mangematin, V. (1998), "Coordination et incitations dans les contrats de recherche: le cas des accords public/privé", *Revue Economique*, July 1998.

Kreiner K. and Schultz M. (1993), "Informal collaboration in R&D", *Organization Studies*, **14**, issue 2, 189-209.

Macdonald, S. (1995), "Learning to change : an information perspective on learning in the organization", *Organization Science*, **6** (5), 557-568.

Macdonald, S. (1996), "Informal information flow and strategy in the international firm", *International Journal of Technology Management*, **11**, 1/2, 219-232.

Lane D., Malerba F., Maxfield R. and Orsenigo L. (1995), "Choice and Action", Santa Fe Institute WP 95-01-004.

Roessner, D. and Bean, A. (1994), "Patterns of industry interaction with federal laboratories", *Journal of Technology Transfer*, December, 59-77.

Roessner, D. (1993), "What companies want from the federal labs", *Issues in Science and Technology*, Fall, 37-42.

Schrader, S. (1991), "Informal technology transfer between firms: cooperation through information trading", *Research Policy*, 153-170.

Senker, J. (1995), "Networks and tacit knowledge in innovation", *Economies et Sociétés*, 9/1995, 99-118.

Steward, F. and Conway, S. (1996), "Informal networks in the origination of successful innovation", in R. Coombs, A. Richards, P. Saviotti and V. Walsh (eds), *Technological collaboration: the dynamics of co-operation in industrial innovation*, Aldershot Edward Elgar.

Szarka, J.(1989), "Networking and small firms", *International Small Business Journal*, **8**, (2), 10-22.

Van Dierdonck, R. and Debackere, K. (1998), "Academic entrepreneurship at Belgian universities", *R&D Management*, **18**, 4, 341-353.

Von Hippel, E.(1987), "Cooperation between rivals: informal know-how trading", *Research Policy*, **16**, 291-302.

Von Hippel, E. and Schrader, S. (1996), "Managed informal information trading: the oil scout system in oil exploration firms", *International Journal of Technology Management*, **11**, n°1/2.

8. Networks and Trust in Transition

Cécile Borzeda and Yorgos Rizopoulos

1. INTRODUCTION

This chapter is based on the survey data of 71 Polish enterprises. The findings relative to the importance of network interactions shed light on topics like the structuring of markets through environment stabilising strategies, the impact of long-lasting relations on investment and development decisions, the conditions of emergence of cooperative behaviour, as well as their evolution.

The information gathered enforced the Richardsonian hypothesis according to which interdependencies – tangible and intangible – are the basis of these long lasting relations but, given the multitude of relations, a typology was necessary in order to rigorously define durable interaction and co-operation. Moreover the development of these interdependencies is based on trust, we had to clarify this concept, taking account of the "non-disinterested" character of the actors' actions, their own dynamics, the asymmetries of their positions, the evolution of their environment and the pursuit of multiple objectives.

The origin and the characteristics of the relations built up by the sample enterprises will be explained, after a brief presentation of the inquiry methodology. Next, we will deal with the diversity and the specific features of various network interactions, as well as with the attributes and the emergence conditions of trust. Lastly, some propositions will be formulated about the intricacy of trust and of "non-disinterested" strategies.

2. METHODOLOGY OF THE SURVEY

The survey was carried on a set of 86 industrial enterprises (construction included), through "face to face" interviews, between February 1998 and September 1998. Because of the insufficiency and inadequacy of the obtained information obtained, 15 questionnaires were left out. The remaining data concern 71 enterprises, situated in three regions of Poland reflecting regional disparities in the country: around the towns of Poznań in western Poland (37 enterprises), Łódź in the centre (24 enterprises) and Białystok in the east (10 enterprises).

On account of the difficulties inherent in the constitution of a representative sample of the whole industry (temporal constraints, refusal to answer, no access to competent persons, and so on), the various branches have been gathered in two large categories according to the intensity of production factors: labour intensive and capital-intensive. In this field, the sample accurately represents the structure of Polish industry[1] (annex 1). Our initial idea was to observe, through this classification, a correlation between inter-enterprise links and the type of activity, but no statistically significant difference could be noticed. We essentially contacted enterprises, which already existed in the planned economy because generally, new enterprises are still too small. In addition, privatised enterprises are more numerous than state-owned ones in the sample, as we wished to focus on supposedly more market-oriented strategies.

A questionnaire was submitted to a manager in each enterprise (head of marketing, production or finance department) during an interview which lasted 2 to 4 hours and took place in the enterprise itself. It contained about 30 "closed" questions – with nevertheless the possibility to choose an open modality for each one – and some more qualitative questions, which were asked during the interview. Further information was also asked by fax to part of the enterprises, in order to complete or clarify the data obtained.

Although we regret that data collected are simply cross-sectional, impeding from relating the dynamics of the relations studied, the cross-checking and verifying of the obtained answers allow us to assert that beyond the usual problems of interpretation, the information given in this research is reliable.

3. STRATEGIC INTERDEPENDENCIES AND THE FORMATION OF LONG-LASTING RELATIONSHIPS

For the main part, the Polish enterprises interviewed devote a great deal of energy to networking. Indeed, long-lasting relations are considered as an investment in specific intangible assets, which contribute to competitive advantage and resolve production or marketing problems.[2] Dissolution of these relations or the damage to them are perceived as generating constraints and high costs which might lead to withdrawal from the market on these points. This inquiry emphasizes empirical and theoretical work on organisational networks in general[3], and in transition economies in particular

(Grabher and Stark, 1997; Johnson et al., 1999; Recanatini and Ryterman, 2000; Rizopoulos 1997a and 1999).

The density of relations formed by the sample enterprises questions the idea according to which cheating and defection are the dominant strategies in the relations between economic agents.[4] Indeed, enterprises outline goals and develop a perception of their own needs, but they have limited resources and skills. They have then to "bargain" for the conditions necessary to achieving their objectives, which means negotiating access to assets they cannot control directly by themselves in a satisfactory way (Pfeffer and Salancik, 1978).

Enterprises do not know what they will gain or lose by adopting respectively an aggressive attitude or a cooperative one, because it is impossible to anticipate precisely the evolution of the environment and the behaviour of the other actors. They do not know either whether they can themselves satisfy the expectations of their possible partners, as they are also aware of the eventuality of opportunistic behaviour on the part of the other actors. Nevertheless, radical uncertainty and bounded rationality produce commitment and benevolent reciprocity (Ménard, 1994; Brousseau, 1996). In a context of strategic interdependencies, enterprises build up permanent relations with actors who have a direct impact on their capacity for action, in order to reduce uncertainty and to be able to predict outcomes. A mix of conflicts, mutual dependence, tolerance, bargaining, loyalty, trust and betrayal; network links constitute a determining factor as to the evolution and survival of each individual actor. They range from mere mutual acquaintance to complex cooperation agreements and form the basis for collective learning, values and rules approved by consent (Rizopoulos, 1997b). These systems of action shape the perception that each enterprise has about problems and stakes (Johanson and Mattson, 1987), they generate formal or informal rules and collective knowledge, which lead the actors' interests to converge.

The strategic interdependency evokes the idea of complementarity, already raised in Richardson's precursory works (1959 and 1972). Yet it is necessary to enlarge this scope to integrate into it – beyond downstream or upstream activities – other economic or strategic synergies (co-ordination in order to improve bargaining power, access to raw materials, market sharing, flexibility of the production process, implementation of diversification policies, and so on). Moreover, it turns out that long-lasting interaction does not constitute an alternative, but is combined with hierarchical and market co-ordination for the same activities. This coexistence seems to indicate that the sample enterprises look for a satisfying articulation of distinct coordination modes, answering to different types of problems, instead of choosing among them the one, which would ensure greatest efficiency as transaction mediator. If we notice that boundaries are blurred and evolve among coordination modes, the entire process depends on strategic considerations and environmental constraints. Transformation of the relative importance of market hierarchies and networks occurs without any necessarily apparent modification of asset specificity or of transactions frequency.

Networks do not have only beneficial effects. They are "costly" and rigidify the context in which each enterprise evolves, eliminating part of its decisional autonomy. Keeping up a long-lasting relationship also means that other relations become unreachable. This opportunity cost of relational assets can be combined with irreversibility and give rise to lock-ins (David, 1985). Nevertheless, these costs and constraints are perceived by interviewees as being an integral part of entrepreneurial activity. Thus, their minimization does not necessarily constitutes a priority – contrary to hypotheses drawn up by the transaction costs approaches (Williamson, 1985) – and they do not seem to be a central preoccupation for the sample enterprises.

Lastly, the absence of formal subordination inside these networks must not give an impression of harmony and equity. As products of historic evolution, relationships in which sample enterprises are inserted are characterized by strong asymmetries (see also, Umbhauer, 1998). Thus, a greater number of links (centrality) in relatively homogeneous networks can mean power and influence (we observed such situations in the construction sector). Furthermore, the density of relations and the quality of the links can be altered at the level of the different clusters, which make up each network. Compared with others, some partners can benefit more from externalities created by the interaction. Depending on the circumstances, market power, vertical dependence or size difference can favor or hinder the formation of long-lasting relations. This way, an enterprise sometimes can exert power by refusing to cooperate. Without direct prejudice to other agents, this attitude engenders losses of development opportunities for them. Besides, a partner who stands in a relatively unfavorable position can prefer proceeding with the relation (see also Elgu and Johansson, 1997), because he fears that a breach could exacerbate its position ("failing anything better"). Then, in some unbalanced relationships, apathetic behavior helps *de facto* to maintain the stability of the network links.

Several questions were asked about the stability of the relations with the main supplier. It turned out that 55% of the sample enterprises had kept the same supplier for more than 10 years. Then, the duration of these relations becomes, in itself, the main reason for systematic recourse to this supplier (Table 8.1). It is characteristic that oral agreements or long-term contracts constitute the preponderant forms of commitment in about 48% of cases

(Table 8.2). Nevertheless, long-lasting relations with the main supplier can be based on periodically repeated contracts. This practice can be linked to the nature of the product, but also to the bargaining power of the customer *vis-à-vis* the supplier.

Table 8.1. Main reason for systematic recourse to main supplier (percentage of the sample enterprises)

Privileged relations	62%
Best quality	14%
Monopolistic position	14%
Lower price	6%
Others	4%
Total	100%

Interesting information has been drawn up about relations among competitors. About 42% of the enterprises in the sample declare that they produce, regularly or sporadically, for other enterprises in the same branch of activity, while about 39% of them recognize that they resort to competitors for part of their production[5].

Table 8.2. Types of contracts with the main supplier (in percentage of the sample enterprises)

Oral engagement	23,9%
Long term contracts	23,9%
Short term contracts	25,4%
Periodically repeated contracts	26,8%
Total	100,0%

4. THE VARIOUS FORMS OF LONG-LASTING RELATIONSHIPS

The forms of long-lasting relations observed during the inquiry are very much varied: exchanges of intermediary products, specialisation, coordination to put pressure on mutual suppliers, informal exchanges of information, technical cooperation, and so on. This plurality – the usual problem which empirical or theoretical research on cooperation has to face

(Rullière and Torre, 1995) – imposes a stylised description and a typology of long-lasting relations, so light can be shed on their main features.

In the various attempts seeking to resolve the contradiction between a theory which predicts generalised opportunistic behaviour on one side, and frequent attitudes of goodwill on the other, the emergence of long-lasting relations is often transcribed by a generic term "cooperation", which is used to define very different situations: implicit negotiation (Schelling, 1960), relations between closely complementary but dissimilar activities and, also, knowledge of competitors intentions (Richardson, 1972, 1995), tolerant behaviour (Axelrod, 1984), "relational quasi-rent" (Aoki, 1988), Williamson's hybrids, strategic alliances, and so on.

Generally, the duration of relations is considered a synonym for cooperation. It seems nevertheless necessary to delimit the different types of interactions with respect to their explicit or implicit character, their density, their complexity and the degree of mutual dependence of participants. In this perspective, four types of long-lasting relations may be distinguished: implicit interaction, explicit interaction, cooperation and alliance (Table 8.3). The most evolved and complex forms of interaction contain elements of the most primary forms, but it does not work the other way round.

Implicit interaction must be understood as the conditions prevailing in organisational fields (markets, sectors, territories), where mutual acquaintance of actors and social embeddedness contributes to the formation of an atmosphere favourable to both the exercise of an economic activity and the formation of rules and conventions allowing the coexistence and the mutual observation of behaviours, without necessarily implying tighter cooperation or explicit reciprocity. All sample enterprises are involved in this type of interaction.

Table 8.3. Types of long-lasting relations

Implicit interaction	Explicit interaction	Co-operation	Alliance
Mutual acquaintance, mimetic behaviour, rules allowing coexistence, social embeddedness	Recurrent relations, exchanges of money, product and information, mobilisation of tangible and intangible assets	Complementarity of assets, co-ordination of some decisions and actions.	Joint projects, sharing of assets, benefits and risks.

With the establishment of direct relations, formal links and organisational arrangements, interaction becomes *explicit*, and the degree of interdependence increases. Producing for a competitor when a temporary lack of production capacities or a special requirement from a customer occurs, exchanging information on the conditions offered by suppliers or about the financial health of customers and the management of raw materials in short supply, are all part of these explicit interactions. In the sample, 24 enterprises among 71 (34%) are implicated in explicit interactions, without reaching cooperation, as defined here.

Cooperation intervenes from the time when actors tempt to exploit jointly tangible and intangible assets (equipment, knowledge, relations, and so on), by co-ordinating some of their activities and decisions. In this case, the mutual dependence becomes strong. Among interviewed enterprises, 19 built relations of this type. Counter-cyclical and diversification strategies often motivate asset sharing and specialisation. Indeed, diversification entails the acquisition of new assets and the problem of under-utilisation of production capacities appears (see also Zuscovitch, 1998). To get out of this vicious cycle, enterprises co-ordinate their activities, by specialising in limited stages of the production process and by acquiring complementary equipment. Numerous physical, monetary and information flows stem from this coordination (trade in products and spare parts, co-ordination committees, information exchanges, joint training sessions for employees, and so on). In some cases, production and transport cost considerations push enterprises not only to produce for each other but also to mutually recommend customers. The fear of the effects of an opportunistic behaviour – that could imply a final loss of the customer – does not discourage these practices,[6] which are anyway combined with cautious attitudes (avoiding wide-range competitors as partners). Cooperation also concerns regrouped purchase of some inputs and collective pressures on suppliers for benefit from lower prices, discount and extra services. Generally speaking, being in competition in some parts of the activities does not prevent cooperative strategies. Reciprocity and fairness reduce the uncertainty relative to the outlets, and in the same way, get round the problem of assets rigidity.

Enterprises that belonged to the same supervisory authority, or had formed a single enterprise during the period of the planned economy, are very often involved in co-operative relations. For the most part, they are now autonomous[7] and very often have complementary activities, as well as, for some of them, similar productions. Their complementarity can thus be observed either at the production level or through the geographic distribution of market share.

Finally, an *alliance* refers to an association for a peculiar project in which resources and skills are pooled and risks, benefits and losses are shared. This is the most evolved form of durable interaction and only one relation of this type was detected in the sample.

5. DURABLE INTERACTIONS AND TRUST

The trust the sample enterprises grant each other constitutes an essential parameter in the long-lasting and cooperative relations that they build.

Trust can be defined as subjective anticipation concerning actions in accordance with expectations of interdependent agents (Gambetta, 1988). It depends on the judgements passed on the propensity of other actors to have deliberate opportunistic behaviour (to "cheat" with regards to their commitments) and on their capacity to mobilise the necessary means and skills to fulfil the terms of an agreement.[8] Some scholars distinguish different levels of trust: "systemic" or institutional trust, trust related to a strong identification to a social group, and trust based upon experience of interaction (Zucker, 1986; Brousseau et al., 1997; Humphrey and Schmitz, 1998).

It can be inferred from the typology of durable relations presented above that implicit interaction requires a minimal expectation of adhesion to some values or rules which make coexistence possible. This type of trust refers to the credibility and the permanence of the rules of the game (North, 1990; Williamson, 1993), or stems from a feeling of belonging to a community with common environmental and organisational constraints (town, region, ethnic minority, industry sector). Thanks to the reputation effects, these macro or meso types of trust strongly reduce uncertainty due to the fear of intentionally disloyal behaviour; thereby the contact and the formation of explicit interactions is facilitated. These types of trust do not constitute, however, sufficient nor necessary conditions for behaviour of reciprocal commitment to develop (Granovetter, 1985 and 1992). Indeed, on account of the complexity of relations and of the existence of contradictory interests, the two levels of trust do not eliminate undetermined attitudes and the leeway of strategic interaction (North, 1990; Scott, 1994). They cannot constitute a sufficient warranty against divergent interpretations of the terms of a complex contract, the modification of the scale of preferences or the failures due to poor appraisal of available resources. From the time when interactions become an important and specific stake for the actors (resource dependence, investment or intense mobilisation of assets, decisions relative to a joint action) arises the problem of trust based upon experience of interaction. We shall focus now on this micro level trust.[9]

In the theoretical framework of non-cooperative games, trust rests on the substantive rationality of the players, because, as a common reference, it allows for the calculation of the maximum utility which incites partners to meet their commitments (for the critics, see Schmidt, 1997 and Billand, 1998). The perspective of future exchanges (Wintrobe and Breton, 1986) or reputation (Kreps, 1990; Kreps and Wilson, 1982) are likened to incentive mechanisms and the existence of extra-legal sanctions constitutes the foundation of trust. Yet, the anticipation of a recurrent game or a good reputation do not seem to be able to solve the problems which arise at the level of specific agreements. Actors would have had to be equal, future transactions identical to past ones, products homogeneous and unchanging, markets transparent and information symmetrical. These conditions are too demanding for the incentive structure to sanction defection (see also Williamson, 1993; Brousseau, 1996; Meidinger and al., 1999), and therefore, micro-trust cannot rely on these elements.

According to Williamson (1993), the commitment would be the outcome of a reasonable calculation in terms of risks and comparative returns. The institutional context and peculiar environment in which the transaction takes place constitute guides for this calculation and when interests converge, cooperation will emerge. In this view, recourse to the notion of trust does not bring anything on the analytical level and is misleading. This thesis, which is valuable for at least attracting attention on the unconsidered use of the notion of trust has been criticised.[10] When hypotheses of substantive rationality and of predictable future are removed, trust cannot be reduced to a calculation problem of gains and losses. According to Orléan (1994), trust is an autonomous interaction mode, which cannot be brought down to calculations of sole economic interests and, as Cordonnier (1997) observed, even clearly identified and powerful interests are not always sufficient to promote co-operation. On the other hand, the confusion between the pursuit of interested strategies and strict economic calculation must be avoided, first because "interest" includes multiple human, social and organisational dimensions (Hirschman, 1980; Elster, 1989) and then because the satisfaction of individual interests is operated through structures of groups and relational networks (Granovetter, 1985).

Some authors (Burchell and Wilkinson, 1997; Lyons and Mehta, 1997) situate the foundations of trust at an intermediary level: it would be neither the quest for an immediate interest, nor an altruistic attitude in actors, who left aside their own interests. Livet and Reynaud (1995) consider there is a "reasonable equilibrium" between the restrictions that express commitment and the justifications – in other terms, the perceived interest – that give a positive sense to these restrictions. If the balance is modified, the commitment will be broken off. Indeed, the multilateral character of relations beetween a great number of agents makes parallel or alternative co-operative and aggressive strategies possible. Each actor can select his partners, co-operate with some of them, be in conflict with others or break off his commitments without necessarily fearing a sanction, according to the new opportunities or modifications within his relevant environment.

Therefore, the emergence of trust cannot be apprehended outside the relational story of the actors concerned. If, without prior explicit interactions, X and Y think they are able to satisfy their respective needs,[11] first they are going to send out signals to enter a process of trust building in the sense of C. Sabel (1992).[12] However, the attraction that a partner can exert because of his declared skills and for benevolent signals cast towards the other must not be confused with trust. Taking these signals into account, X and Y adopt risky but cautious attitudes (they "neglect" the uncertainty inherent in each relation). Through negotiations and mutual adjustments, they commit themselves in a first co-ordinated action. From the moment when the results of the interaction are judged satisfactory, its repetition contribute to the emergence of trust[13]. Cooperative relations characterised by the constitution of specific assets, the coordination of actions or the sharing of sensitive information then become possible. Yet under no circumstances can micro-trust exist by anticipation, nor is it a necessary condition for starting a relationship. It appears most unlikely that cooperation will emerge between parties that do not trust each other, as that trust cannot be apprehended outside a process of repeated interactions. In this perspective, trust stems from long-lasting relations and not the reverse.

The dynamics of trust can then be formulated as follows: Y thinks that the relation with X can be beneficial to the achievement of his (her) goals. Y considers that X is in a position to satisfy his (her) expectations, all the more since, by doing that, X thinks he (she) will be serving his (her) own interests; he (she) then invests cautiously in the building of trust, which will be reinforced or weaken as interactions between the partners are repeated and new opportunities or constraints appear.

This proposition delimits the trust encountered in economic activities, which corresponds to the situations studied during the inquiry. Indeed, we observed that relations implying a strong interdependence result for the main part from the period before 1990 and trust frequently find its roots in ties formed in the context of the planned economy's institutional and organisational constraints (branch structure, subordination to the same central authority, geographic concentration, informal relations to face up to shortage, and so on). Actors remember their past interactions and these links are generally maintained and developed.

On the other hand, if the weight of relational networks, formed historically, is considerable, such relations undergo deep changes and are reshaped according to the recombination of property rights, the redefinition of powers inside the enterprises and foreign investment. Changes of managerial teams can break up the personal relations on which an important part of trust was founded, and, on which exchanges rested. Simultaneously, because of exacerbated competition, some enterprises seek to increase the scope of their activity by extending their market or by enlarging their specialisation range, which throws their past relations into question. Foreign direct investment plays a preponderant role in this process. Investors bring funds, modernise the production system, improve competitiveness and, very often, redefine positioning and strategic orientations. Enterprises under foreign control generally stand in a position of strength *vis-à-vis* their traditional partners and often wish to loosen the links with them to reach new markets. Simultaneously, they are involved in new networks (foreign owners usually impose new suppliers) or integrated fully and exclusively into the hierarchical structure of the foreign firm.

Because of these evolutions, network relations are formed and broken up according to the strategic orientations of the enterprises and changes that affect the compatibility of their mutual interest. In the sample, at least 14 enterprises had recently brokn off long-term relations, while preserving others. Consequently, it seems difficult to apprehend trust, durable interactions and cooperation, when "non-disinterested" behaviours are left aside.

6. CONCLUSION

The density of durable relations observed among the enterprises interviewed impedes the hypothesis of pure individualistic behaviour. Leading non-disinterested strategies in an uncertain context entails attitudes of commitment, perceived as a means of diminishing environmental uncertainty and opening new opportunities. Because of self-interest, actors in unequal positions are inserted in a framework of long-lasting relations. They are essential for their survival and constitute a world of conflicts and mutual adjustments, where bargaining and mistrust coexist with reciprocity and friendly behaviour.

The uncertainty concerning inputs and outlets, the rigidity of production processes and the impossibility of adjusting assets rapidly because of the irreversibility that characterises economic activity, incites enterprises to stabilise informational and physical flows. Firms are ready to accept a dependence *vis-à-vis* known partners. Enterprises protect these relations because they condition their capacity to act and their perception of opportunities, problems and solutions. This attitude, based on the memory of past interactions, is reasonable and interested, but does not result from a strict calculation of gains and losses, which would in any case be unreliable.

The fear of undergoing the effects of opportunistic behaviour does not prevent the formation of such relations. Avoiding the creation of production capacities through a single-handed investment strategy, on which it is hard to make returns because, exerts a much stronger influence on the decisions of enterprises than the risk of disloyal attitudes. Moreover, the possibility of being locked up in disadvantageous relations does not seem to be integrated in the actors' strategic thought process.

The goals of enterprises and their trajectories being different, the forms of the links which unite them are characterised by great diversity. Nevertheless, it seems possible to distinguish four generic types of long-lasting relations – implicit interaction, explicit interaction, cooperation and alliance – according to their density, complexity and degree of mutual dependence of actors.

The duration of the relation, the deepening of mutual acquaintance and the satisfying outcome of interactions can give birth to trust between the parties and reinforce it. Although a central element in the relations studied, trust is not blind; it cannot exist *a priori* and is evolutionary. It can increase or diminish until it disappears, according to the modifications of the positions, representations and assessment criteria of actors, to the emergence of new opportunities and to the unforeseeable evolutions of the environment. It rests on repeated contact, past experience and the compatibility of the perceived interests of the parties.

NOTES

1. Energy and mining sectors have been excluded because of their monopoly structure and the large size of enterprises. Trade companies have also been left out. Meanwhile, because of ambiguities in sector qualification and recurrent changes in the field of activities, five enterprises proved to have brisk trading activity. Eleven sectors are represented in the sample: food industry (12 enterprises), clothing (11), textile (10), chemistry (8), printing (8), machinery and equipment (3), electrical machinery and appliances (3), metal products (2), rubber and plastic products (1) and construction (12).
2. It is interesting to highlight the gap between the discourse of managers, who glorified competition and "individualistic" behaviour, and their tendency to commit themselves to durable relationships with other firms.
3. The importance of the "affiliation network", as a reserve of resources and factor of flexibility, is mentioned by G. Richardson (1972), (see also Granovetter, 1985; Contractor

and Lorange, 1988; Powell, 1990; Nohria and Eccles, 1992; Axelsson and Easton, 1992; Grabher, 1993; Langlois and Roberston, 1995).

4. In neo-institutionalist approaches, only the incentive devices (principal-agent model) and the mechanisms of coercion and control (theory of transaction costs) allow the eviction of opportunist behaviour. In the framework of the game theory, this *ad hoc* postulate stemmed from the hypotheses of the strictly rational and individualistic behaviour of actors – who are supposed to be informed about the gains obtained from each situation – and common knowledge. Meanwhile, even in a "prisoner dilemma" game with more than two players, aggressive strategies are stable only under the conditions that cooperative strategies arise one by one (Axelrod, 1984). If the co-operative actors present in a group – even in a limited number – they could be "in average" more efficient than the selfish actors (the free-riders "punish" themselves). Besides, by introducing simultaneous interdependence of the players, a problem of multiple equilibrium arises and the game theory is not able to explain the result of the negotiation (Elster, 1989).

5. These percentages are underestimated because of commercial considerations (business secrets) and the willingness not to appear dependent on others. Often, negative answers have been disproved by competitors or partners.

6. Sub-contracting could appear less risky, because it avoids a direct link between the customer and the competitor. It can be argued that too high transaction costs impede such a solution. Meanwhile, this argument would be plausible only if enterprises were able to compare transaction costs with the cost of the risk of losing the customer. Without operating such complicated and hazardous calculations, enterprises rely on informal codes of fairness that are considered a sufficient warranty against opportunistic behaviour on their partners' part.

7. Some of them still belong to the former central authority, which may have been converted into a holding company (but this is rather rare). More often, they still bear the same name, followed by their location, so they can be distinguished from one another.

8. In the economic literature on trust, it is above all the first dimension which is dealt with. The central position occupied by opportunism is bound to an ahistorical and asocial perception of economic activity.

9. Casson (1997, pp. 120-123) propounds a typology of inter-enterprise networks according to the degree of trust and identifies five types: ordinary market, organised market, private network, communal network and commitment network. His notion of trust – securing quality of information at lesser costs – is "strictly rational", considering, however, that moral commitment is based on the prospect of "emotional reward".

10. According to Karpik (1998), this disqualification of trust is bound to the dualism of hierarchy/market, which characterises the transaction costs theory.

11. This presentation is voluntarily linear in order to make it clearer. In reality, the goals of actors are defined on account of the relational networks that could make realisation easier. Besides, one relation between actors can develop from a constraint without any previous desire or quest for it on the actor's part.

12. Casson (1997, pp. 119) also underlines that trust emerges thanks to actors' investments.

13. The emotional relation is certainly the most difficult element of trust to apprehend, but not the least considerable: "...The behaviours of agents rest on emotional relations tied in the framework of common repeated actions and that appeal to principles of equity and solidarity..." (Ménard, 1994, pp. 202). Also see Casson, 1997, pp. 135-136.

ANNEXES

Table 8.4. Structure of the sample

	Enterprises (number)	Enterprises (%)	Employees (1,000)	Employees (%)
Labour-intensive activities, Of which :	*51*	*71.8*	*29,092*	*75.5*
Food industry	12	16.9	5,267	13.7
Electrical machines and appliances	3	4.2	918	2.4
Clothing, lather, shoes	11	15.5	10,139	26.3
Printing	8	11.3	1,588	4.1
Metal products	2	2.8	1,600	4.1
Machinery and equipment	3	4.2	846	2.2
Construction	12	16.9	8,734	22.7
Capital-intensive activities, Of which :	*20*	*28.2*	*9,425*	*24.5*
Textile	10	14.1	6,962	18.1
Chemicals	8	11.3	1,243	3.2
Rubber	1	1.4	1,000	2.6
Construction materials	1	1.4	220	0.6
Total	71	100.0	38,517	100.0

Table 8.5. Structure of Polish industry

	Enterprises (number)	Enterprises (%)	Employees (1,000)	Employees (%)
Labour-intensive activities	44,513	84.5	3,142.7	77.8
Capital-intensive activities	8,175	15.5	896.0	22.2
Toyal	52,670	100.0	4,038.7	100.0

Table 8.6. Structure according to property

	Sample			
State and "corporatised" enterprises	Privatised enterprises	Cooperatives	New private sector	Total
15	41	6	9	71
22.5%	56.3%	8.5%	12.7%	100%
Population of the Polish Enterprises (industry and construction) 1998				
2145	1745	3273	44460	51623
4.2%	3.4%	6.3%	86.1%	100%

Table 8.7. Size structure according to the number of employees

	sample				
	less than 100	100 to 499	500 to 999	more than 1000	Total
Number of enterprises	9	36	16	10	71
%	12.7	50.1	22.5	14.1	100
Employees	1461	7410	7610	16948	33429
%	4.4	22.2	22.8	50.7	100
Polish manufacturing enterprises (1)					
Number of enterprises	43.3	46.1	6.5	4.2	100
Employees (1997)	10.89	37.7	17.4	34.06	100

(1) More than 50 employees, excluding mining and energy.

Source: *Rocznik Statystyczny (1998), GUS.*

REFERENCES

Aoki, M. (1988), *Information, incentives and bargaining in the Japanese economy*, Cambridge University Press, New York.

Axelrod, R (1984), *The evolution of cooperation*, Basic Books, New York.

Axelsson, B. and Easton, G. (ed) (1992), *Industrial networks : A new view of reality*, Routledge, London-New York.

Billand, P. (1998), "Rationalité et coopération : le rôle de la confiance en économie, *Revue d'Economie Industrielle*, **84**, 2e trimestre, 67-84.

Brousseau, E. (1996), "Contrats et comportements coopératifs : le cas des relations interentreprises", in J.-L Ravix (ed), *Coopération entre les entreprises et organisation industrielle*, CNRS Editions, Paris, 23-51.

Brousseau, E., Geoffron, P. and Weinstein, O. (1997), "Confiance, connaissances et relations inter-firmes" in B. Guilhon, et al. (eds), *Economie de la connaissance et organisations*, L'Harmattan, Paris, 402-433.

Burchell, B. and Wilkinson, F. (1997), "Trust, business relationships and the contractual environment", *Cambridge Journal of Economics*, **21** (2), March, 217-237.

Casson, M. (1997), *Information and organization. A new perspective on the theory of the firm*, Clarenton Press, Oxford.

Cohendet, P., Llerena, P., Stahn, H. and Umbauer, G. (1998), *The economics of networks, interaction and behaviours*, Springer, Berlin-Heidelberg.

Cordonnier, L. (1997), *Coopération et réciprocité*, PUF, Paris.

Contractor, F. and Lorange, P. (eds) (1988), *Cooperative strategies in international business*, Lexington Books, Massachusetts.

David, P. (1985), "Clio and the economics of QWERTY", *American Economic Review*, **75** (2), May, 332-337.

Elgu. and Johansson U. (1997), "Decision making in inter-firm networks as a political process", *Organization Studies*, **18**(3), 361-384.

Elster, J. (1989), *The cement of society. A study of social order*, Cambridge University Press, Cambridge.

Gambetta, D. (ed) (1988), *Trust: Making and breaking cooperative relations*, Basil Blackwell.

Grabher, G. (ed) (1993), *The embedded firm. On the socioeconomics of industrial networks*, Routledge, London et New York.

Grabher, G. and Stark, D. (eds) (1997), *Restructuring networks in post-socialism*, Oxford University Press, New York.

Granovetter, M. (1985), "Economic action and social structure: The problem of embeddedness", *American Journal of Sociology*, **91** (3), 481-510.

Granovetter, M. (1992), "Problems of explanation in economic sociology", in *Nohria et Eccles (1992)*, 25-56.

Hirschman, A. (1980), *Les passions et les intérêts*, PUF, Paris.

Humphrey, J. and Schmitz H. (1998), "Trust and inter-firm relations in developing and transition economies", *The Journal of Development Studies*, **34** (4), April, 32-61.

Johanson, J. and Mattsson, L.-G. (1987), "Interorganizational relations in industrial systems: A network approach compared with the transaction cost appproach", *International Studies of Management & Organization*, **XVII**, (1), 34-48.

Johnson, S. and McMillan, J. and Woodroof, C. (1999), "Contract enforcement in transition", CEPR, Working Paper n° 20/2081, January.

Karpik, L. (1998), "La confiance : réalité ou illusion ? Examen critique d'une thèse de Williamson", *Revue Economique*, **49** (4), July, 1043-1042.

Kreps, D. (1990), "Corporate culture and economic theory", in J. Alt and K. Shepsle (eds), *Perspectives on Positive Political Economy*, Cambridge University Press, Cambridge.

Kreps, D. and Wilson, R. (1982), "Reputation and imperfect information", *Journal of Economic Theory*, **27** (2), 253-279.

Langlois, R. and Robertson, P. (1995), *Firms, markets and economic change. A dynamic theory of business institutions*, Routledge, London, New York.

Livet, P. and Reynaud, B. (1995), "La confiance indécidable et ses versions en économie", Séminaire interdisciplinaire *"Confiance, apprentissage et anticipation économique"*, UTC, 23-26 janvier.

Lyons, B. and Mehta, J. (1997), "Contracts, opportunisme and trust : self-interest and social orientation", *Cambridge Journal of Economics*, **21** (2), March, 239-257.

Meidinger, C., Robins, S. and Ruffieux, B. (1999), "Confiance, réciprocité et *cheap talk*", *Revue Economique*, **50** (1), January, 5-44.

Menard, C. (1994), "Comportement rationnel et coopération : le dilemme organisationel", *Cahiers d'Economie Politique*, 24-25, 185-207.

Nohria, N. and Eccles, R., (eds) (1992), *Networks and organizations: Structure, form and action*, Harvard Business School Press, Boston, Massachusetts.

North, D. (1990), *Institutions, institutional change and economic performance*, Cambridge University Press, Cambridge.

Orlean, A. (1994), "Sur le rôle respectif de la confiance et de l'intérêt dans la constitution de l'ordre marchand", *Revue du MAUSS*, **4**, second semester, 17-36.

Pfeffer, J. and Salancik, G. (1978), *The external control of organization: A resource dependence perspective*, Harper and Row, New York.

Powell, W. (1990), "Neither market nor hierarchy: Network forms of organization", in B. Staw and L. Cummings (eds), *Research in organizational behavior*, **12**, JAI Press, Greenwich-London, Connecticut-England, 295-336.

Recanatini, F. and Ryterman, R. (2000), "Disorganization or self-organization ? ", SSRN Electronic Library [http://papers.ssrn.com/].

Richardson, G.B. (1959), "Equilibrium, expectations and information", *The Economic Journal*, vol. 69, n° 274, June, 223-237.

Richardson, G.B. (1972), "The organization of industry", *The Economic Journal*, **82**, (327), September, 883-896.

Richardson, G.B. (1995), "The theory of market economy", *Revue Economique*, **46** (5), 1487-1496.

Rizopoulos, Y. (1997a), "Socio-economic networks and economic transformation. The Russian case", *Economic Systems*, **21** (4), December, 365-369.

Rizopoulos, Y. (1997b), "Marchés, organisations, réseaux : alternatives ou complémentarités ? ", in C. Palloix and Y. Rizopoulos (eds), *Firmes et économie industrielle*, L'Harmattan, Paris, 369-387.

Rizopoulos, Y. (1999), "Stratégies organisationnelles et réseaux post-socialistes en Russie", *Revue d'Etudes Comparatives Est-Ouest*, **30** (2-3), June-September, 283-302.

Rullière, J.-L. and Torre, A. (1995), "Les formes de coopération inter-entreprises", *Revue d'Economie Industrielle*, special issue, *Economie industrielle : développements récents*, 215-246.

Sabel, C. (1992), "Elaborer la confiance : de nouvelles formes de coopération dans une économie volatile", in D. Foray and C. Freeman (eds),, *Technologie et richesse des nations*, Economica, Paris, 419-450.

Schelling, T. (1960), *The strategy of conflict*, President and Felows, Harvard College.

Schmidt, C. (1997), "Confiance et rationalité. Sur quelques enseignements de la théorie des jeux", *Revue d'économie politique*, **107** (2), Mars-April, 183-203.

Scott, W. R. (1994), "Institutions and organizations. Toward a theoritical synthesis", in W. Scott and J. Meyer (eds), *Institutional environments and organizations*, Sage, Thousand Oaks – London, 55-80.

Umbhauer, G. (1998), "Introduction", in P. Cohendet et al., (1998), 1-13.

Williamson, O. (1985), *The economic institutions of capitalism*, The Free Press, New York.

Williamson, O. (1993), "Calculativeness, trust and economic organisation", *Journal of Law and Economics*, **XXXVI**, April, 453-502.

Wintrobe R. and Breton A. (1986), "Organizational structure and productivity", *American Economic Review*, **76** (3), June.

Zucker, L.G. (1986), "Production of trust : Institutional sources of economic structure, 1840-1920", in B. Staw and L. Cummings, *Research in organizational behavior*, **8**, JAI Press, Greenwich-London, Connecticut-England, 53-111.

Zuscovitch, E. (1998), "Networks, specialization and trust", in Cohendet et al. (1998), 243-264.

9. Environmental Change and the Evolution of Cooperative Behavior

Anne Plunket

---

1. INTRODUCTION

The literature on the evolution of inter-firm cooperation concentrates on the internal aspects of this dynamic. Two issues are particularly emphasized. The first one considers the impact of contractual arrangements on the incentives to cooperate (Bureth, et al. 1997). The second one considers how institutionalization processes and the creation of resources affect the internal dynamic of agreements (Ciborra, 1991; Ring and Van de Ven, 1994; Lazaric and Wolff, 1993).

This chapter adopts a complementary view. It focuses on the role of exogenous factors in the evolution of cooperation. We show that the agreement's external environment is a strong source of selection for its economics viability and thus its evolution in terms of adaptation and continuation. Two sources of exogenous factors are distinguished: first, the agreement's economic and institutional environment, which affects its goals and results; second, each partner's environment and internal situation. In most of the literature it is implicitly and wrongly assumed that the agreement perfectly fits each partner firm. In fact, the greater the firm, the more likely it is for the agreement to become a suborganizational component. Thus, the external environment as well as the corporate and internal situation of each firm impact on the agreement's evolution as they determine their incentives to cooperate.

This analysis sheds a new light on the issue of the agreement's stability. Stability is most often equated with success understood as the quality of inter-firm learning and interaction, as well as the achievement of common goals. If these endogenous aspects are indeed essential for the continuation of agreements, the major contribution of this chapter is that the relation between success and stability is not so straightforward. We suggest that these internal factors are necessary but not sufficient conditions of stability for the continuation of the agreement, which also depends on exogenous factors.

The first section proposes a typology of environments, in so far as it has an impact on cooperation. In the second section, we specify the impact of exogenous factors on agreements. The last section discusses the implication of external factors on the evolution of cooperation. This paper draws on the results of 25 case studies.

2. TYPOLOGIES OF ENVIRONMENTS INFLUENCING THE EVOLUTION OF COOPERATION

This section discusses the way exogenous forces influence the behavior of firms and their organizational structure. Among the theories studying how environmental factors shape organizational structures, contingency theory has contributing to determining the organizational forms that are best suited to face particular contexts. This theory proposed various typologies most relevant for analyzing firm's behavior given the various degrees of environment complexity and stability (Emery and Trist, 1965; Burns and Stalker, 1961). Nevertheless, these approaches are rather ill-adapted for analyzing cooperative issues. For this reason, we propose a specific typology for the impact of environmental changes on the firms' incentives to cooperate.

Firms' Adaptation to Unexpected Changes

The literature on cooperative agreements has emphasized the role of uncertainty as a reason for cooperation. This chapter shows that unexpected events are also a major source of destabilization. If the agreement is chosen for technological, industrial, legal or economic reasons, changes in these conditions should reduce the partners' incentives to collaborate.

As agreements have to be managed actively, the partners will adapt their behavior through strategic reorientation. Gulati et al. (1994, p. 67) illustrate this situation with the breach of the alliance between Digital Equipment Corporation (DEC) and Tandy: "Tandy was to be the sole source of low-cost PCs for DEC's entry into the market, whereas DEC's installed customer base would allow Tandy to increase its production volume and achieve greater scale economies. (...) the benefits of the alliance changed when Compaq forced the market toward performance, rather than price orientation. (...) DEC felt it had to offer higher-performance PCs to remain competitive in the industry, and the value of its alliance with Tandy suddenly diminished."

The adaptations suggest that the instability of an agreement is not necessarily a sign of failure regarding the quality of cooperation, knowledge creation, and so on. External factors may also change the incentives to cooperate, as illustrated by Gomes-Casseres (1987) in his paper on the relation between the industrial dynamics and the instability of joint ventures.. He shows that variations in the initial conditions have lead to changes in the proprietary structure of a joint venture (for example, through a merger or an acquisition). In this respect, the cooperative agreement is a temporary solution, which represents a strategic option on the future (Kogut, 1991): that is to say that the partners keep the possibility to transform the organizational form of their activities if needed. Thus, there is a critical difference between a sequential view of this transformation and of qualifying it as a failure. The sequential view suggests that the initial choice was good despite necessary adaptation whereas an interpretation in terms of failure suggests that it was wrong to ignore these changes. The modification of the proprietary structure shows an adaptive move, in the first case, but it is a corrective action in the second case.

When agreements involve several partners the number of environmental forces and the sources of destabilization are multiplied. Furthermore, partners very often have different, though not necessarily conflicting, objectives and strategies that may become a source of divergence. Consequently, it is important to specify the agreement's environment, that is what lies outside the boundaries of the agreement. In this view, each partner's corporate situation and economic context represent the agreement's environment.

Multiplicity of Environments

The sources of unforeseen events may be twofold: (1) changes in the economic or institutional context of the agreement, (2) changes in the corporate and economic situation of each partner firm. This distinction is relevant because, most of the time, agreements are only a sub-part of each partner firm. They are therefore considered here as exogenous factors for the evolution of cooperation. Though formal, this distinction is important because it emphasizes the fact that alliances and partner firms are different entities, although interrelated, and partly overlapping. The agreement cannot be completely equated with them: it has its own objectives, resources and rules. In other words, it has its own dynamic that is more or less independent from that of the partner firms.

Three types of environment may be distinguished.
(1) The agreement's specific economic and institutional[1] environment has a direct impact on its goals and results.

(2) Each partner's specific economic and institutional environment: firms have a variety of products based on different technologies and processes sold on different markets. Thus, partners are not necessarily acting on the same market or context. Environmental changes affecting one firm in particular may modify its strategy, and subsequently its incentives to cooperate. Said differently, changes that have apparently no link with the agreement may nevertheless have an indirect impact on its evolution and continuation.

(3) Each partner's specific corporate situation: internal changes in the organization, the strategy, and so on of each firm may also have an indirect impact on the agreement.

These changes may be either negative or positive as they may lead to a breach of the agreement or, conversely, they may strengthen it.

Though formal, the aim of distinguishing three types of environment is to highlight that the agreement's rationale does not only depend on its own goal and results but also on each partner's environment, overall corporate strategy and internal situation. Each firm has a set of strategies and projects, and usually the agreement covers only one of these projects and how they can be implemented.

Empirical Analysis

This analysis draws on 25 case studies of R&D agreements in the area of biotechnology and new materials. The desire to investigate cooperative agreements whilst generating comparative data led to case studies involving interview-based methodology. The interview schedule was in four parts: division of labor, strategy, unexpected events internal and external, results and termination. The investigation was aimed at generating reasonable indications and details on history, problems, expectations and results. The interviews were semi-structured with a minimal use of prompts for open-ended questions. Important issues were addressed from a number of different angles so that any inconsistency or ambiguity could be examined. Interviews were conducted with project heads, often R&D managers and engineers. Each lasted at least two hours and was transcribed immediately afterwards. When possible we tried to interview two persons in a firm. Nearly all the firms are European-based and mostly French. Foreign partners were interviewed by phone and e-mail.

The 25 case studies are R&D Eureka agreements (bar 2) in biotechnology and new materials. The two domains were chosen for their similar characteristics: they both cover a wide range of technological fields and applications in a more or less developmental phase. If biotechnology is relatively homogeneous because of a common technological paradigm, new materials are very heterogeneous and cover different technologies and materials: polymers, paper recycling, ultra high strength concrete, aluminum alloys and so on. The table 9.1. proposes some basic information on the case studies. More information on the agreements cited in this chapter such as the aim, financing and origin of partners, may be found in the Eureka database at [http://eureka.belspo.be/].

Table 9.1. Partner strategies (markets, activities), individual objectives relating to cooperative project and the purpose of the agreement

Firms	Markets	Firms' incentives to cooperate	Purpose of the agreement
Vertical agreements			
*Biosepra	Chromato-graphy	Purification of albumin	
*Smith Kline Beecham	Infectious pathologies	Vaccine (whooping-cough)	To develop dyes for the chromatography
*Vilmax	Dyes	Dye	
*Applexion	Process engineering	Dvlp. of a refining process	Application of membrane technology separation for sugar purification
*RAR	Sugar refinery	Optimization of production process	
*Tech-Sep	Research	Dvlp. of membranes (generic input)	
*Industrial Quimica	Production of naphthalene	To optimize their production process	Dvlp. of a process and construction of a factory
*Befs Prokem	Engineering of process	Dvlp. of a process	
*Adler	Equipment supplier	Devlp. new machines	Dvlp. of a very resistant concrete pipe to compete with other varieties of pipes.
*Bouygues	Engineering	Valorization of a resistant concrete	
*Eurobéton	Cement manufacturer	Look for new materials	
*Benalu	Vehicles of transport	Dvlp. of transport vehiculs in aluminium	Dvlp. of light material for the "rail-road" transport systems
*Pechiney	Aluminum	New markets for aluminum.	
*Genset	Biotechnoloy firm	Dvlp. of diagnosis based on molecular biology	Dvlp. of a kit of diagnosis
*Nunc	Chemistry, pharmacy	Markets for plastics (input)	

*Gist Brocades France	Producer of enzymes	Dvlp. new enzymes (input)	Production of fruit juice with new enzymes
*Nufri	Fruit juice producer	To increase productivity and quality	
*Fiberweb	Producer of non-woven materials (output)	New non-woven material	Dvlp. of biodegradable non-woven materials
*Neste OY	Chemical industry (input)	New markets for polymers	
*Vetoquinol	Veterinary pharmaceuticals (market)	New applications	
*Eurocable	Producer of lathes	To find cheaper materials, which can be recycled (European legislation)	Recycling the polyurethane from the recycling of refrigerators
*Hecker und Krosch	Equipment supplier	Production of equipment for lathes	
*R&t Umwelt	Recycling of refrigerators	Polyurethane supplier (input)	
Horizontal agreements			
*Jouveinal	Gastro-enterology	Valorization of a jouveinal molecule	Clinical development of a drug
*Sigma Tau	Gastro-enterology	Co-development (1/2 costs + risk)	
*Serbio - Stago	Thrombosis	Dvlp. of common technologies:	Dvlp. of two diagnosis
*Alpha Biotech	Infectious pathology	division of costs and risks	
Sanofi	Production of heparin	To develop their activity	Synthesis of heparin for pharmaceutical applications.
Organon	Extractive chemistry	Valorization of a know-how Co-develop. (1/2 costs and of the risks)	

Table 9.1 illustrates the differences between the firm's strategies (that is, incentives to cooperate) and the agreement's goals for some of the cases studied. Its analysis shows the following points:

(a) The purpose of the agreement most often covers only the aim of the partner who originated the project and who is usually the leader, the other firms being suppliers or users. In this case, the environment of the agreement overlaps only one partner's environment.

(b) In vertical agreements, the partners' environments are usually different: they do not necessarily act on the same markets, or have the same activities. They cannot therefore have the same corporate strategies.

(c) In horizontal agreements, firms usually seek to avoid direct competition among them. Thus, even in horizontal agreements, firms usually act on separate markets, although they sometimes have similar competencies. When partners initiate an agreement for sharing costs and risks in activities that require a critical size, their environment may overlap more widely. The co-development usually results in common patents that may lead to conflicts at the end of the cooperation when partners decide to share markets.

3. THE IMPACT OF EXOGENOUS FACTORS ON AGREEMENTS

The aim of this section is to specify how exogenous factors act on the internal dynamic of the agreement and its continuity.

Agreement's Stability: Between Economic Legitimacy and Corporate Coherence

The agreement is a way of implementing the partner firm's objectives. Thus, the sources of change that destabilize the agreement are not only due to its internal dynamic including problems of interaction and coordination between partners, problems related to technical and commercial feasibility and profitability and so on. The destabilization of agreements may also be due to changes in each partner firm's corporate projects and strategies.

In other words, three different types of legitimacy may explain the continuation of the agreement:

(a) The agreement's profitability that sanctions its returns on investments: this legitimacy is sanctioned, first of all, by internal aspects already mentioned, and also its external environment, the market in particular.

(b) The coherence between the agreement's objectives and each partner's corporate strategy sanctions the capacity of the agreement to implement each firm's own corporate strategy. This legitimacy is assessed, first of all, within each firm. In that case, the selection criteria are not strictly economic but also political, in the sense that the evolution of the agreement depends on the balance of forces between the managers inside each firm and the evolution of each firm's project priorities.

(c) The legitimacy of each firm's corporate strategy and thus each particular project, including the agreement. Behind this idea lies the fact that strategies, just like projects within firms, are in competition for the allocation of resources (Warglien, 1995). This competition depends on the amount invested, the expected returns, its duration and so on. In this case, the selection criteria are largely economic and dictated by the market, although political dimensions (power relations inside the firms) cannot be excluded.

The distinction introduced between these different types of legitimacy explains that the unexpected events that may touch the agreements do not simply sanction their profitability. They also sanction the agreement's coherence with each firm's objectives and their capacity to implement them. Consequently, it is essential to highlight the changes that affect the partner's situations as they may end up affecting their involvement in the cooperation.

Environmental Impact on the Agreement's Purpose

Agreements may serve various goals such as the development of a specific good, a process or new equipment goods, the creation of know-how, the implementation of a distribution channel etc. An environmental shock concerning these goals may modify the agreement's profitability, the expected returns and thus the resources originally allocated to the project.

In the case of the Serbio-Alpha Biotech agreement, the purpose was to develop a diagnosis of infectious and thromboembolic diseases. It illustrates the impact of two external factors: public policies and changes in the corporate strategy. This agreement lasted for 5 years between 1991-1996. Its aim was to develop fast diagnoses (with almost instantaneous results) for infectious and thromboembolic diseases by using two types of tests (an individual test and a laboratory test). Serbio is the research center of Diagnostic Stago, which is a leader on the market of diagnosis tools in the field of heart diseases. Alpha biotech produces diagnosis kits for infectious diseases such as herpes, rubella and hepatitis.

Origin of the project: In the early nineties public authorities in charge of health policies in Europe were particularly interested in early diagnosis and preventive treatments for reducing the social cost of cardiovascular diseases. Serbio and Alpha Biotech decided to pool resources together for the development of specific technologies needed for the development of these diagnoses. They were not competitors since their relevant markets were different.

The partners divided the work among them after having defined their means and objectives. Regularly, they discussed the advancement of the work done. Every six months, a meeting of the management committee was organized to evaluate the research and to allocate the resources.

External factors:

- *Market problems*: the market quickly evolved, in particular because of a wave of concentration and drastic reduction in public health budgets.

- *Strategic reorientation* : The company Alpha Biotech (formerly known as "Ismunit"), was acquired by the Schiapparelli group two years after the beginning of cooperation. The project continued although the new group was not particularly interested; they imposed more controls, stricter profitability criteria. Finally, the new group let the project continue and then dropped it without seeking a particular result.

Results: the objectives were partially achieved: a test leading to cross licenses and joint patents was developed. The agreement also enabled learning processes and led to new working methods and routines that are still being used.

Activity after the agreement: in 1997 (during the first interview with Serbio project's manager), the project given up in 1996 was started again in-house. Serbio would have liked to resume the cooperation with Alpha Biotech but the Italian group's new objectives did not integrate these developments, with the regret of the former partners ("the *staff from both companies became very good friends*" said the person interviewed on the Italian side). In 1998 (during a second interview with Serbio's finance manager), the project was stopped for good: the membrane technology successful. Moreover, the former project manager had moved to another company.

Changes Affecting the Partner's Environment and Internal Situation

This point is based on the dichotomy between the firm's environment and that of the agreement. Two types of unexpected events are considered: the external changes that modify the firm's situation and the internal transformations that result in new corporate strategies and organizational structures.

The aim is to show that events that have apparently no direct link with the agreement may nevertheless have major impacts on its continuation, although the project may still be profitable. Firms are continuously subject to incremental changes in their values, strategies, structure of power, their structure and control as shown by Tushman and Romanelli (1985). These core elements define the internal selection environment of firms. When changes in these elements do not lead to sufficient levels of performance, they induce more radical reorganization of their activities. These reorganizations imply fast successive changes and discontinuous strategies,

systems of values and so on. In other words, they result in reexamining the
structures of governance used to implement the objectives, strategies and
underlying projects, and thus its organizational practices and competencies.
This last point is particularly important in restructuring situations where
firms decide to externalize certain activities.

Table 9.2. Indirect impacts on the evolution of agreements

Changes concerning the firm	Possible impact on the agreement	
Economic situation	Market drop, reduction in resources allocated and the scope of the project.	Contract is stopped or frozen when the situation is temporary
Strategy	Re-evaluation of the agreement	Breach of contract is a function of: • Adequacy of the agreement to the new strategy • Sunk costs and degree of advancement • Financial repercussions • Generic character of resources
Organization • Sale and dismantling of firm's divisions	Destruction of competencies and resources	Rescission, if not delays and problems of reorganization
• Displacement of personnel	Breaks the dynamics of institutionalization and confidence	Rescission, if not delays and problems of reorganization

These changes affect the partner's incentives to cooperate and thus the
evolution of the agreement. Three types of changes are emphasized: the
modification of the economic situation, the firm's strategies and internal
organization (see Table 9.2):

(1) *The economic situation* of a partner can change during the contract.
Changes in the sources of provisioning, in demand, in production process, in
prices, etc. affect performance and thus lead firms to reassess their activities,
their markets and their current projects. During the Benalu-Pechiney
agreement, for example, a serious recession reduced the resources available
for the project, leading Benalu to dismiss one-third of its employees and stop
cooperation. Both companies decided to suspend the agreement and even
consider terminating it. The project was resumed after a market rebound, two
years later.

(2) *Strategic reorientation* in firms usually leads them to re-examine their
organization and projects. Mergers or acquisitions may or may not induce
this type of reorientation. In some firms, the selection of projects, among
which cooperative agreements, depends on their coherence with the corporate

strategy or the strategy of the group to which it belongs. Reorientations may thus end up stopping a project (Sodern-IABG-Vought on the accelerator of protons to detect early erosions on certain materials such as the fuselage of planes) or reinforce it (Fiberweb-Neste Oy-Vetoquinol).

(3) *Modifications to internal organization* can hamper the continuation of an agreement, in particular because of the local aspect of the learning and institutionalization processes (Plunket, 1999). These reorientations can result in:

  (a) *Outsourcing or shutting down divisions*, which reduces the firm's activities or competencies as part of the equipment and the employees are no longer available for the project's implementation. This was the case with Neste Oy in its contract with Fiberweb. The outsourcing caused various delays since Neste had to re-examine its organizational structure and the role of a certain number of its employees.

  (b) *Employee or manager turnover*: when there is trust in an agreement, it is most often inter-individual rather than an inter-organizational one. It depends largely on the size of the firm. When the firm is very large, it is likely that the agreement involves only a small number of people inside the firm. Thus, when trust is inter-individual, it is difficult to continue an agreement after the departure of a project manager who usually defends the project within the firm. The Pica-Sara Lee agreement on decaffeinization is a striking illustration of such situations. The new manager who was in charge of the project, at Sara Lee did not seem to have the same interest as his predecessor and eventually, the agreement was stopped.

The Fiberweb-Neste Oy-Vetoquinol agreement emphasizes the need for a tight coherence between the agreement and the strategy of the group. This agreement lasted three years between 1993-1996. Its aim was to develop biodegradable non-woven materials. Fiberweb is the world's third largest producer of non-woven material. Neste Oy partakes in the oil industry, in energy and chemistry and develops biopolymers, that is biodegradable plastic starting from renewable resources. Vetoquinol is a veterinary pharmaceutical laboratory, a potential user of biodegradable non-wowen material.

History of the project: the Fiberweb company wished to develop a biodegradable non-woven material. The constraint was to find a raw material and the competencies specific to the project. Fiberweb proposed its project to its polymer suppliers, which directed it towards Neste Oy, a Finnish polymer producer with which Fiberweb had never been in a relationship before. Neste Oy wanted to diversify its markets in polymers and, more particularly, it wanted to develop environment friendly polymers. Vétoquinol was a

Fiberweb customer in charge of testing the various product applications for the veterinary surgery.

Organization of the agreement: the partnership was organized and divided into products. Quarterly meetings were organized; the modifications to be implemented were discussed according to the expectations and the difficulties encountered.

Unforeseen events:

(a) Fiberweb was acquired twice during the project. At the start, Fiberweb (formerly Sodoca) became Fiberweb Sodoca after the first acquisition. Then, after a second acquisition by BBA, an English group, it became Fiberweb France. With each new acquisition, the strategy was fully overhauled and all the projects reevaluated. The project manager at Fiberweb had, each time, to show the coherence of his project with the group's strategy, while insisting on the return on investment and the differentiation of the product compared with that of the competitors (positioning compared to competition). The project represented part of the company's first three priorities.

(b) Neste Oy also went through a strategic and organizational reorientation after a merger and the sale of certain activities. The agreement underwent some delays because of the outsourcing of the laboratories, which carried out the tests for Neste Oy.

Results: The non-woven product is a technical success as it has reduced the costs of processing waste by better valorization. Waste can now be degraded without generating toxic residues for the environment and calling upon resources of natural origin.

4. IMPLICATIONS FOR THE EVOLUTION OF COOPERATION

This chapter has raised the question of the impact of the exogenous factors on the evolution of cooperation. It has proposed a typology of these various factors and a discussion of the way they affect the agreement's purpose and the partner's corporate and internal situation. This last section discusses the role played by the exogenous factors compared to the internal dynamic of agreements.

The internal dynamic depends on a complex interaction between the resources invested by the partners and the agreement's outcome (expected or confirmed), which has a major impact on the partners' incentives to cooperate. As it is not the aim of the chapter to discuss the internal aspects of the evolution of cooperation, it will give some elements without going into major detail.

Invested resources concern the transfer, the creation and appropriation of technological know-how through interactive learning processes. Learning is the key driving force to this internal dynamic (Bureth, et al., 1997). The partner's commitment may be reinforced if the project's outcome satisfies their expectations, otherwise they will redefine their objectives and the means to implement them. If the gap between their new and prior objectives is too wide, the partners may reduce their commitment or stop cooperating. Given this setup, the stability of the agreement depends on the quality of partner interaction and the capacity to generate value through innovation. In other words, it depends on its profitability.

The major contribution of this chapter is to show that the way the agreement may evolve can be very different when one adds the exogenous dimension. The approaches in terms of internal dynamic emphasize the role played by partner interaction and organizational learning processes. It is often assumed that learning processes affect the whole firm. Yet, the key point, however often ignored, is that the agreement is usually a suborganizational component of the partner firms. Actually, the greater the firm and the more likely it is for learning to be localized at sub-levels of the organization in charge of implementing the project. Thus, it is necessary to distinguish two levels of decision and action; the top management in charge of the strategic decision and an operational level, that is, the team which is in charge of implementing the project. Yet, the top management may not be able to assess the real value or difficulty of the cooperative process. The top management may undervalue or underestimate the importance of developing common routines and competencies.

The idea here is that, in each firm, disagreements may exist between the top management in charge of corporate strategy and the operational level. Thus, the agreement may lead to different levels of assessment and divergence. For example, the divergence may concern the level and speed of project advancement. At the strategic level, the work may not advance sufficiently quickly whereas work seems very fruitful at the operational level. The opposite situation is also true: cooperation seems impossible at operational levels (for example, because of incompatible routines) whereas it seems viable for the top management from a strategic point of view. This remains valid for both internal and external changes. However it still applies when changes occur at the corporate level. Strategic reorientation, whatever the reason, will lead to a reconsideration of the agreement's interest of the firm and thus its incentive to cooperate.

The key point, here, is that the evolution of cooperation will not only depend on its own efficiency and profitability but also on the coherence between the goal of the agreement and the strategy of the group. Thus, exogenous changes that lead to a greater coherence with the group's strategy generates the agreement's reinforcement. On the other hand, if the project lies at the edge or outside the boundaries of the new strategy, the partners can decide to stop it. The very survival of the agreement should depend on various factors such as sunk costs, the degree of advancement of the project, the expected financial returns and the generic character of the resources involved.

(1) *The gap between the purpose of the agreement and corporate strategy*: when technological opportunities and the market become relatively less important, firms are forced to focus on niches requiring specific competencies while reaching critical sizes necessary for financing their activities. Thus, firms get rid of activities and stop projects that are not directly similar (see Richardson, 1972) to their core activities (that is that contribute more to their added value). In the case of Sodern-IABG-Vought on the accelerator of protons, as both companies were bought up by the Loral group, IABG and Vought stopped their commitment to the current agreement because the agreement's purpose was not consistent with the new strategy. This point may nevertheless be moderated in certain cases.

(2) *The importance of sunk costs and the degree of advancement of the project*: When the project is well advanced, firms may find it beneficial to continue the agreement until its end, especially when the committed costs are irreversible. This is particularly true when there are intangible investments in R&D activities as was the case with Serbio-Alpha Biotech. This agreement was already well underway when Schiapparelli, an Italian group, bought over Alpha Biotech. The cooperation was continued, although stricter constraints of profitability and management were imposed. However, when Serbio wanted to launch a new agreement with Alpha Biotech, the Italian group refused against the opinion of its employees. By contrast, if the agreement is uncertain, the chances to end it up earlier are higher.

(3) *The importance of expected financial returns*: as suggested, when the project is long term and requires much investment for uncertain results, the agreement runs a higher risk of being dropped. On the other hand, if the project concerns large markets with reasonable chances of considerable profits, the firm can be interested in continuing the agreement, even though the corporate strategy has changed.

(4) *The specific or generic character of the resources*: the incentive to cooperate does not rely only on expected returns on investment, but also on indirect benefits and spin-offs that the firm can obtain. For agreements based on generic technologies and know-how, that is applicable to several activity domains, firms will have a higher incentive to continue the partnership.

5. CONCLUSION

The evolution of cooperation depends on a complex combination between internal and external forces. These selection mechanisms not only sanction the agreement's economic and organisational legitimacy but also its coherence with the corporate strategy to which it belongs. In other words, it goes far beyond the simple issue of the agreement's continuation. Events and external shocks enhance the complexity of this issue. The outcome of the agreement may thus depend on (1) the dimension that is favoured by each firm and the capacity to generate short-term financial returns or the long-term capacity to develop competencies; (2) the nature of the environmental shocks that affect the agreement of each partner firm.

More fundamentally, the stabilizing effect usually ascribed to the learning process, and more generally to the institutionalisation process, should be specified. If this effect is a necessary condition for the agreement's success, it is, above all, localized at the level of the cooperating teams that implement the projects. These teams should not be assimilated into the whole firm. Thus, the future of the agreement also depends on the strategic decisions about the definition of activity portfolio and the allocation of resources. These decision levels are often too distant, in hierarchical terms, to assess the economic potential of this learning process. Therefore, in response to modifications affecting firms, the external events of the agreement may lead to termination though the economic viability has not changed. Finally, it may be concluded that for understanding the evolution of agreements it is fundamental to distinguish between the internal dynamic on which the agreement relies and the external factors, which contribute to determining and explaining its evolution.

NOTES

1. The economic environment may be characterized by market (growth, extent) and industrial conditions (products and processes), and so on. Institutional factors may be characterized by public policies (R&D policy, infrastructure development, the financing of health policies, and so on) but also legal rules, consumption and production norms, the procedures for launching new products, and so on.

REFERENCES

Bureth, A., Wolff, S. and Zanfei, A. (1997), "The two faces of learning by cooperating: the evolution and stability of inter-firm agreements in the European electronics industry", *Journal of Economic Behaviour and organization*, **33** (2).

Burns, T. and Stalker, G.M. (1961), *The Management of Innovation*, Tavistock.

Ciborra, C. (1991), "Alliances as learning experiments: Cooperation, competition and change in hightech industries", in L.K. Mytelka (eds), *Strategic Partnerships, States, Firms and International competition*, Pinter Publishers, London.

Emery, F.E. and Trist, E.L. (1965), "The casual texture of organizational environments", *Human Relations*, **18** (1)

Gomes-Casseres, B (1987), "Joint venture instability: is it a problem?", *Columbia Journal of World Business*, Summer 1987, 97-102

Gulati, R., Khanna, T. and Nohria, N. (1994), "Unilateral commitments and the importance of process in alliances", *SLoan Management Review*, Spring 1994.

Kogut, B., (1991), "Joint ventures and the option to expand and acquire", *Management Science*, **37**(1), january, 19-33.

Lazaric, N. and Wolff, S. (1993), "La dynamique organisationnelle des accords inter-entreprises dans les technologie de l'information et de la communication : une approche en termes de flexibilité et d'apprentissage", Cahier de recherche n°13 de l'Université Technologique de Compiègne.

Plunket, A. (1999), "Evolution de la coopération. Contribution à l'étude des déterminants des processus d'évolution et de sélection de la coopération technologique", Thèse de doctorat en Sciences économiques, Paris Sud.

Richardson, G.B. (1972), "The organisation of industry", *The Economic Journal*, **82**, 883-896.

Ring P. and Van de Ven A. (1994), "Developmental processes of cooperative interorganizational relationships", *Academy of Management Review*, **19** (1), 90-118.

Tushman, M. and Romanelli, E. (1985), "Organization evolution: a metamorphosis model of convergence and reorientation", *Reasearch in Organizational Behavior*, **7**, 171-222.

Warglien, M. (1995), "Hierarchical selection and organizational adaptation", *Industrial and Corporate Change*, **4** (1), 161-186.

PART III

Industrial and Research Networks

10. Inter-institutional Collaboration and the Organisation of R&D

Pier Paolo Saviotti

1. INTRODUCTION

Innovation networks became a very widespread phenomenon starting from the early 1980s (Chesnais, 1986. Mytelka, 1991; EC, 1997, Ch. 11). They are constituted by a set of heterogeneous and independent institutional actors that enter into some kind of collaborative relationship in order to create new knowledge and innovations. They are part of a larger class of inter-institutional collaborative agreements (Mytelka, 1991). In fact, collaborative ventures between independent firms had always existed, but they were previously used for quite different purposes. For example, joint ventures were used to establish productive facilities in less developed countries (LDCs) to exploit technologies previously developed in industrialised countries (Amin, 1996). Examples of inter-firm collaboration used to create new knowledge are a novelty of the 1980s.

When they first appeared, innovation networks were considered by economists as a temporary phenomenon. The theories of industrial organisation generally adopted in the early 1980s considered that only markets and hierarchical organisations were stable. Twenty years after their emergence innovation networks seem to have become a standard component of industrial organisation whose stability, if not eternal, seems to be guaranteed in the short to medium term. A considerable amount of research has been done on this topic, but a full theoretical understanding of innovation networks still escapes us.

In what follows we will focus on innovation networks in biotechnology, although most of the considerations developed here will be of considerable generality. In particular, we will review the explanation initially given of the roles played by different members in innovation networks and we will argue that these roles alone would not be enough to guarantee the continued stability of these networks. The approach adopted in this chapter will be based on a number of concepts recently emerged within the economic analysis of knowledge.

2. EMPIRICAL EVIDENCE ABOUT INNOVATION NETWORKS

Innovation networks are part of a larger class of inter-institutional collaborative agreements (Mytelka, 1991). No standardised classification exists to describe either innovation networks or other types of collaborative agreements. In spite of the uncertainty arising from this lack of a rigorous classification it seem that the number of innovation networks has been constantly increasing since the early 1980s (EC, 1997, Ch. 11). These networks can be found in many industries, but their frequency is greater in industries linked to high technologies (IT, biotechnology, new materials, and so on). Amongst the factors that are generally associated with the formation of networks are the shortening of product life cycles and the higher rate of creation of new knowledge.

The emergence of networks has been accompanied by the creation of small firms specialised in the emerging technology, generally called new technology firms (NTFs). In biotechnology they are called dedicated biotechnology firms (DBFs). Perhaps more so than in other industries, DBFs played a crucial role in the emergence of new biotechnology based industrial practices (Grabowsky and Vernon, 1994).

It is to be stressed that NTFs or DBFs were not just another type of SMEs. In general SMEs exist and are stable under particular conditions. For example in sectors where economies of scale are not very large. Another role that SMEs frequently play is that of supplier of spare parts to LDFs. In the 1970s most R&D was performed by large diversified firms (LDFs), although a considerable amount of innovative activity took place in SMEs. Yet it was not common for SMEs to be pioneers of a completely new technology. As had already happened before in a few cases in IT, in biotechnology DBFs were the first firms able to understand and use the new technology.

Biotechnology innovation networks include public research institutions (PRIs) amongst their members. University-industry collaborative agreements have existed for a long time. However, the participation of DBFs in these networks introduced a significant difference in the way LDFs interact with public research institutions. DBFs had the capacity to understand both the new technology and its potential industrial applications. They could bridge the gap between the competencies and interests of PRIs and of LDFs. It seems as if the knowledge gap between PRIs and LDFs had grown wider, making their direct interaction more difficult. In these conditions DBFs could become the required catalyst for the adoption of the new biotechnology by LDFs. DBFs became intermediaries between PRIs and LDFs.

In summary, we can consider that innovation networks are constituted by three types of actors: DBFs, LDFs and PRIs. This is not to say that no other types of institutional actors take part in or influence networks. In the next section we deal briefly with the main types of actors and with the main factors influencing innovation networks in biotechnology.

The Main Factors Affecting Innovation Networks in Biotechnology

Dedicated biotechnology firms (DBFs) are an entirely new phenomenon emerging in the USA in the second half of the 1970s. Modern biotechnology was born in that period from a small number of discoveries that transformed the scientific developments of molecular biology into industrial applications. Recombinant DNA and monoclonal antibodies opened the way to a whole stream of industrial applications, at first mainly in the pharmaceutical industry, although it was immediately evident that important potential applications could exist in other areas (agriculture, environment, and so on). Thus we are referring here to what has been called third generation biotechnology, that is to the biotechnology that depends in an essential way on being able to modify the genetic make-up of organisms. However important these potential applications, equally important barriers to the adoption of these technologies by firms existed in the second half of the 1970s. First, pharmaceutical and agrochemical firms, the firms that were more likely to benefit from the adoption of biotechnology in that period, had a knowledge base depending on disciplines different from molecular biology, for example organic chemistry. The knowledge base of incumbent pharmaceutical or agrochemical firms was then qualitatively different from the knowledge base of the emerging biotechnology. To put it differently, incumbent pharmaceutical and agrochemical firms had a limited absorption capacity (Cohen and Levinthal, 1989, 1990) for the new biotechnology. A second important barrier existed at the international level. In the early 1970s molecular biology had achieved a much greater level of development in the USA than anywhere else. Even in Europe and in Japan scientific capabilities in molecular biology were very limited with respect to those of the USA. A third barrier that made adoption of biotechnology relatively more difficult in Europe was the virtual absence of a venture capital industry. In the early 1970s venture capital firms (VCFs) were an institution existing almost exclusively in the USA. VCFs were not just another type of bank. They were very important in the development of biotechnology, of information technology and of other high technologies because they funded the development of very young firms in as yet unproven technologies or, sometimes, of groups of individuals with a project, that could become a firm. None of these firms or projects could be evaluated by means of the criteria normally used by banks. VCFs had an intimate knowledge of the activities of the NTFs and DBFs that they funded and could assess the potential for their future development even when a firm was not yet present. To stress the difference between VCFs and banks even further we could say that VCFs evaluated a firm's future potential based on its activities while banks evaluated the past performance of a firm based on a series of financial indicators. VCFs were thus a new type of institutional actor which funded the creation of firms which in the same conditions would not have been funded by banks. VCFs are a combination of knowledge and financial capital more appropriate to the emerging knowledge-based economy than traditional banks. The simultaneous scarcity of scientific capabilities and of venture capital firms in Europe considerably delayed the emergence of European DBFs.

The creation of dedicated biotechnology firms (DBFs) represented a way to accelerate the development of industrial applications. DBFs were often created by research scientists and generally located in the proximity of important research centres. DBFs thus had a very rapid access to all the important developments in the new biotechnologies. Of course, in spite of the importance of their academic origins and links, DBFs also included managers. Even if their founding team was constituted only by scientists, the requirement of subsequent development generally led to the employment of managers. Thus, in the second half of the 1970s the actors that could participate in the creation and diffusion of biotechnology were a few DBFs, a number of research institutions and several LDFs, where the first two types of actors were very asymmetrically located in the world economic system, that is in the USA.

At this point a number of possible scenarios could have been envisaged. In one of them LDFs would have been incapable of absorbing the new biotechnology and would have been replaced by DBFs, who would have become the new generation of LDFs. This scenario resembles that foreseen by Schumpeter (1912, 1934), according to whom the producers of locomotives and railway equipment were unlikely to be the same that produced horse-drawn carriages. Of course, this is not what happened and we can understand why.

3. SOME CONSIDERATIONS BASED ON THE ECONOMIC ANALYSIS OF KNOWLEDGE

The intensity of knowledge in most industrialised countries increased so much recently that many commentators hypothesise that we are moving towards a knowledge-based society (David and Foray, 1994).In such a society we can expect that processes of knowledge creation and utilisation will become the fundamental factors determining firm competitiveness and economic development. Human capital would then be expected to play a growing role in the economic performance of firms and countries (Romer, 1990; Lucas, 1988). It has been hypothesised that not only we use more knowledge to create new goods and services, but that the very same mechanisms of creation and utilisation of knowledge are changing. According to Gibbons et al. (1994) a new mode, called Mode 2, is emerging in addition to the traditional Mode 1. In Mode 1 the creation and utilisation of knowledge took place in separate institutions, each having its own criteria for evaluation. In Mode 2 the creation and utilisation of knowledge happen simultaneously and they are sometimes performed in the same institution. As a consequence, hybrid evaluation criteria have to be used in Mode 2. The change from Mode 1 to Mode 2 has a number of important implications that we need not discuss here. For the purposes of this chapter it suffices to say that the mechanisms of creation and utilisation of knowledge are very rapidly changing.

This growing knowledge intensity, although appreciated only recently, is not a completely new phenomenon. Its roots can be found in the institutionalisation of R&D, first in German universities in the second half of the nineteenth century, and then in industrial firms, starting from the beginning of the twentieth century. The institutionalisation of R&D introduced a completely new activity into the economic system and can rightly be considered a revolution (Freeman, 1982; Freeman and Soete, 1997).

In spite of the recognised importance of knowledge, economics is still ill equipped to analyse it. In what follows some very general concepts useful for the economic analysis of knowledge are introduced. R&D can be considered an example, although the most important, of *search activities*. Search activities can be defined as all the activities that explore unknown subsets of the external environment, trying to understand them and to prepare new routines that could potentially replace existing ones (Saviotti, 1996). Routines are repeated patterns of operations that are systematically performed in response to environmental stimuli falling within a pre-determined range. Routines represent a form of habitual behaviour because they are not changed unless the stimuli start exceeding the allowed range. Routines show some inter-temporal stability, that Nelson and Winter (1982) consider as the organisational analogue of the genetic heritage of biological organisms. With some degree of approximation it is possible to classify all economic activities as either routines or search activities.

The organisation of R&D that has been prevalent so far is based on a distinction between publicly and privately funded R&D. Basic or fundamental research is usually publicly funded because its output is considered to be a public good and to have limited appropriability. Public funding is justified because in these circumstances basic research would be underfunded by the private sector. Privately funded R&D is usually applied research or development and it is generally performed in vertically integrated firms. However, recently this form of organisation of R&D has been challenged by an alternative form, innovation networks.

Firms have a knowledge base. However, at any time the external knowledge available to them is much greater than their internal knowledge base. We can consider that this external knowledge pool has two important properties that determine the ability of a firm to internalise it: its rate of change and its degree of complexity. Furthermore, the ability of firms to learn external knowledge depends on their absorption capacity (Cohen and Levinthal, 1989, 1990). In other words, a firm has a greater probability of learning a given piece of external knowledge, the more similar this knowledge is to the one on which the firm has previously done R&D. Furthermore, at least large diversified firms (LDFs) have the capacity to combine different competencies, assets, and so on. Thus a pharmaceutical firm has the capacity to combine chemical and biological research with drug testing, protection of intellectual property rights, marketing, and so on. An LDF has core and complementary assets (Teece, 1986).

Knowledge generation is characterised by important discontinuities. Concepts such as scientific paradigms (Kuhn, 1962), technological paradigms (Dosi, 1982), dominant designs (Abernathy and Utterback, 1975), technological regimes (Nelson and Winter, 1977) are examples of these discontinuities in both scientific and technological knowledge. Furthermore, knowledge is cumulative. Thus, in order to learn the latest element within a given field of knowledge all the previous elements with the same field have to be learned. The more knowledge progresses within a given field, the greater the barrier a potential entrant has to face with respect to an incumbent. Thus the mechanisms of knowledge creation and utilisation tend to create barriers to entry as knowledge advances within a given field. However, such barriers are only intra-paradigmatic. When a new paradigm qualitatively different from the previous one and capable of leading to important industrial applications emerges, the economic value of the knowledge corresponding to the old paradigm falls, sometimes dramatically. The absorption capacity of incumbent firms is high with respect to the old paradigm but very low with respect to the new one. On the contrary, the barriers to entry into the new paradigm would be very low for the small, specialised new firms constituted largely by researchers having previously done R&D on the new paradigm. Thus, the emergence of a new paradigm can dramatically change the barriers to entry into an industrial field.

Discontinuities in knowledge creation could potentially lead to the replacement of incumbent firms by new emerging firms. This is not necessarily the case and innovation networks point rather to the co-existence of incumbent and of new firms in the industrial sectors concerned. This co-existence can be explained by the fact that although new firms may have a much greater absorption capacity for the new paradigm, the complementary assets required to produce the final output are still held by incumbent firms. In these conditions the most likely outcome is a co-existence of incumbents and of new firms, in which the two types of firms play complementary roles.

The situation described above could be temporary if incumbent firms, although slower to react than small specialised firms (DBFs), could gradually construct an absorption capacity for the new paradigm. If that were to happen incumbent LDFs could do without any form of alliance or collaboration with DBFs. Innovation networks would then have a temporary existence limited to the period required by incumbent LDFs to construct an absorption capacity for the new paradigm. Let us observe here that the possibility that DBFs replace LDFs depends on the resources that the former need to acquire complementary assets which together with the new technology allow a marketable output to be produced.

The temporary character of innovation networks was hypothesised as soon as they were observed (see Teece, 1988). About twenty years later their emergence innovation networks seem to have acquired a relative stability as an important form of industrial organisation, although their decline cannot be excluded over a longer period. Thus we have to come to terms with their existence and to try and understand why their predicted decline has so far not taken place.

A specific role has been identified before for DBFs, that of identifying novel elements of knowledge and of communicating them to LDFs. This role of DBFs will be called the *translators'* role. As pointed out above, the translators' role could be only temporary and limited to the period required for LDFs to acquire an absorption capacity for the new paradigm. The temporary existence of DBFs and of innovation networks would not follow if either LDFs were not capable of acquiring an absorption capacity for the new paradigm or if DBFs were to play different roles in innovation networks. That LDFs are capable of acquiring an absorption capacity for the new paradigm has now been proved (see Grabowsky and Vernon, 1994). Thus we turn here to the possibility that DBFs can play different roles in innovation networks. In order to explore this possibility we go back to an analysis of routines and of search activities.

As was previously pointed out, we can in an approximate way classify all existing economic activities as routines or search activities. In this context search activities can be considered activities aimed at scanning the external environment looking for alternatives to the routines presently used. We can consider routines as the set of activities that correspond to what Schumpeter (1912,1934) called the circular flow. In Nelson and Winter (1982) the routines used by a firm were considered to be stable up to the point where the targets that the firm set were not achieved. Failure to achieve the targets would trigger the adoption of new routines. In turn, the new routines would have been created based on the results of search activities. Perhaps the initial conception of search activities was unnecessarily limited. It seems as if firms carry out search activities all the time and use the results to create new routines, irrespective of the failure to achieve established targets. Thus, although threats and failure are undoubtedly powerful inducements to the change of routines, anticipation of the productive potential corresponding to a new subset of the external environment can lead to the creation of other routines.

Search activities are one of the most important modes of learning for firms and organisations, but they differ very much from other modes of learning. If we compare them to learning by doing, that occurs as a given activity is performed repeatedly, we can see that search activities can be considered as a form of *learning by not doing*. If we were faced with the problem of improving the performance of an industrial plant we could either try to use learning by doing or to study the reactions taking place in the plant in a more fundamental way, for example at a very reduced scale in a laboratory experiment, or by means of simulations and so on. The advantages of search activities with respect to learning by doing are obvious: (a) the cost of a laboratory experiment or of a simulation is much lower than that of building and operating a full scale plant; (b) the range of conditions that can be explored in a laboratory experiment or in a simulation is much wider than the one possible by changing the parameters of an operating plant. Of course, if instead of improving the performance of an existing plant we need to create a new good or service there are no alternatives to search activities. Thus if doing refers to actual processes of transformation of inputs into outputs, search activities consist in exploring the relevant parts of the external environment in order to define the conditions required to create a given type of output and to improve the efficiency with which the transformation is achieved The institutionalisation and diffusion of R&D that took place during the twentieth century represents a shift away from learning by doing and towards learning by not doing.

Search activities thus represent a central feature of the emerging knowledge-based society. In spite of their recognised importance, it is not easy to measure them. The most common, although not the only, example of search activities is constituted by R&D. Statistics about R&D have been available for a long time, but some of the classifications used are increasingly problematic. For example, the distinction between basic and applied research and development is increasingly difficult to use. Although some extreme cases are clearly distinguishable (for example, the development of a theoretical model of a physical or chemical system vs the construction of a pilot plant to test and implement a new process), in other cases the same activity could equally be labeled basic or applied research, depending on the motivation that led to its performance or to the institution where it was carried out.

Figure 10.1. Basic (a-b), applied (c-d) search and development (e-f) represented by means of the range of search and probability of success

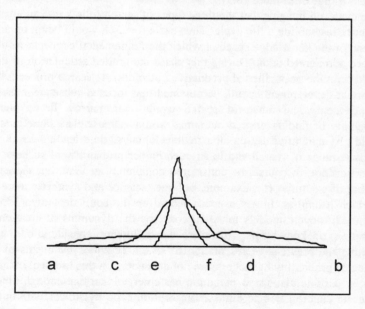

Dasgupta and David (1994) stressed the importance of the property rights regulating the production of knowledge. While undoubtedly property rights have a powerful influence on the dynamics of creation and utilisation of new knowledge, we maintain that there are types of knowledge that are intrinsically different. Yet these differences are not those implied by the classification of basic and applied research and development. To overcome this problem we adopt here a representation of search activities by means of two variables, the range or span of the external environment that is explored and the probability of finding a desired outcome. An example of such an outcome would be the development of a new product or process. If, for simplicity, we assume that the external environment can be represented as a mono-dimensional space on which the corresponding variables are placed, we can represent search activities as a distribution of the probability of obtaining a desired outcome over a range or subset of the external environment. Any two types of search activities can then be characterised by the range of search and by the probability of obtaining the desired outcome. In this framework basic research would have a very large range and a low probability of success (range a-b, Figure 10.1), applied research would have a narrower range and a higher probability of success (range c-d, Figure 10.1) and development an even narrower range and an even higher probability of success (range e-f, Figure 10.1).

We can even imagine that the three types of search follow one another in a sequence resembling a life cycle. Thus basic research would begin on a wide portion of the knowledge space in which the fundamental concepts would be defined and agreed upon. During this phase the limited articulation of theory would limit the possibility of productive outcomes. As search proceeds some important developments could be obtained that focused subsequent research around them. The range of search would then narrow down and the probability of finding desired outcomes would increase. The same tendency would be magnified by passing to development, thus leading to an even narrower range of search and to an even higher probability of success. This pattern cannot, of course, be considered completely general, but there are a number of examples (for example, polymer science and synthetic materials) to which it applies. In a sense this would be the equivalent of product or industry life cycle models for what concerns the dynamics of creation and utilisation of knowledge. However, the following considerations, while adopting the previous representation of search activities by means of their range and probability of success, are not dependent on this life-cycle view.

Let us assume that a new paradigm has emerged and that enough time has passed to enable LDFs to build an absorption capacity for it. Even in these circumstances LDFs and DBFs would not be equivalent. LDFs can generally be expected to have a comparative advantage in 'combining' the assets required to produce a final output (for example, a pharmaceutical product). If the rate of growth of new knowledge within the paradigm is low, LDFs can be expected to be able to innovate without the collaboration of DBFs. In these conditions most DBFs would be expected to disappear. If, however, the rate of growth of knowledge within the new paradigm is very high, LDFs might not be capable of acquiring the resources required to learn the new knowledge internally. Observed rates of growth for LDFs are much lower than for DBFs. We would not normally expect an LDF to double its personnel from one year to the next, while such high rates of growth are observed for DBFs. For an LDF to rely on external alliances with DBFs can be considered a less risky and more reversible strategy. In these alliances DBFs would explore portions of a rapidly expanding knowledge space on behalf of LDFs. The latter could then indirectly monitor this new knowledge space and be ready to invest if new and promising productive applications were to emerge within it. In these networks the role played by DBFs would be substantially different from the one previously described, that of translators. While translator DBFs had a much higher absorption capacity than LDFs, *explorer* DBFs owe their existence to the lower "cost" of exploration and to their willingness to enter into contractual arrangements that are more flexible and reversible than the construction of an adequate internal R&D capability by LDFs. The role of explorers can then survive in the intra-paradigmatic phase and co-exist with LDFs that have acquired a high absorption capacity for the new paradigm, provided that the rate of creation of new knowledge within the new paradigm is sufficiently high. Networks would then have a long-term stability because the possible decline of the translator role would be compensated by the rise of the explorers' role.

The stability of innovation networks observed so far could be explained by the emergence of multiple roles for DBFs. Of course, the role of explorers as described here is a possible one, but a confirmation of its existence would require a more analytical treatment of the problem, which is outside the scope of this chapter. A simulation model that approaches the problem of the stability of innovation networks in biotechnology, and of the different roles played by DBFs in them, can be found in Pyka and Saviotti (2000). What seems more likely from the previous reasoning is that if DBFs were to play only the translators role their probability of survival would be expected to decline from the inter-paradigm transition phase to the subsequent intra-paradigmatic phase.

On the basis of these considerations we can in principle expect that innovation networks will continue to be a component of industrial organisation for the near future (~5 years) and probably for longer than that.

Of course, this does not mean that the same firms will continue to be members of the innovation networks. The rate of entry and exit can be expected to be much higher amongst DBFs (Hannan and Freeman, 1989) than amongst LDFs. Thus both failures of DBFs and their acquisition by LDFs are going to provide exit routes for DBFs, which would lead to a reduction of their number if this was not compensated by the entry of new DBFs. The population of DBFs is in a very dynamic equilibrium, characterised by a high rate of entry and by a high rate of exit. Thus even at a constant size distribution of the total population of firms (LDFs + DBFs), the identity of the firms and the composition of the networks would continuously change. At a constant number of DBFs network density and connectivity can be expected to change. Both empirical observations (Catherine, 2000) and simulations (Pyka and Saviotti, 2000) show that density and connectivity increase in the course of time. Thus, innovation networks are a standard component of industrial organisation, but their structure may change in the course of time.

Competition, Collaboration and Innovation Networks

Innovation networks are an important component of industrial organisation. This raises a number of general questions. First, does the emergence of innovation networks lead to a lower intensity of competition by replacing some competitive interactions with collaborative interactions? Undoubtedly in networks there are collaborative interactions. All members participating in a network derive benefits from it, although the distribution of benefits is unlikely to be egalitarian. Thus, if a DBF makes an important advance in technology that is subsequently transformed by an LDF into a successful product, both benefit. In general collaboration is likely to be easier if the members of a network perform complementary roles. That would be the case if DBFs were the only firms able to understand and internalise the new technology, as they did in the role of translators, and LDFs had the complementary assets required to produce a marketable output. As long as the members of a network have complementary functions they are not going to compete amongst themselves (see Richardson, 1972, for an early analysis of the role of complementary interactions). Although not all interactions within networks are complementary, the majority of them are. The predicted decline of innovation networks coincided with the acquisition of an absorption capacity for the new technology by LDFs and thus with LDFs and DBFs becoming substitutes or competitors. Even in the new potential role of explorers DBFs are not substitutes of LDFs. Although at this stage LDFs have acquired an absorption capacity for the new technology, they cannot explore the whole knowledge space available and they have to rely on faster, nimbler DBFs. Yet, if the rate of growth of new knowledge were to slow down, LDFs and DBFs would become competitors because they could both to the same thing.

If most of the interactions amongst members of an innovation network are of a complementary nature that does not mean that competitive interactions have disappeared. First, the formation of networks has displaced the "locus" of competition. Once the first few networks have been formed and prove successful, other firms will imitate them and form themselves networks. Now different networks compete amongst themselves. Thus, inter-firm competition has been transformed into inter-network competition. Second, although firms now rely on networks, they do not completely loose their individuality. Any important LDF competes against similar LDFs by participating in networks. The choice of "good" networks becomes a competitive device. Likewise, participation in "good" networks becomes an important step in the development of DBFs. The ability of these firms to obtain further funding depends largely on their participation in successful networks. Thus LDFs compete amongst themselves for their final output markets and for the participation of the best DBFs in their networks, and DBFs compete to enter into LDF centred networks. The formation of innovation networks then relies on a mixture of collaborative and competitive interactions. In fact, all the competitive interactions that were in a pre-network economy are still there, but new interactions have emerged between new actors (DBFs) and pre-existing ones (LDFs, PRIs). Whether the intensity of competition in the economy as a whole has increased or decreased is a question that requires an analytical and quantitative answer. In absence of this answer we cannot state with any certainty that the emergence of innovation networks has lowered the intensity of competition. Second, what are the boundaries of industrial organisation? Traditionally they have coincided with the boundaries of the industrial sector concerned. However, as we saw previously, public research institutes (PRIs) are very often members of innovation networks. The growing interactions of science and technology are reflected in the increasingly fuzzy boundaries of industrial organisation, that can now be considered to overlap with those of pubic research institutions. I a knowledge-based society it seems logical that the boundaries of industrial organisation are defined as much by the knowledge base used as by the nature of the outputs produced. For example, the so called life-science companies were so defined by means of heir knowledge base and not by the markets in which they sold their products. The fact that at present most of these firms are busy selling or separating their agrochemical divisions is due to a sharply increased heterogeneity of their markets (for example,

pharmaceuticals and agrochemicals) and not to a decreased or changed role
of their knowledge base. Even if we can expect that the heterogeneity of
markets will continue to demand some specialisation at the output level, we
can also expect that the growing importance of knowledge will make the
boundaries of industrial organisation increasingly fuzzy.

We can conclude this section by observing that the emergence of
innovation networks can be represented by means of division of labour and
co-ordination. The emergence of DBFs (or in general of NTFs) adds a new
role and a new actor to the economic system and it is an example of an
increasing division of labour. New forms of coordination are required
between the new actor and pre-existing ones. If there were a market for the
output of DBFs we could expect coordination to occur through it. However,
the main output of DBFs is knowledge and markets for knowledge are
notoriously very imperfect. Traditionally this co-ordination problem was
solved by the internalisation of R&D activities within LDFs. The growing
inability of LDFs to internalise all new knowledge limits the usefulness of
this mode of coordination. Innovation networks can be considered an
alternative mode of coordination more appropriate to a situation where a high
rate of creation of new knowledge predominates. A full analysis of this
situation is outside the scope of the present chapter, but it has to be the
necessary background for this type of analysis.

4. SUMMARY AND CONCLUSIONS

Innovation networks emerged in the early 1980s as a new mode of industrial
organisation. At the beginning of their existence they were considered to
have only a temporary existence, limited to the period of transition between
two paradigms. They should have disappeared once the new paradigm had
established itself. The relative stability they have acquired in the following
twenty years seems to imply that their existence is more than temporary. This
chapter discuses the roles of the actors participating in innovation networks
and attempts to explain why such networks have so far been stable
components of industrial organisation.

Innovation networks are characterised by three types of actors, large
diversified firms (LDFs), small new technology firms (NTFs), that in the case
of biotechnology are called dedicated biotechnology firms (DBFs), and
public research institutions (PRIs). Of these actors, NTFs or DBFs are a new
type of actor, substantially different from traditional SMEs.

The temporary nature of innovation networks would be explained if DBFs
were to play only the role of *translators*, that is of firms capable of

understanding the technology of a new paradigm and of communicating it to LDFs. Assuming that LDFs are slower in internalising the new paradigm DBFs could play this role in the period required for LDFs to build an absorption capacity for the new paradigm. Once this happened DBFs would become redundant and the prevailing form of industrial organisation could be expected to go back to vertically integrated organisations. A second role is hypothesised in this chapter for DBFs, the one of explorers. In this role DBFs would scan parts of the external environment that LDFs cannot explore, although they are in principle capable of doing it since they have now acquired an absorption capacity for the new paradigm. This new role of DBFs would enable them and innovation networks to survive as long as the rate of creation of new knowledge is so high that LDFs cannot explore the whole new knowledge space themselves. The role of *explorers* is compatible with the acquisition of a high absorption capacity by LDFs and can explain the persistence of innovation networks.

Although they involve collaboration, innovation networks do not eliminate competition. By adding a new actor (NTFs or DBFs) to the economic system they increase the number of inter-actor interactions. The new interactions are in part competitive and in part collaborative. Thus networks compete amongst themselves. Furthermore, within networks LDFs and DBFs conserve their individuality and keep competing with similar firms by means of their participation in networks. Thus innovation networks have increased the total number of interactions and added some cooperative and some competitive ones. The question of whether the intensity of competition in the economy has increased or decreased due to innovation networks does not have a simple answer but demands an analytical treatment.

The existence of NTFs, of DBFs and of VCFs can be considered the result of an increased division of labour. They are new institutional actors that have been added to previously existing ones. Of course, the presence of new institutional actors involves the coordination of these actors amongst themselves and with those that already existed. Thus an increasing division of labour is accompanied by an increasing extent of coordination required in the economy. Competition and collaboration are two types of interaction that help achieve that coordination. The emergence of new types of actors that are not substitutes of pre-existing ones leads to an increasing complexity of the economic system, that can be considered the counterpart of an increasing variety of output. In this context innovation networks can be considered a new form of industrial organisation which is being added to the pre-existing ones (markets and hierarchical organisations) and which is better adapted to a complex, rapidly changing and qualitatively evolving knowledge base.

REFERENCES

Abernathy, W.J. and Utterback J.M. (1975), "A dynamic model of product and process innovation", *Omega*, **3**, 3-22.

Amin, M. (1996), "Understanding strategic alliances: the limit of transaction cost economics", in R. Coombs, A. Richards, P. Saviotti and V. Walsh (eds) *Technological Collaboration: The Dynamics of Co-operation in Industrial Innovation*, Aldershot, Edward Elgar

Catherine, D. (2000), "Les réseaux d'innovation en biotechnologie", Thèse, Université Pierre Mendès-France, Grenoble

Chesnais, F. (1986), "Technical co-operation agreements between independent firms, novel issues for economic anlysis and the formulation of national technology policies", *STI Revue*, **4**, 51-121.

Cohen, M. and Levinthal, D. (1989), "Innovating and learning: the two faces of R&D", *Economic Journal*, **99**, 569-596.

Cohen, M. and Levinthal D. (1990), "Absorptive capacity: a new perspective on learning and innovation", *Administrative Science Quarterly*, **35**, 128-152.

Dasgupta, P. and David, P. (1994), "Toward a new economics of science", *Research Policy*, **23**, 487-521.

David, P. and Foray, D. (1994), "Accessing and expanding the science and technology knowledge base", Paris OECD, DSTI/STP/TIP(94)4

Dosi, G. (1982), "Technologicam paradigms and technological trajectories: a suggested interpretation of the determinants and directions of technical change", *Research Policy*, **11**, 147-162.

EC (1997), *Second European Report on S&T Indicators*, Brussels.

Freeman, C. (1982), *The Economics of Industrial Innovation*, London, Pinter

Freeman, C. and Soete, L. (1997), *The Economics of Industrial Innovation*, London, Pinter.

Gibbons, M., Limoges C., Nowotny, H., Schwartzmann, S., Scott, P. and Trow, M. (1994), *The New Production of Knowledge-The Dynamics of Science and Research in Contemporary Societies*, London, Sage.

Grabowsky, H. and Vernon, J. (1994), "Innovation and structural change in pharmaceuticals and biotechnology", *Industrial and Corporate Change*, **3**, 435-49.

Hannan, M.T. and Freeman, J. (1989), *Organisational Ecology*, Cambridge, Mass., Harvard University Press.

Kuhn, T. (1962), *The Structure of Scientific Revolutions*, Chicago, Chicago University Press.

Lucas, R.E.B. (1988), "On the mechanics of economic development", *Journal of Monetary Economics*, **22**, 3-42.

Mytelka, L. (Ed), *Strategic Partnerships and the World Economy*, London, Pinter (1991)

Nelson, R. and Winter, S. (1977), "In search of useful theory of innovation", *Research Policy*, **6**, 36-76.

Nelson, R. and Winter, S. (1982), *An Evolutionary Theory of Economic Change*, Cambridge, Mass, Harvard University Press.

Pyka, A. and Saviotti, P.P. (2000), "Innovation networks in the biotechnology based sectors", presented at the Conference of the International Schumpeter Society, Manchester, June.

Richardson, G. (1972), "The organisation of industry", *Economic Journal*, **82**, 883-96.

Romer,P. (1990), "Endogenous technical progress", *Journal of Political Economy*, **98**, 71-102.

Saviotti, P. P. (1996), *Technological Evolution, Variety and the Economy*, Aldershot, Edward Elgar,

Schumpeter, J. (1934), *The Theory of Economic Development*, Cambridge, Mass, Harvard University Press, (original edition 1912).

Teece, D. (1986), "Profiting from technological innovation", *Research Policy*, **15** 236-305.

Teece, D. (1988), "Technological change and the nature of the firm", in G. Dosi, C. Freeman, R. Nelson, G. Silverberg and L. Soete, *Technical Change and Economic Theory*, London, Pinter.

11. Public Knowledge, Private Property and the Economics of High-tech Consortia: Case Studies in Bio-medical Research[1]

Maurice Cassier and Dominique Foray

1. INTRODUCTION

Since the early 1980s a twofold development affecting the research economy has been observed. First, a trend towards the privatization of knowledge: through the extension of exclusive rights on new areas of research such as biotechnology or information technology; the adoption of industrial property policies by scientific institutions, and the takeover of basic research by the private sector – such as part of genome research by start-ups in the US – often through the privatization of public research institutions (like the Plant Breeding Institute in the UK). Secondly, a parallel trend towards cooperation has occurred through the high growth rate of formal R&D networks, particularly research agreements between universities and industrialists, or between firms and research consortia, university-industry research centers – as in the US – or mixed laboratories or institutions. To what extent does collective invention offer a solution to excessive privatization of knowledge? (Heller and Eisenberg, 1998, refer to the tragedy of anticommons, related to the excessive fragmentation of ownership of knowledge in genome research, which tends to slow down bio-medical innovations.)

Collective invention, whether spontaneous (industrial districts studied by Allen (1983) and know-how trading networks studied by Von Hippel (1987) and Appleyard (1996)) or collusive (high-tech consortia), creates a sort of third sector between the public and private research domains.[3] Research consortia represent explicit coordination between economic and scientific actors. They aim at increasing interaction between knowledge to create new technological resources through reciprocal openness and the coordination of research investments and learning. The idea is to devise contexts for the socialization of knowledge and collective learning, in a concerted and collusive way (unlike the industrial districts studied by Allen where processes of collective invention are primarily spontaneous and informal). It is to control research externalities simultaneously (to regulate relations between members and non-members, between special users and all users). Thus, the economy of research consortia can be analyzed along three axes, which describe the process and procedures of collective invention: the first corresponds to the production and circulation of knowledge (which is, to varying degrees, distributed and collective); the second to the attribution and appropriation of results (with various modes of appropriation, from the establishment of collective property rights to the maintenance of private rights); the third to the composition of the group (purely academic or mixed consortia with industrial partners) and to the management of knowledge externalities (internalisation versus dissemination of results). The communities, which support collective invention, do not all meet these criteria to the same extent (production and circulation of research, attribution and diffusion of results). Some consortia are characterized by very little mutualization of research and small knowledge pools, whereas their results are appropriated disjointly by participants. Others promote the sharing of research tools and the conjoint production of knowledge and even of collective property rights.

R&D consortia create spaces for the sharing of knowledge, in which there is a break from technological secrecy and the retention of knowledge by laboratories. They generate a new category of knowledge, of collective data, shared between the participants but not accessible – at least not immediately – to all users. As such, these common goods have a hybrid nature made up of both private and public goods. The creation of pools of knowledge between partners and the definition of collective property rights on the results are local solutions to the fragmentation of knowledge and to restrictions on its dissemination (in other words, a way of averting the tragedy of anticommons). It is, however, clear that R&D consortia can have different characteristics from the point of view of research production – that is, the exploitation of positive externalities by partners (Cohendet, 1995) – and that of the attribution and diffusion of results – that is, control of the externalities generated by the consortium. Finally, the degree of openness of R&D consortia as regards the public domain is an important element. There is a proliferation of fairly closed cooperative spaces, dominated by a few major partners who control pools of knowledge.

The analysis presented here draws on eight monographs[3] on biotechnology research consortia. Six of these consortia are European, supported by Community programmes, and two are international academic consortia organized on an ad hoc basis by researchers. They can be divided into three categories. In the first group the consortia are composed of public laboratories which have no industrial members but have relations with clubs of industrial users established on the periphery of the consortium (industrial platforms set up by the EEC to facilitate knowledge transfer). These consortia work on the sequencing and functional analysis of yeast, and on Bacillus Subtilis and Listeria bacteria. The second group consists of mixed consortia in which industrial firms participate in the work alongside public laboratories, and sometimes manage research projects (for example, the lipases consortium comprising five industrial leaders – all rivals – in this domain). In this case, the consortium members opposed the creation of an industrial platform for non-member firms. The third group comprises international academic networks (international consortia working on breast cancer and melanoma) without any specific ties to the industry.

In the first section of this chapter we consider the apparatus used for producing and circulating research within the consortia in question. The second section is devoted to the ways and means of distributing and attributing the results of work carried out jointly. We then look at the control of the consortium's research externalities and, finally, at processes for regulating the management of knowledge.

2. FORMS OF DIVISION OF LABOUR AND DEGREES OF COLLECTIVIZATION OF RESEARCH

The R&D consortium economy generates not only the control of negative externalities, through systems of controlled diffusion, but also the exploitation of positive externalities (Cohendet, 1995) through the division of labour, the sharing of resources and the coordination of learning.

As regards the production and circulation of research, R&D consortia aim, to varying degrees, to coordinate learning and share data among the participants, and thus to create new knowledge. The production of collective research is based on diverse forms of dividing labour, on the use of tools for coordinating learning, and on practices and rules for sharing and circulating resources. These practices and rules facilitate the creation of knowledge pools of different sizes, and mobilize knowledge in various degrees of strategic importance.

With collective research, three properties of knowledge systems can be exploited.

First, consortia exploit the divisibility or modularity of certain scientific or technical objects. For example, genomes are highly divisible objects which can be shared between several participants for faster decoding. European networks working on yeast and on Bacillus Subtilis, created in the late 1980s and early 1990s, accelerated sequencing before this work was automated. The division of labour organized in parallel (each laboratory is allocated sections of a chromosome to be decoded and sends its data to a central data processing laboratory) requires the standardization of data and the establishment of quality control procedures so that the data can be assembled. The network facilitates mutual learning as the laboratories exchange protocols and know-how. However, this trading does not eliminate specialization and disparities between laboratories (the most experienced laboratories produce by far the most numerous sequences).

Secondly, R&D consortia are set up to exploit the complementarity of the participants' knowledge and expertise. Whereas in the preceding case the division of labour was based on the similarity of tasks entrusted to the different participants (each one is responsible for the sequencing of a piece of genome), here the idea is to take advantage of the different laboratories' specializations and systematically to combine them (each of them tests genes in relation to their particular specialization). No single laboratory has all the expertise required to study the functions of thousands of genes in an organism. European consortia set up to study the functions of yeast and Bacillus Subtilis genes combined a wide range of specialities to produce an initial characterization of the functions of genes and construct a knowledge base, including a bank of biological material and a data bank, that was subsequently to be made available to all potential users. The difficulty lies in coordinating the work of laboratories which have widely diverse competencies as regards genome sequencing (the quality of results is sometimes very different and some laboratories' lack of experience causes delays).

Thirdly, R&D consortia are set up to unite and exploit collections of objects and data. By putting together a large enough collection of samples, knowledge of a better quality, or knowledge which could not be obtained otherwise, can be produced. This is the main aim of the European lipases enzyme consortium: "New knowledge on a number of these enzymes will make it possible to understand why they are lipases and how they function as such" (article 1 of the consortium guidelines). This is possible owing to the comparisons and syntheses that will be facilitated. The international breast cancer consortium has the same aim. The networking of a large number of laboratories has made it possible to select and test markers on a vast collection of families which, put together, far exceeded the immediate capacities of any one group. The consortium's added value stems from the standardization of markers and the statistical analysis carried out on a large collection: "Thus the claim put forward by a single research group that there is a gene on 17 q able to predispose mankind to early onset of breast cancer, was overwhelmingly confirmed by an international consortium in less than a year's time. This produced important spin-offs such as an estimate of the genetic heterogeneity and approximate location of the gene".

Apart from the definition of data standards, the sharing of knowledge and, in particular, the constitution of a pool of resources within the consortium is a key element in the process of collective invention. There are various degrees of difficulty in the pooling of data, depending on the former nature of the resources used. For example, strains of yeast or Bacillus Subtilis mobilized in the European sequencing consortia are public data, which circulate fairly freely in academic networks (the yeast strain was initially made available to the European network by an American researcher). Issues are quite different when private material, belonging to different owners, is to be pooled. Some partner firms in the lipases consortium were reluctant to disclose confidential information on the strains they used in their industrial processes. These difficulties were partly overcome. First, the circulation of biological material was strictly compartmentalized, either within small teams with no industrial rivals or between owners who made them available to public laboratories temporarily for research purposes. The owners then had the possibility of communicating reference material that was of a less confidential nature but was sufficiently close to their industrial strains to allow the acquisition of transposable knowledge.

The circulation of data concerns not only resources existing prior to the creation of the consortium, but also data produced during its activity. Data sharing becomes crucial when the aim is to exploit interdependencies between data so as to progress faster in the elucidation of similar objects, to locate a site on a map (a gene) or to produce a synthesis or a common result. Thus, the accessibility of a consortium's data bases (biological material banks and data banks) for participants is in itself a sensitive question. The participants may decide on explicit rules for sharing knowledge. That is the case in virtually all research consortia studies, with the exception of the international breast cancer consortium where no rule on knowledge trading has been written. The consortium's guidelines on lipases, like those of the yeast network, define an original category of data, that of pooled or collective data. These data are shared between the members of the network while the research is underway and are then made publicly available. Their existence is the result of a compromise between collective invention and the individual priorities of the participants who want exclusive rights for a certain period. Thus, the consortium agreement organizes the controlled dissemination of data. They define first a closed circle of individual rights for a certain period

(3 or 6 months), then the data sharing in the collective space of all the consortium members (for 3 or 6 months) and, finally, the transfer of the data to the public domain. Pooled data have a hybrid nature: they are shared between all the members of the consortium but are not accessible to outsiders. Their existence is limited upstream by individual participants' rights, and downstream by the diffusion of data in the public sphere.

The scale on which pooled data exist, and the longevity of these pools, varies depending on the academic or industrial competition between participants and the limits of the technical systems used to circulate the data. In the international breast cancer consortium, established in 1989, data shared within the network are strictly delimited (markers are selected for tests and results of analyses carried out by each participant in the network). The most strategic collections of genetic material and markers are excluded. The consortium is a bench for validating the latest results, while the most advanced research is done in groups of rival laboratories. Thus, horizontal knowledge trading within the consortium is relatively limited, while trading within sub-groups is essential (exchange of DNA and markers). Several participants are either involved in negotiations with pharmaceutical laboratories or else in the process of creating a new business. We could consider this a relatively weak collective, even if participation in the consortium provides information enabling partners to remain in the genes race. The collective process is far stronger in the European breast cancer consortium, where 15 laboratories have been working together as part of the BIOMED programme since 1994. In order to locate predisposing genes, this programme involves the collection of vast families, but the division of labour is subject to more extensive planning and hierarchy (one laboratory is responsible for the statistical analysis of data and several laboratories are responsible for analysing mutations). Circulation concerns selected markers, samples, and data, which are centralized by the laboratory in charge of statistical analysis. However, the sharing of data is by no means complete. The laboratories retain the DNA of the families and, in parallel with this cooperation, compete fiercely with one another to identify the second predisposing gene. Each of them privately analyses mutations and keeps the results confidential. Finally, the process of collective research, highly structured hierarchically, produces an asymmetry between the laboratory which centralizes the data for statistical analysis and the other laboratories which produce their results. The central laboratory will patent the gene.

In yeast and Bacillus Subtilis sequencing consortia, the division of labour produced a collective entity, a chromosome map or the entire genome. However, the circulation of data between participants while the research was underway was not problem-free. In both cases, the data produced by the laboratories were centralized by a coordinating laboratory responsible for assembling them and creating a data base. The Bacillus Subtilis consortium agreement stated that these data were to be kept confidential for nine months by the data processing coordinator. This period was justified by the need for quality control. Members of the network were denied direct access to the registered sequences although they periodically received a list of the registered data. This procedure failed to function as intended and some laboratories were granted access to data only a few weeks before complete publication of the genome. The period of existence of the pooled data was therefore substantially reduced, to the detriment of interaction between the knowledge produced. The switch from "private" to "public" data was direct.

Thus, a continuum can be drawn from the least to the most collective circulation of data. The international breast cancer consortium is a fairly weak consortium as regards research production (it is an authority for validating results obtained elsewhere). The lipases consortium, in which strong tension exists between 6 rival firms in partnership with 16 university laboratories, has tried mainly to coordinate the participants' work and to mutualize data. Whereas strategic resources like enzyme strains have circulated very little among sub-groups, data pooling really does exist, especially on kinetics. These data were produced for all the participants by a CNRS laboratory and were shared for a period of a few months within the consortium. The European consortia for the functional analysis of yeast or Bacillus Subtilis have organized intense division of labour and a substantial circulation of data (for example, each laboratory participating in the network for the functional analysis of Bacillus Subtilis receives a complete collection of the 1,000 mutants created by all the laboratories and has immediate access to the consortium's data base). Moreover, the research results stem in this case from the combination of a series of tests carried out by the various laboratories so that it is difficult to tell who produced a particular functional datum.

3. SOLUTIONS FOR DISTRIBUTING AND ATTRIBUTING RESULTS

Contexts of collective invention create original situations for the attribution of results. In our sample we identified four systems for the attribution of property rights, from systems of disjoint or divided ownership, which constitute a large proportion of individual property rights, to systems of co- or collective ownership. Property rights systems are generally formalized in contracts or "consortium agreements", except for the breast cancer consortium where the appropriation process was spontaneous (as we have seen, there was little coordination between participants).

With the lipases consortium, disjoint property rights are granted. While the participants agreed to collect a set of enzymes belonging to different and rival owners, and to exchange research results (pooled data), they also set up a system of separate ownership in which each firm retained control over its confidential biological material, its technological know-how and its inventions. At first, the consortium focused on the acquisition of basic data and excluded biotechnological processes that involved highly sensitive know-how. The consortium was then divided into five sub-projects that were shared out among the firms. This organization guaranteed the compartmentalization of sensitive material. Because firms were spread out among separate contracts, they would not be forced to grant licenses to their rival partners, as in typical European contracts. Each one controlled its territory and filed patents on the inventions developed in-house. This system can be explained by the presence of rival firms within the consortium, by the collection of objects which belonged to different owners prior to the project, and by the nature of the collective invention process, which mutualizes research data only while materials and technological developments remain the exclusive property of their owners.

European yeast and Bacillus Subtilis sequencing consortia grant participant laboratories temporary ownership of the fragments of chromosomes they receive and decrypt for the duration of the research programme: "Each segment granted to a participant and accepted by that participant becomes his 'property' for the duration of the chromosome sequencing programme. No other participant can lay claim to it during that time" (Perfect Gentleman Sequencer). During this period, the laboratory may publish, communicate or patent data concerning its fragments. The right to do so lapses once the sequencing of the chromosome of the genome is finished and the data have been validated and published. This system is obviously facilitated by the divisibility of genomes and by the fact that work division is based on individual research carried out in parallel. It is therefore easy to grant individual rights on clearly differentiated fragments (each participant has a segment). For this purpose a specific tool for sharing property rights is used, namely a physical or genetic chromosome map.

We identified three consortia (out of eight) which established a regime of collective property rights, for different reasons.

In the listeria consortium, which consists of ten participants – eight university laboratories and two small genome sequencing firms – the partners chose a system of collective property because they had no tool for sharing their research object, the bacterium genome, or attributing limited fragments to the different participants. Thus, in this case the object is perfectly divisible but the participants have no cadastre, that is, no genetic or physical maps enabling them to grant well-defined pieces to particular partners. The genome will be divided into fragments, but these will not be ordered and located in relation to one another. For example, a given gene will be identifiable through the fragments of all the participants. It is therefore not possible to grant it to a particular firm: "Because of the strategy used, it is not possible to grant part of the sequencing to a single partner. For these reasons, each partner accepts that any patentable result obtained during the project will be the joint property of all the partners" (consortium agreement). The share of each participant will depend on their participation in the work, remunerated on a piece basis: "The share of co-ownership granted to each partner will be determined on the basis of funds received by each partner during the project" (consortium agreement).

In consortia working on the analysis of gene functions, the problems of individual property rights are due not to the absence of tools for sharing the object, but to the profoundly collective nature of the research product (these consortia are set up to exploit the complementarity of the participants' knowledge and expertise). Data concerning the function of a gene are the result of the combined work of n participating laboratories (the laboratory which constructs the mutants and those which carry out the multiple tests). Because the information obtained on a gene is the product of several laboratories' work, the yeast and Bacillus Subtilis consortia have decided to introduce collective property rights. The results are thus defined as indivisible.

The establishment of a system of collective property poses particular management problems. The Eurofan consortium has created an ad hoc institution for managing its collective property, a Charity Trust governed by English law: "Individual laboratories and institutions participating in the Eurofan project relinquish their property rights and transfer all rights acquired in the Eurofan project to a legal entity, the Eurofan Trust or the Trust" (guidelines of the yeast industrial platform). It is the Trust that will be responsible for transfer contracts with users and that will then pay the laboratories a pro-rata amount based on their participation in the project: "Only the Trust will be in a position to negotiate licences on the results of the Eurofan project or to facilitate collaboration with Eurofan laboratories ... Contracts with individual laboratories in the project cannot be entered into without the intervention of the Trust". The creation of a specific institution in charge of intellectual property rights raises problems of delegation for some partners who refuse to relinquish their individual rights. Management of the consortium's collective ownership of the Listeria bacterium was entrusted to the project coordinator, the Pasteur Institute. This organization has expertise in industrial property rights the other academic partners in the project do not have.

The international breast cancer consortium was formed in 1989 to accelerate research on the location and identification of predisposing genes. Collective invention is relatively limited here and the most intense trade takes place within rival sub-groups (for example, an American clinician gives a group of French laboratories exclusive rights to his own collections of families affected by family cancers; he will not grant access to them to rival laboratories). The consortia members also have ties with pharmaceutical laboratories interested in genes, but these transactions are bilateral and secret. One of the consortium partners, an American academic who established a biotechnology start-up – itself in partnership with a major pharmaceutical laboratory – identified the first predisposing gene and patented it. The appropriation process is spontaneous and each participant is engaged in bilateral transactions outside the consortium. Thus, the community was relatively weak from the outset. Although it signed joint publications, it never drew up any specific agreement on industrial property rights.

4. MANAGEMENT OF RESEARCH EXTERNALITIES: DISSEMINATION OF THE DATA PRODUCED BY THE CONSORTIUM

Consortia try to control the research externalities which they generate by managing tension between delayed and immediate dissemination, complete and partial dissemination, and privileged users and all other users.

Research consortia must first and foremost solve an initial dilemma between immediate and delayed dissemination of their results.[4] The question is particularly acute in consortia consisting of university laboratories. All the European consortia studied, whether they are composed exclusively of public laboratories or include universities and industry, have adopted a policy of delayed dissemination of their results (from 3 to 12 months). The idea is to be able to control processes concerning the transfer and appropriation of results. First, in the absence of a grace period in the European patent system, and given the application of absolute novelty criteria, an invention that is immediately published is considered to be in the public domain and therefore unpatentable. The reservation of results for a certain period preserves the possibility for the members of the consortium or privileged users to file for patents. Pressure in favour of delayed dissemination is exerted by clubs of users, industrial platforms established on the fringe of R&D consortia to organize and control knowledge transfers to European industry. In the race for priority of publication this type of policy has a cost. It creates asymmetry in relation to the US researchers with whom the laboratories collaborate and to the European institutions that have opted for immediate disclosure of their data in the public domain. That is why researchers want the establishment of a grace period in European patent rights, whereas European firms are fiercely hostile to this idea, for they consider it a source of insecurity. One solution lies in the selective dissemination of certain results, namely partial information.

R&D consortia can decide to send signals either to their members or to outside users that give them an idea of the results obtained and encourage them to cooperate. That is what the yeast and Bacillus Subtilis consortia decided to do to inform laboratories of the sequences that had been entered into the central data bank: "This procedure favoured direct contact between the members of the network interested in the sequences" (technical annex). It is the way consortia operate as regards industrial platforms. Within a short space of time (one month) or as soon as the sequences have been entered into the consortium's data base, the coordinator sends a confidential document to the platform members, containing derived information (for example, notes, a list of similitude, significant facts) but not the sequences themselves. Dissemination may be immediate in so far as it is only partial. The advantage is, for the producer and the user, twofold. The consortium immediately publicizes its results but maintains their confidentiality. It is thus in a position to negotiate access rights. As for the firm, it receives early signals on research underway and can establish direct cooperation with the laboratories that own the data. Sending signals enhances the dissemination system of research data by combining accessibility and exclusivity.

European research consortia strive to control the externalities of their work by creating platforms of industrial users on their periphery. The firms that belong to these platforms are the first to receive information in exchange for a modest access fee. The partial information enables them to establish early contact with the laboratories that possess relevant data. The advantage of being a member of a platform is twofold: in terms of appropriation (the firm benefits from priority access to the data) and in terms of learning (it benefits from a degree of familiarity with the research underway). We have identified three different situations, depending on the degree of the firms' inclusion in the research consortia: (1) In the first situation – also the most frequent in our sample – the consortium is composed solely of public laboratories and industrial firms are grouped together on the periphery, in platforms. "Consortium agreements" govern the trade relations between the consortium and the platform. All the members of the platform are the first to receive information. If a firm is interested in the transfer or development of a result, it must enter into a separate agreement with the owner of that result. (2) In the second configuration, the industrial platform becomes a contracting party within the consortium (that is the alternative chosen by the yeast industrial platform). This form of organization aims at strengthening interaction between laboratories and industrial users, who participate at least in the definition of programmes and the discussion of results, if not in the research work itself. (3) The third situation covers consortia in which industrial firms are members of the consortium as individual partners in their own right. That is the case of the lipases consortium in which the firms play a major role in the production and industrial use of these enzymes manage research projects. They are opposed to the creation of industrial platforms for outside firms because such an arrangement would undermine the competitive advantage they gain from the project.

Industrial platforms try to deal with the dilemma between appropriation and learning. In situation 1, there are relatively few problems of appropriation within the consortium (user firms are on the periphery). However, during industrial platform meetings, because firms fear they may divulge industrial secrets they say very little about their center of interest, thus limiting exchange with scientists. Some bilateral cooperation between member firms and laboratories has been noted, but on the whole interaction is considered far too weak. In situation 3, problems of appropriation are acute (the consortium is divided into sub-projects and member firms have refused the creation of a platform for outside users), but interaction is strong (co-patents, development of prototypes in partnership with academics and industrial researchers, and so on). Situation 2 (inclusion of the platform in the consortium) is the intermediate solution.

5. REGULATION PROCESSES

High-tech consortia are areas of high level institutional creativity. The actors have to devise rules for sharing and appropriating knowledge, which can be used to manage multiple tensions between individual priorities and collective learning, between members and non-members, and between privileged users and all users.

All the European consortia studied drew up consortium agreements or guidelines to complete standard EEC contracts, on sensitive points of cooperation, particularly the circulation of data and the granting of property rights. These rules are usually written by the researchers themselves, sometimes in cooperation with the industrial property department of the research organizations or firms to which they belong. There is of course a sound legal framework in the form of standard contracts concerning research and categories for the management of intellectual property rights, drawn up by the European Commission.[5] But the participants in the consortia have to deal with particular and sometimes unusual contexts of collective invention, with highly specific technical objects (objects and data relating to genomes) and diverse configurations of actors (mixed consortia with rival firms, or very large ones such as EUROFAN that consists of 138 laboratories). Thus, coordination constraints differ when data and products are divisible or indivisible when they result from the assemblage of individual work or from their combination, or were originally of a public or private nature. Consortium agreements meet this need for specificity. They are often appended to the standard contract, which they either extend or amend.

All the consortium agreements have been drawn up directly by researchers, sometimes with the assistance of European Commission scientific administrators and legal experts from the scientific institutions. The yeast network's guidelines were written by an academic, formerly a scientific administrator with the European Commission, and improved by a researcher from the Pasteur Institute. The lipases consortium guidelines were drawn up by two groups of researchers, one for the circulation of the kinetic data obtained on lipases, and the other for the circulation of structural data,[6] without involving the industrial property services of the research organizations or firms working on the project. The Bacillus Subtilis and listeria networks' consortium agreements were written by researchers and endorsed by the industrial property services of the coordinators, INRA and the Pasteur Institute.

Justification for this self-regulation is based primarily on the highly specific nature of the knowledge local actors have of their objects. Thus, researchers, perfectly aware of the eminently collective nature of information obtained on gene functions, conceived a system of collective property rights for the Eurofan consortium. The same applies to the listeria consortium where the collective property policy is directly justified by the "shotgun" sequencing strategy, which decodes the genome without a cartographic tool. Direct involvement by local actors facilitates subsequent coordination because all the partners know the rules, which have been discussed and negotiated. It also facilitates the application of the rules since specialists are often best qualified to interpret the situations of dispute involving technical knowledge. There is, however, a weak point: the endorsement of these rules by the industrial property services. The researchers participating in the lipases network, industrial researchers included, short-circuited their legal services to avoid delays. In this case the guidelines remain an agreement between professionals, without any formal commitment by the contracting parties. There is consequently a factor of uncertainty in case of dispute over property rights.

6. CONCLUSION

Collective invention is an original institution, as suggested by Allen (1983). It creates spontaneous or collusive areas of knowledge trading so that, for a limited period, industrial secrecy or the retention of data by laboratories is no longer practiced. This is achieved by organizing reciprocal exchanges of data, by coordinating work and learning, and by creating pools of knowledge. For Favereau (1991), cooperation amounts to a temporary and local "suspension" of competitive relations in the market, which will be resumed more satisfactorily at a later stage. We have identified more or less accomplished communities in regard to the following criteria: (a) the production and circulation of research; (b) the attribution and appropriation of results; (c) the composition of the group (purely academic or mixed consortia with industrial partners) and the scope and level of final dissemination of knowledge. We can thus define relatively weak communities, such as the international breast cancer consortium, for which horizontal data trading is limited because the work coordination concerns only the validation of results, and for which the distribution of industrial property rights is spontaneous, based on asymmetries between partners and the vertical alliances they have formed outside the consortium. There are also, by contrast, fairly strong communities such as the listeria consortium or the consortia for the functional analysis of yeast and Bacillus Subtilis. These are bound by the collective production of knowledge and by the horizontal exchange of resources and intermediate data. They have devised formulae for the collective ownership of results. In between there two consortia such as the lipases consortium, within which pools of knowledge have a real existence, despite the relative compartmentalization of research and the fragmentation of industrial property. When the consortia are purely academic (for example, the yeast and Bacillus Subtilis consortia), the ultimate problem is one of spin-offs and transferability of results to industry and users. An important practice here is the building of an industrial platform, which includes certain privileged users. In this design, however, industrial partners do not participate in the consortium's agenda. When industrialists are integrated within the consortium (the lipases consortium), the question of spin-offs is less relevant. The basic principle here is the controlled dissemination of data which can lead to more gradual processes of diffusion.

Collective or shared property rights among participants in consortia are of particular interest as regards the "tragedy of the anticommons" studied by Heller and Eisenberg (1998). They avoid the fragmentation of results among multiple owners, in contexts where attribution would be costly or even impossible to establish. Users also find this reduces the costs of negotiating rights when management is entrusted to a single institution (Charity Trust for the Eurofan consortium, or the Pasteur Institute for the listeria consortium). They thus facilitate potential users' access to a large knowledge base (the complete genome of an organism and the associated material). Several authors have considered comparable solutions to the problem of fragmented property rights. In the information technology domain, Breese (1996) proposes a collective patent to cover inventions that are to become standards and will therefore have a quasi-public status. The collective patent formula could be said to be comparable to that of the collective trademark used by economic partners. Use of the trademark implies affiliation with the partnership and compliance with the rules for using such a trademark: "Thus, without depriving the inventor of just remuneration, it provides access to the patented invention with a minimum amount of formality, and in particular, avoids any need to negotiate and grant a license". Heller and Eisenberg (1998) make a comparable proposal for biomedical research: "Recent empirical literature suggests that communities of intellectual property owners who deal with one another on a recurring basis have sometimes developed institutions to reduce transaction costs of bundling multiple licenses". They refer to the pools of patents set up in certain industries, sometimes with government help, to facilitate access to knowledge covered by multiple patents with a view to developing new products. The continuation of our work on a larger and more diversified collection of high-tech consortia, and the extension of the category of collective data and divided or shared property, should enable us to enhance our understanding of new forms of industrial cooperation.

NOTES

1. The research presented here was carried out as part of the COLLINE project, supported by the EEC TSER programme.
2. Allen (1983) asserts that collective invention, in the form of know-how trading networks between industrial firms, is an original institution likely to support research and innovation, along with scientific institutions, industrial research laboratories and individual inventors.
3. In each case we collected the contracts and consortium agreements written by researchers, and the access rules to industrial platforms set up by the EEC. We conducted in-depth interviews with scientific coordinators, researchers, scientific administrators in charge of contracts, and the Yeast Industrial Platform secretary. We also collected joint publications

by the consortia. We furthermore hold a copy of the statutes of the Charity Trust created as part of the EUROFAN project to manage that consortium's collective property.
4. See also Hilgartner (1995), Joly and Mangematin (1997) on the dissemination policy adopted by the European yeast network.
5. The general conditions of Community contracts define: categories of knowledge, either basic or new; property and knowledge transfer rules; access rights, and so on.
6. In so far as the morphology of the network and the types of data produced were not the same: there are five productive sources for structural data and only one for kinetic data.

REFERENCES

Allen, R. (1983), "Collective invention", *Journal of Economic Behavior and Organization*, 1-24.

Appleyard, M. (1996), "Knowledge sharing in the semiconductor industry", Department of Economics, Berkeley, 30 pages.

Breese, P. (1996), "Monopoly standards in conflict", *Les Nouvelles*, March, 8-10.

Cohendet, P. (1995), "Formes de gestion des externalités de la recherche par la puissance publique", Colloque CNRS "Innovations technologiques et performances : approches interdisciplinaires", 65-67.

Favereau, O. (1991), "Règle, organisation et apprentissage collectif : un paradigme pour trois théories", paper presented at the conference "L'économie des Conventions", Ecole Polytechnique, 27 and 28 March 1991, Paris.

Heller, M. and Eisenberg, R.S. (1998), "Can patents deter innovation? The anticommons in biomedical research", *Science*, **280** (1) May, 698-701.

Hilgartner, S. (1995), "Data access policy in genome research", Cornell University, 39 pages.

Joly, P-B. and Mangematin, V. (1997), "A qui sont ces séquences... ", *Biofutur*, **173**, December, 18-21.

Von Hippel E. (1987), "Co-operation between rivals: informal know-how trading", *Research Policy*, **16**, 291-302.

12. Technological Needs and Networks

Vincent Giard

---

1. INTRODUCTION

In order to survive, companies must transform themselves to adapt their goods or services to market requirements, striving to increase their competitiveness and reactivity. This generates new organizational forms and management tools, facilitated or made possible through new techniques.

The coverage of the network model has been spreading throughout the last few years. It is thus interesting to question the potential impact of some characteristics of this organizational mode observable in network companies created a few years back on "classically" managed companies interested in this approach. The evolution of techniques generates opportunities that could broaden the applications of "network" approaches and also bring about the evolution of management tools.

This chapter puts a few salient features of this evolution into perspective and asks a few methodological questions. The viewpoint taken in this chapter is of course partial, and even partisan, but the ideas expressed here present one of the possible angles from which to renew management tools. We will first position the problem before examining the emergence of new technological need, which are partly influenced by the extension of the network model.

2. PROBLEM DEFINITION

First of all, one must clarify the network and technology concepts at the heart of this chapter before stating the profound mutations occurring in economic, technical and managerial environments that force companies to reorganize.

Definitions

Technology

We will select here the acceptance of the term proposed by Morin (1985) who defines technology as "the art of implementing, in a local context and for a specific purpose, all sciences, techniques and fundamental rules used in the design of products and manufacturing processes, management methods or information systems of a company". Three significant characteristics stem from this definition.

- First, technology interdependently combines, on the one hand, engineering sciences for the coordinated design of products and production processes, including equipment design and, on the other hand, managerial sciences for structure design (organization charts, task distribution, and so on) and control of the production system (definition of procedures for command, control, design and access to management information).
- Technology is considered as an art, not a science. This leads to the development, on a largely intuitive basis, of adequate combinations of engineering and managerial requirements.
- Technology is contingent in two ways. By assigning technology to meet a specific need, the resulting efficiency criterion obviously impacts on the selected combination of engineering and managerial requirements. Also, this implementation of technology is carried out in a given local and dated context, which generates a selected solution designed to meet a specific need that cannot be universal.

This image of technology must be linked to the one proposed by reengineering pioneers (Hammer and Champy, 1993; Davenport, 1993) who relate technique and management to a contingency and organizational innovation theory designed to create leeway by quashing implicit hypotheses on which the organization is based. The rationale, summarized in Figure 12.1, is simple: at any time, the available techniques induce a certain number of constraints that largely influence the organization. It is clear that technique evolution modifies organizational constraints, but nothing induces it to transform itself in order to take this constraint modification into account. One of the strong reengineering principles is to search among emerging techniques, especially among information and communications techniques, those that modify some strong constraints that weigh, often implicitly, on the organization and, by doing so, give transformation opportunities. It is pertinent to note that this technological approach has all of the three characteristics mentioned above, but it introduces a certain dissymmetry in the relations between engineering sciences and managerial sciences.

Once technology has been defined as shown above, it becomes obvious that technological needs depend both on the available techniques and their evolution as well as on the instrumentation in use and its foreseeable transformations in a changing socioeconomic context. One of the trends we can observe in the new organizational forms is the focus on the network concept.

Figure 12.1. The reengineering approach

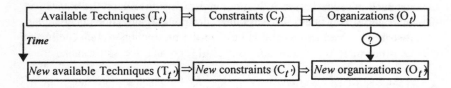

Compagny and network

Curien et al. (1992) consider *network companies* from two angles. The *engineer* focuses on the "spatial interconnection of complementary equipment, cooperating to transport matter, energy or information fluxes and send them from an origin to a destination", while the *economist* focuses on intermediation, the function of these companies being to "establish a link between suppliers and consumers of certain goods and services".

Characterization of the productive resources selected in the first design helps classify, without ambiguity, the merchandize or person transportation companies as part of the network company category. The function approach is much less discriminating as it encompasses almost all companies in the distribution field. In medium and large companies, functional specialization is the reason why there is always one or several production units exclusively in charge of logistics, which meets Curien's first definition. We can thus expect that any moderate-sized company will meet the few problems facing network companies "in the strictest sense", whose main specificity is that logistics activity is a *main activity*, and not a secondary one.

A third network design is based on the precept that any complex production system can be analyzed as a network of production units linked by exchanges of products or services. From this point of view, the *company boundary* differs when seen either from a legal point of view ("property" of production means) or from an economic point of view (set of production units concurring in a given production). The production of intermediate goods can often be replaced by supply or subcontracting (or co-contracting) and most service activities, especially support activities (personnel management, information system management, transportation, etc.) can also be subcontracted (or co-contracted).

We are witness to the ascendancy of more or less stable alliances leading to the creation of *networks of companies* or to what Paché and Paraponaris (1993) call *networked company*, which they characterize as being a "flexible and adaptive structure mobilizing - and no longer owning - a set of coordinated and stabilized skills". Compared to network companies, the interconnection is more organizational than spatial, which poses new coordination and control problems related to a partial integration of management by the partners. Also, certain specificity characteristics in network companies "in the strictest sense" are found although slightly diluted, in networked companies "in the largest sense" or in networks of companies (see Giard, 1994).

A Deeply Modified Context

The evolution of technological needs and the interest of network organizations is better understood when put into perspective with major transformations in company environments, characterized by a radical market transformation, by technical mutations with heavy consequences and, finally, by a significant renewal of management tools.

Radical market transformation

Changes over the last few years are relatively well known:

- a clear *hardening* of *competition*, which translates into a significant shortening of both the useful lives and the development periods of products;
- changes in *customers*, who became *choosier* and more *volatile*;
- interesting modifications to *attributes of the exchanged object*:
  - for a very long time, these attributes were exclusively attributes of *price* and "vaguely" of *technical specifications*;
  - customers' increasingly desired specifications such as *variety* of the offer and *quality* of products or services were added to these attributes;
  - competition spread by the inclusion of *additional services limiting the risk* (after-sales service, exchange or reimbursement, consideration of risk of theft or damage, and so on) *or the discomfort* (home delivery,

courtesy vehicle, direct assumption of formalities or of some expenses in case of litigation or accident), translating into a more global view of the needs to be met;

- finally, relatively strong recent competition can be observed regarding the *time* required for a product or service to be available; time elasticity (as price elasticity) plays an increasing role, which explains that the *availability date of the object* or service has become a new attribute explaining certain transformations in organization and competition modes.

Hardening competition and transformation in customer requirements *has become the standard*, whatever the company's field of activity.

Technical evolutions with far-reaching consequences

It would seem that from a technical point of view the pace of innovation has not decreased over the last few decades. We are not dealing with innovations for companies in a given field, but with those all companies can use and, more especially, those innovations known as New Information and Communications Technologies (NICT).

Acquisition, storage, processing and restitution of information are becoming increasingly economic and performing and thus open new management angles. Within the company, they allow real-time monitoring of products and services production as well as the use of human and equipment resources. Traceability impacts on the performance of production systems, which can be managed in a more efficient and reactive manner, but it also impacts on the quality of processes and products in a total quality perspective. Moreover, because they overcome proximity constraints in the collection and processing of certain information, they authorize transient work, which was impossible until then. Finally, they allowed the use of certain management tools, which is to be discussed later.

Transaction dematerialization possibilities brought on by NICT will also transform inter-company relationships and those between certain companies and their customers. Inter-company commercial relationships are progressively switching from a "paper" logic to a dematerialized logic when transmitting information: commercial exchanges are made through EDI (Electronic Data Interchange) and large development projects of new complex products are carried out by a network of companies using the CALS approach (Computer-aided Acquisition and Logistic Support). Commercial relationships between certain companies and their customers are also affected by NICT. E-business is progressively replacing mail-order selling, giving the vendor extraordinary scale savings because there is no need of hard copies (electronic catalogue) or clients visiting the company, as the company is not looking for potential clients.

In short, NICT disregard frontiers in a world where added value is increasingly based on information.

Management tools renewal

Managerial techniques have never stopped evolving since the industrial revolution, so discussing renewal may seem a tad unreasonable. Nevertheless, from the early 1980s on, three major evolutions need to be emphasized to better point out the technological perspectives of network or networked companies.

Process rehabilitation

In the early 1980s, new movements based on a process-focused reflection came into being. They were designed to capture the process in order to consider it globally and improve on it: Activity Based Costing, TQM, Kaizen, project management reengineering. In each of these various approaches, the process must first be identified before being modified.

The main disincentive to process identification normally lies in the analysis of goods or services production conducted on the basis of the consolidation of tasks by services to which the individuals performing these tasks belong. This "vertical" view has long been considered as adequate, but it must be completed or replaced by a horizontal view, the process approach. This implies that, when depicting a company, we must complete the classical descriptions of the organizational charts, BOM and routings with flow charts, while process charts still present a limited usage.

A flow chart shows as a simplified representation of an existing production system (a plan visualizing main production stations) the flow of matter (or of files) passing through the various processors to be processed, before arriving in its final or intermediate state of finished product or completed service. This representation differs from the graph of a routing chart, which represents the sequencing of operations, because it focuses on the sequencing of mobilized production stations and the absence of detailed information on the operating modes used.

The process chart is more extensive as it allows features relating to several points of view:

- multiple ratings for each operation: operation with or without added value for the client of the process, time spent waiting or processing, nature of the operation from a decisional or a materiel point of view;

- multiple ratings for each process in a general process map: for example, main or support process, with the possibility of breaking down either category;
- multiple ratings for each mobilized resource: assignment to a functional entity or, for people, role played in the process, rating or hierarchy level.

These multiple points of view of course complicate our representation of reality and only present an interest as they allow better understanding of the process so it can be improved; this implies the use of the "relevant level of details" for the analysis.

The cause of reengineering

Until recent times, the evolution of production systems observed in response to the transformation of the competitive environment consisted in an *emphasis* on *process fragmentation* and in the *specialization of actors*. This movement, justified by the search for a "local" reduction of complexity, induced increasing needs for coordination, which were tentatively met by using ever increasingly sophisticated managerial techniques. The assumption behind reengineering is that this organizational response revealed itself to be less efficient, to a point where it can now really generate significant scale diseconomies.

Concerning this trend, with roots in scientific work organization and value analysis, process defragmentation and simplification now seem to be efficient means to reduce the coordination work of productive activities. This process revision procedure seeks to breach the implicit hypotheses on which the organization is based, which are "false constraints", by resorting to an inductive procedure (which stems from the technical solutions of seeking the problems to which the solutions could apply) and to NICT.

The application of this procedure leads to a transformation of the processes and can be seen as a compression of the structures, both vertically (reduction of the line of command mainly due to the fusion of the roles of analyst, decision maker and operator) and horizontally (simplification of processes to widen the circle of actors responsible for a process).

Introduction of new resolution approaches for complex problems

It is evident that the progress in micro-computing allowed the development and use of processes that could not have been foreseen twenty years ago or that, for economic reasons, would only have known limited developments.

- With the arrival of *relational databases* and extremely fast and efficient tools that can create prototypes and update and operate these ergonomic and user-friendly bases, we have, at acceptable cost, easy to use raw material to analyze and make more-or-less structured decisions. This has allowed the development of meccano-type integrated architectures based on the same relational databases with ERP (Enterprise Resources Planning).

- This computer progress leads the way for the solution of *Operations Research* problems that describe complex decisional situations. When doing this, the difficulty of defining problems of a certain dimension in an operational manner and the modification of such problems led researchers to propose an innovative approach, that of *Algebraic Modelling Languages*, that relies on the separation between the description of the model and the units it uses; this gives rapid fine tuning and an immediate generalization of the formulation obtained to a class of problems (Giard, 1997 and Rosenthal, 1996). In a related field, this computer evolution favored the development of several, economically affordable, specific tools: *Expert Systems*, *statistical processing software* (the most recent, based on the Exploratory Data Analysis approach or the Data Mining one, help users understand their data and formulate hypotheses), and so on. Of course, *spreadsheets* must be placed in this category owing to their basic functionalities totally different from those available about a dozen years ago. They have been increased tenfold by the various add-in possibilities (especially the ones that facilitate sensibility analyses in both a given or random universe).

- Interests for the Monte Carlo management approaches was underscored in the early 1960s. The first formal approaches allowing *simulation* of problems of a certain complexity go back to the early '70s but they are based on programming languages that are fairly closed. During the 1990s, new software generations came into being, which were based on graphical approaches. They greatly reduced the difficulty of describing a complex process. These last few years, for little more than the cost of a spreadsheet, easy to use simulation software can be purchased. Their performance places this class of tools within the grasp of managers who can now think differently on the transformation of the rules controlling a complex production system.

- The *DSS* (Decision Support Systems), dating back to the 1970s focus on helping to formulate a problem that is part of a complex category of problems and on helping to operate systems. The solution of the stated problem, which can rest on sophisticated tools of operations research, is generally carried out without the intervention of the *DSS* user, who can now concentrate on formulating the problem and on applying the proposed solution.

- For about ten years now, Groupware tools have been developed for mixed-initiative work, on poorly-structured problems that do not require the players in a workgroup to be all at the same place at the same time. Progress in micro-computing and the generalization of networking has led to an interesting extension of these approaches when formulating and solving poorly-structured and very complex problems.

On the whole, the manager's toolbox has expanded considerably. We now have means that the 1970s managers could only imagine with difficulty. The problem presently facing us is the development of new "decisional models" that take advantage of these possibilities to decision-making in strategy that are more or less structured (designing productive systems, and so on) tactical (defining typical organizations) and operational (real-time control, and so on).

3. NEW TECHNOLOGICAL NEEDS

The technological needs taken into consideration here pertain to the necessity of the development of new managerial techniques and a new "meccano" based on NICT because of changing issues for the manager. The emergence of new approaches will be illustrated by an innovative example of complexity processing for network companies.

Changing Issues for the Manager

Placing this into perspective is undoubtedly debatable and reductive but, according to us, it translates the prioritization of the efforts required in the coming decade, if we want to be able to adapt the managerial techniques to the new market requirements. It seems first necessary to facilitate the passage of a process decoupling logic to a logic of process integration. It then seems necessary to improve the knowledge and the mastery of complexity. These research axes are not exclusively linked to network or networked companies. Yet the attractiveness of the network model is closely dependent on the innovations realized in these fields.

Switching from a decoupling logic to a logic of integration

The observation of complex productive processes, both for designing products (or services) and their manufacturing routings, and for producing and distributing these products (or services), evidences the successive use of a certain number of productive sub-systems. Several means are available, outside the continuous efforts taken to make the processes reliable, ensure decoupling between the sub-systems and avoid problems occurring in a sub-system from spreading to adjacent systems. The oldest is undoubtedly the building of stocks at the boundary of these sub-systems. The size of these *stocks* corresponds implicitly to a time period available to locally solve the problems before they spread to adjacent sub-systems. Other means are classically mobilized to solve the problems more rapidly and thus allow a decrease in stocks, considered as a source of inertia and waste. This is mainly about having *surplus resources* (mainly as equipment and tools) and the search for minimal *multipurpose* resources (personnel, equipment).

We now understand the importance of a final decoupling technique used implicitly, namely the *sequentiality* of the processes. Thus, until quite recently, the industrial organization of mass production clearly separated the definition of project specifications for new products, the design of these products and the design of the manufacturing routings of these products. This sequentiality has the advantage of a precise determination of roles and responsibilities. It also facilitates the local optimization of each process. The transformation of companies' environments and especially chrono-competition led to questioning this sequential logic and to starting a partial fusion of the processes that question the independence of the productive sub-systems. The disadvantages of sequentiality were known and had led to the installation in large companies of transverse structures, often called matrices but the aim of which was more to improve co-ordination than question, once again, the sequential organization.

This switch from a decoupling logic to an integrated logic raises several problems that are not specific to network or networked companies but have an increased complexity for this type of company.

• Companies that have opted for a *"project" approach* to manage the design of new products implement specific organizations that can go as far as including the merger of services (for example the merger of studies and methods departments at Renault). Most often, integration goes through an organization of concurrent engineering between partners of a global process often belonging, for important projects, to different companies and leading to co-development. This implementation is shown by the creation of project platforms to design new and complex products, which pose relatively new problems (determination of the number of platforms to create, determination of the players to involve in these platforms and for how long, determination of their decisional power, and so on). However, sequentiality allowed relationships of the ownership – contractorship type that is supplanted in part by the concurrent engineering: the definition of certain specifications implies a more collective responsibility and a different approach for the risks encountered. These lead to the implementation of procedures to help the early emergence of problems, and to their solution by instruments that rely on principles ranging from mutual adjustment to contractualization.

- Decoupling systems allow the use and design of independent and heterogeneous *information systems.* The integration of design and production processes does not tolerate well the juxtaposition of information systems implied by carrying out "transcription" tasks without any added value and thus puts a brake on reactivity.

- Switching from a decoupling logic to an integrated logic involves *taking greater notice of the client*, that is, a logic resting on synergy in the value chain. This is how we can observe that suppliers are taking charge of wholesales or retailer stock management. They can thus greatly increase the added value of services that were previously mainly based on time and price. This transformation allows a global decrease in the cost of supplies and gives the supplier more faithful clients when he meets competition. Among the services given to the "integrated" client, there is a whole series of added value services from visits better matching the client's needs (frequency, time window, orders traceability of orders in process, and so on) to a better handling of client logistics (presentation of merchandise in a certain order, and so on), especially in JIT organizations.

- Accentuated coupling generates *new problems* not only for activity *coordination* to ensure a satisfactory synchronization of coupled systems, but also for risk management, and thus bring forth a new problematic.

  - The co-ordination of coupled systems involves increased complexity in production management, better integration of information systems if we want to tend toward a real-time type of collective control and, finally, a transformation of management control practices that can no longer rest on a restricted and stable perimeter. These multiple challenges give rise to several problems, which must be solved on a theoretical level as well as on a practical level.

  - Risk management must also be adapted. Therefore, the supply of optional components to be installed on an assembly line can be done several times a day according to a daily production programming, taking account of the constraints related to the individualization of finished products. In this context, the quality requirements can lead to work being done twice at certain work stations, thus modifying the initial sequencing (the altered product would let the following ones pass by). The change leads to modification of effective demand for these optional components on the production time intervals related to deliveries. This risk is evidently dealt with by a safety stock but this safety stock is determined according to a radically different basis from that classically used in stock theory (Danjou et al., 2000).

- The problem of the economic perimeter brings us back to the debate on the integration or the outsourcing of some processes. This outsourcing of some activities is justified by stating that regulation by the market based on "market" prices is more effective (in terms of efficiency and reactivity) than internal regulation based on the "transfer" price. Such, outsourcing allows to refocus the company's hardcore activity. This type of strategic decision must be conducted rigorously.

  - For value-added activities, such as designing, the decision is more complex because, implicitly, outsourcing involves relationships of the "ownership-contractorship" type, that is, it supposes the definition of a "good" set of specifications independent of the solution to the problem stated. This sequential process often leads to less performing solutions than those based on concurrent engineering.

  - For fairly standardized support activities outsourcing poses, *a priori*, even fewer problems, so it often becomes difficult to economically establish the speed and reactivity characteristics of certain services. This outsourcing movement, often amplified by poor use of management accounting (use of total costs), implicitly rests on a fragmented approach of the processes that could bias strategic thinking. For example, we know that integrating transport logistics to supply the stores of a chain can be the key to a decidedly competitive advantage over the competitors who prefer to outsource this activity. This type of decision must be taken according to analyses that are not based exclusively on some elements retained in a simplistic modeling of the production processes, because it is easy to see the benefits. It is also necessary to integrate in this thinking the fact that the competitive advantage of outsourcing may be attenuated by the commoditization of expertise thanks to efficient and low-cost software and also to savings generated by the integration of modules in the "modern" approaches to management systems that are based on relational data (especially ERPs).

This reflection on the degree of coincidence between economic and legal perimeters is therefore difficult to undertake and must rest on several complementary points of view for which the available instruments must be improved.

Understanding and mastering complexity

Any quest for understanding and mastering complexity is most certainly an impossible goal to satisfy fully. Efforts should be made in two complementary directions: improving process analysis techniques and productive systems design.

If there is a consensus on the necessity to *analyze the process*, there are also multiple approaches to carry this out. The reengineering trend led to the publication of several documents and software to help with the representation of the processes. One can distinguish between the deterministic approaches and the stochastic approaches.

• The deterministic approaches, either computer assisted or not, are mainly designed for multidimensional representation of the processes by selecting several qualifications. The more detailed the information retained, the less directly exploitable it becomes. This leads to the creation of filters allowing to display only the information deemed relevant for the point of view selected. Then there is the question of the detail level of the information that is handled, as one can imagine working on aggregated processes, using all points of view simultaneously, or on detailed processes, using only a very limited number of points of view. The aggregation of a process generates formidable methodological problems as to the transmission/adaptation rules of characterization available on the "entities" available at a detailed level (resources, material or information flow, procedures), on the ones of the aggregated "entities". Solving some of these problems places conditions on the "automatic" supply of information corresponding to the points of view and detail level desired by those who wish to understand the operation of a complex process and improve its control or design.

• Two types of *stochastic approaches* represent the process. Simulators allow to know the response of a productive system to a given or random demand and to calculate a certain number of indicators that play a role similar to certain filters (the possibility of referring to outsourcing programs and the possibility of interfacing with certain spreadsheets now allow to do everything). Certain software also offers the possibility of aggregating production centers that simplify the analysis of a complex process. However, over the last few years, new software has been developed: they combine a flow mapping logic formally close to certain deterministic approaches (explicitation of branch tests for choosing alternate routings, roles, services, and so on) and a stochastic definition of operating time and flow orientation coming from an elementary production center; this approach is due to certain more detailed aspects (especially for the production of services) but it has its limits (calling on multiple resources, for example). In both cases, the software can quite easily study the impact of planned transformations for certain processes but the methodological problems stated for the deterministic approaches are also found in the stochastic approaches.

If these process analysis tools can be improved, the problem of help with diagnosing an existing situation and proposing its transformation stays the same. It is a major field of research for the coming years. To build these universal sets used to facilitate the search for improving the process, managers could benefit from the advantage of the important company modeling work carried out in the last twenty years (Vernadat, 1999) in related fields of study, in the United States as well as in the EU. That said, the multiplicity of points of view to tackle this problem lead to think that the manager using these approaches will be dealing more with some form of art, and for quite a long time yet.

Mastery of complexity also goes through a design improvement of productive systems. This raises two categories of issues:

- the search for better flexibility, reactivity and efficiency of productive systems, right from their design, especially in mass production industries, must be caught upstream within the scope of a strategic inquiry on:
  - the degree of component standardization (Giard, 2000),
  - the interdependence between occupational logic and project logic (respective roles, concurrent design of the manufacturing products and processes, finished and standardized components, ...), but also on the interdependence linking projects for finished products with the ones having largely standardized components,
  - the design of a range of technologically close products that can share equipment and manufacturing or assembly lines during production. This involves taking consideration of certain constraints right from product design, but, on the other hand, it overcomes demand instability on each product routing. Similar problems are also found in the production of small series, with the creation of temporary virtual cells allowing to strike a balance with flexibility requirements.

These transversal problems do not generally stem from a clearly identified direction, they are not independent from one other and pose challenging methodological economic control problems (transfer costs systems, coherence of specific management controls, and so on) that are far from resolved and for which the "network" orientation complicates issues.

- Competition exacerbation drives companies to adopt differentiation strategies. One of them is based on the search for sources of added value for the client through the design of a productive system. For on-demand productions, an improvement in traceability is not only an improvement in physical control, it is also, for the client, a reduction element of the variability in delivery delays and product quality. For stock production, this differentiation can be obtained by moving the limit of the productive system that can "penetrate" the client's facilities by offering value-added services as a complement to products or deliveries sold: specific merchandize conditioning limits handling by the client, helps him manage his stocks, and so on.

These changes in perspective, now made possible by technical evolution, involve decompartmentalization of expertise and are a major challenge for companies.

Example of a Possible Way to Process Complexity

When faced with very complex problems, a manager classically favors the Cartesian approach of dividing up a complex problem into simpler elementary problems, related to one another by a set of constraints ensuring coherence for the whole. This processing of complexity is based on a prior analysis that rests on the joint use of a certain number of analytical grids that structure, sequence and simplify the problems encountered. The productive system is divided into interdependent sub-systems that have a certain decisional autonomy. The decisions that must be taken are structured and sequenced to limit the boundary (object, constraints, degrees of liberty) and to ensure coherence thanks to sequence dividing (pertaining to resources, products, clients and processes) and time dividing logics (distribution among the strategic, tactical and operational levels, and so on).

These problems of dividing up and coordination, more formidable when it concerns network companies or networks of companies, can only receive possible satisfactory answers within a given context. For those who favor reengineering, the usual solutions of "divide/simplify + co-ordinate" have reached their limits. Two remarks must then be made:

- One of the major obstacles found in the traditional approach undoubtedly stems from the lack of foreseeability of the impact of certain planned innovative organizational transformations. Within this perspective, an improvement in foreseeability will push forward the limits of this approach by making it easier to manage the "limit displacements" that allow better management of increased complexity without increasing the fragmentation of processes, even by introducing some defragmentation.

- Reengineering a network organization seems difficult without somehow dividing it up into elementary processes, on the basis of a "client-supplier" type of architecture. From this point of view, we are also faced with "division/coordination" problems, but with a major difference, as we then accept to question the actors' roles and significantly review procedures and services.

In both cases, the search for performing solutions must be based on methodological principles that rigorously favor the problem raised by the design of management systems able to solve more complex situations.

A new approach to the "division/coordination" problem in a network company (*La Poste*) has recently been studied (Giard et al., 2000). Its methodological bases can be used several times to solve either problems of network companies or network of companies and, therefore will be rapidly presented.

It was meant to ease strategic or tactical organizational decision-making concerning the concentration and distribution of the mail between the post office and sorting centers, and to define the level of mail processing carried out by these various production centers. The postal network can be divided into four sub-systems, as illustrated in Figure 12.2; it shows the mail path from the sender to the receiver, as well as the main sub-systems. This logistical organization has been functioning fairly satisfactorily for over a century but the adaptation of the organization to market segmentation (implementation of specialized networks sharing or not sharing certain resources), to the greater requirements in terms of reactivity, and the cost of the variability of the demand to be met (existence of cyclic components and a strong random component) implies that the organization must be able to transform the productive system (modification/network creation; modification of processing locations) but also capable of modulating it according to the time and stochastic characteristics of the demand. The problem stated is challenging as it is evident that each sub-system has a certain decisional autonomy but the decisions still have an impact on the flexibility of the other systems forcing them, in certain cases, to mobilize additional resources. The "division/coordination" problem involves sufficient visibility of the interactions between sub-systems. We shall show the proposed method by analyzing the problem posed by sub-systems 3 and their relations with the adjacent sub-systems (sub-systems 2 and 4), by focusing on the problem of mail concentration.

Figure 12.2. Systemic analysis of the postal system

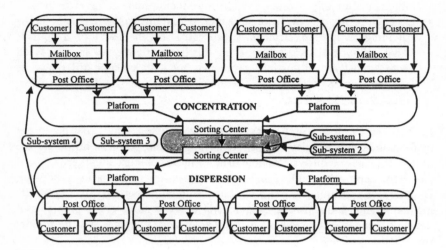

From a system command point of view, the volume of mail to be processed is an exogenous datum and the decisions to be taken concern (1) the allocation of offices to the sorting centers for all or part of their mail, (2) the segregation level of the mail coming from these offices (this involves upstream processing and a segregation level of the tight flows) and (3) the temporal profile of the emitted or received flows (as shown in Figure 12.3 for the receiving sub-system). If the main characteristics of these exchanged flows between sub-systems are considered as constraints by the given sub-system, each sub-system can be considered independent from a decisional point of view. It follows that, for a given "division", "co-ordination" fundamentally rests on a negotiation based on the characteristics of the flows exchanged between the sub-systems.

It is evident that improvement of global performance depends not only on the quality of the decisions taken by the players in each sub-system but also on the characteristics of the flows between sub-systems. These characteristics are the result of compromises between force ratios and the local points of view for several reasons amongst which strongly figures the low predictability of the incidence of foreseeable reforms, due to the players visibility, which is limited by the relative partitioning of the sub-systems.

Figure 12.3. Characterization of the flows between two sub-systems

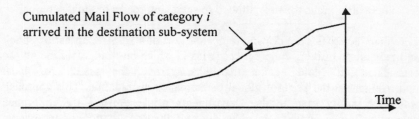

Cumulated Mail Flow of category *i*
arrived in the destination sub-system

Time

To go beyond this local point of view in the transformation of a productive system, it is necessary to set up a constraint negotiation mechanism which is associated with the rapid development of the transformation scenarios (resources, control rules, and so on) of two "adjacent" sub-systems. In a DSS-oriented approach, the DSS must have two properties, as seen in Figure 12.4:

Figure 12.4. Constraint negotiation mechanism between two sub-systems

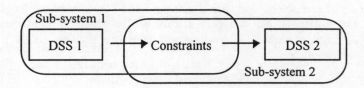

Sub-system 1

DSS 1 → Constraints → DSS 2

Sub-system 2

- As we are in the presence of a negotiation process between sub-systems, each DSS must be able to function under two modes: it has to establish new constraints following the transformation of the given sub-system or take account of the constraints imposed by the other sub-system.
- Constraint negotiation involves a certain reactivity on both sides. The DSS dedicated to one of the sub-systems must be able to find quickly a "good" solution to a problem characterized by a series of organizational hypotheses, different from the implemented ones. DSS operational credibility then largely rests on its capacity to rapidly propose an innovative, efficient and coherent solution. Innovation implies that the DSS can easily define the main hypotheses for contrasted scenarios. Efficiency and coherence imply relying, when possible and if justifiable, on an optimization approach that can solve the "hardest to solve" problem, on the condition that the DSS user can modify the proposed

situation since it rests on modeling that cannot pretend to resolve the complexity of the given constraints and because the man–machine interaction limits the time allotted to searching for an optimal solution.

These characteristics are drawn up in some sort of a DSS specifications book and they allow refining coherent scenarios in which one can avoid the all too classical "Old Maid" game that characterizes the search for local improvement at the price of global performance degradation. This approach was successfully used in the Departments of *La Poste's* Ile de France delegation. On a strategic level, it allowed the construction of innovative organizational scenarios for postal concentration, and on a tactical level, it allowed the modulation of an organization according to seasonal demand characteristics, thus avoiding the inconveniences of over dimensioning due to "peak" demand.

4.CONCLUSION

The adaptation of companies and the displacement of their boundaries is first a question of men and willpower, but in an open economy it is also an adaptation of technology and thus a mastered and coordinated evolution of techniques and tools. For companies, this implies training efforts and a favorable attitude towards innovation and therefore towards research on managerial techniques.

REFERENCES

Curien, N. et al. (1992), *Economie et Management des Entreprises de Réseau*, Economica.

Danjou, F., Giard, V. and Le Roy, E. (2000), "Analyse de la robustesse des ordon-nancements/réordonnancements sur lignes de production et d'assemblage dans l'industrie automobile", *Revue Française de Gestion Industrielle*, **1**.

Davenport, T. (1993), *Process Innovation: Reengineering Work Through Information Technology*, Harvard Business School Press, Boston.

Giard, V. (1994), "Gestion de production et entreprises de réseau", *Le manager des entreprises de réseau*, **5**.

Giard, V., Triomphe, C., and André, R. (2000), "*Organist*: un Système Interactif d'Aide à la Définition du niveau de traitement du courrier des bureaux de poste et des tournées d'acheminement à un centre de tri", Cahier du GREGOR 97.06, presented at the 2ᵉ Congrès international franco-québécois de génie industriel, September 3-5 1997 and adapted for the n°1 of *Cahiers du Génie Industriel*.

Giard, V. (1997), *Processus productifs et programmation linéaire*, Economica.

Giard, V. (2000), "Economical analysis of product standardization", presented at the 2nd Conference IFAC/IFIP/IEEE Management and Control of Production and Logistics, Grenoble, July, Elsevier.

Hammer, V and Champy, V. (1993), *Le Reengineering : réinventer l'entreprise pour une amélioration spectaculaire de ses performances*, Dunod, Paris.

Morin, J.(1985), *L'excellence technologique*, Publi-Union, Paris.

Paché, G. and Paraponaris, C. (1993), *L'entreprise en réseau*, PUF.

Rosenthal, R. (1996), "Algebraic modeling languages for optimization",in S. Gass and C. Yarris (eds), *Encyclopedia of Operations Research and Management Sciences* , Kluwer.

Vernadat, F. (1999), *Techniques de Modélisation en Entreprise : Applications aux Processus Opérationnels*, Economica.

13. Synchronous Production and Industrial Organization

Michel Sapina and Jean-Charles Monateri

1. INTRODUCTION

The automobile sector is greatly concerned with continuous organizational and product innovation. Firms simultaneously improve the way they deal with constraints such as productivity, flow tightening and how they cope with an increasing variety of final products. To capture market share, firms strike in the automobile arena by innovating in the areas of both products and organizations: they frequently renew their product lines and always search for new ways to pilot and coordinate production more efficiently. What complicates their task is that the global process of production is divided more and more between independent firms, managing interdependent processes, and using complementary activities (Richardson, 1972). Here, we will consider complementary activities in a vertical inter-industrial process: complementary issues relate both to product complementarity (such as components of functions to a final product) and to process complementarity (the final outcome of one process gets included in another successive process). Firms must make their production cycles compatible, and they also implement a differentiated tension of flows through the various levels of the global process of car-making.

Also, contractual arrangements and new industrial architectures, dedicated to identified final products, are efficient weapons to create and sustain competitive organizational advantage. We define "industrial architectures » as « sets of lasting, structured and hierarchized industrial relations, enforced by contractual arrangements. Such arrangements are set between complementary firms, to make an efficient industrial system, in an unstable competitive environment, through ensuring proper reactivity between markets and production activities" (Monateri and Sapina, 1998).

Industrial architectures establish rules of coordination that structure durable and complementary relationships between firms. They also stabilize the parameters piloting production. Implementing a system of synchronous production also means utilizing specific or co-specific assets (Teece, 1986a), to articulate production and ensure a coherent articulation between the economic criteria of volume, (scale), flow tightening (speed) and products variety (scope of the product line). Firms must then cooperate to ensure proper coordination in operations management, as well as in contractual and complementary investment issues.

Here, our goal is to assess the empirical impact of a piloting system for synchronous production on structuring and coordinating contractual activities, and its effect on shared, complementary investments in an industrial automobile architecture. Synchronous production is an organizational innovation based on stronger, durable, cooperative and bilateral coordination between firms. Such innovation rests on the interdependence and cooperation of firms and is enforced by co-specific assets (Teece, 1986b) such as EDI, so as to better articulate industrial processes.

First we shall describe a bilateral system for articulating synchronous production between productive units owned by a first-rank supplier and a carmaker. We empirically characterize this system related to synchronous production management, on a short-term basis. Then we shall analyze what determines this articulation, and enlarge our first sight analysis to the coordination of automotive industrial organization. We refer to organizing production contracts through contractual arrangements (Brousseau and Quelin, 1996) between firms, and through sizing common investments in a proper industrial architecture.

2. MANAGING SYNCHRONOUS PRODUCTION: BILATERAL COORDINATION OF PRODUCTION AND LOGISTIC FLOWS

Industrial relationships between carmakers and their first-rank suppliers are a useful observation topic for synchronous production management. We study the specific relationship between Peugeot, a carmaker, and Peguform, a first-rank supplier which processes plastics into differentiated and even customized bumpers for Peugeot cars. Thanks to synchronous production, those firms developed a durable relationship, based on more radical constraints for coordinating production cycles (technical and information-related constraints). Mastering synchronous production ensures better coordination and improved (through increased constraints) production management between the firms' plants. Coordination is short- or medium-term oriented, focusing on final products and peripheral variety coherence (Fisher, et al. 1995). It also relies on implementing complementary competencies, specific to one industrial relationship.

Empirical Characterization of Synchronous Production

To characterize synchronous production, we must first clearly define its basic criteria, and examine how firms allocate competencies inside the "synchronous supply chain".

Basic criteria about synchronous organization
In the industrial relationship established between firms, a synchronous production system relies on three main elements:

- The tightening of product flow's intensity. The final assembly line owned by the carmaker sets the pace of first-rank production. It also sets the time constraint, called "requisition time", by which the first-rank supplier brings products onto the final assembly line. With synchronous procedures the first-rank supplier pilots its activities according to the equilibration needs of the final assembly line.
- Variety of options (peripheral variety) is also imposed on the synchronous suppliers by the carmaker. Variety forecasts are made using downstream estimations on product-demand, from final customers. Equilibrating the final assembly line is strongly related to the organizational response from the carmaker to demand focused on identified and individualized products. Cars and their customized options are paired during the assembling process, so that peripheral variety is individually linked to one car only.
- Managing product variety depends on late product differentiation. Late differentiation applies both to the firms' internal processes (production and assembly lines) and to the organization of productive relationships between firms. The coordination of variety and flow tightening generates a process of progressive and individualized customization of cars. This process is also made to accelerate in order to secure product flows and ensure proper individual variety for final products.

These elements define a specific type of inter-firm coordination. They imply a specific twofold relationship between carmakers and their synchronous first-rank suppliers. Both co-dedicated products and co-specialized assets are concerned.

Products made by the synchronous supplier are identified and specified downstream by the carmaker's assembly line. The carmaker imposes its differentiation strategy to its suppliers through the constraint of final product coherence. This constraint expresses in technical as well as "visible", differentiation aspects, articulating final, individual demand, and customized options, on a one-to-one correspondence basis. Options produced by the supplier are individually attributed to identified, specific cars: total coherence is achieved on the final assembly line. Products (options and body-frames) are also co-dedicated to one another, with a perfect bilateral fit. Because of synchronous production, options and frames must correspond on the final assembling line. One red car with a high customization level must be coherent with its own options, designed for "cockpit dressing" (cockpit plastic color or technical options) or for external "sight-seeing" differentiation ("red" colored bumpers, wing-tips). Synchronous production matches the supplier's internal production with the car assembly line, at an individual rate.

Co-dedicated products and flow tightening impose specific and even co-specific production assets that improve coordination between the plants of the carmaker and those of the synchronous supplier. Those specific assets are shared systems for information and logistics management, designed to ensure a complete identity between one car and its peripheral, dedicated options, all along the flows between productive units (production plants or lines). To reach a perfect balance between the production rates, both supplier and carmaker must produce and share precise, reliable short-term information, so they can finely pilot and synchronize their processes. The information relates to characteristics and assembly order of products and options.

Implementing such specific assets creates new capabilities on production and also on logistics and coordination. Those capabilities are shared between the carmaker and its synchronous supplier. The new allocation of assets and competencies induces a new allocation of firms' boundaries and core processes in the value chain. The synchronous value chain can also be considered as an extension of the value chain concept from internal organization to inter-firm process organization.

A new allocation of competencies between carmakers and synchronous suppliers

Owning assets dedicated to synchronous production implies specializing the productive competencies of both carmakers and their synchronous suppliers. Firms focus on their core competencies and mainly on productive and design capabilities for which they can improve their competitive advantage and create an efficiency differential with their direct competitors. They adopt a logic of vertically specializing activities through the whole supply chain (Dyer, 1995). Productive competencies are core competencies and define the main business of the firms in synchronous relation.

Carmakers and their suppliers share competencies for coordination too. Their goal is to make common information reliable so that industrial and logistical performances are continuously improved thus, better product quality as reduced direct product costs and inter-organizational costs are achieved. This is closely linked to the implementation of a shared synchronous process. It relies on the capability of firms to use relational competencies for inter-process coordination (Sapina et al., 1999).

As coordination comes from the carmaker's piloting of the inter-firm value chain, one needs landmarks to understand the basics of that coordination.

Industrial Landmarks for Piloting Synchronous Value Chain

Organizing synchronous production means articulating a triplet of economic principles: product scope (variety), speed (flow tightening) and volume (production scale). After explaining this triplet, it becomes possible to give allows for a precise definition of the main ways of synchronizing production, which permits a better understanding of their implications for industrial processes management.

Managing the "Speed-Scale and Scope" (SSS) triplet to structure the automotive value chain

The synchronous organization uses the triplet of economies of speed, scope and scale, focusing on two simultaneous aspects to coordinate flows and activities: late product differentiation and progressive product flow tightening between the firms' plants.

Figure 13.1 analyzes the triplet and its implications for the industrial organization associated to synchronous production. The position of the location point and the length of the lines in the triangle induce priority for one or two criteria: the criteria of speed and scope are much favored in a triplet designed for synchronous production.

Inside the Speed Scope and Scale triplet, two economic principles regulate the creation of competitive advantage in relation to synchronous production. The first one is progressive tightening of product flow, which increases in the downstream of the process (speed criterion), near the final assembly line. The second one is linked to the carmakers' strategy of late product differentiation (individual parts' variety criterion). Scale criterion is secondary here: it is relocated to upstream processes, and never intervenes in the synchronous process itself where lot-size is the unit, that is, at the very downstream of the automobile assembly line.

Figure 13.1. Triplet "Speed Scope and Scale", and production organization

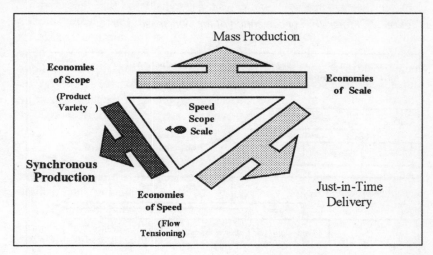

Figure 13.2 exhibits the breakdown of activities, economic principles and individual processes in the synchronous, bilateral value chain. Applying speed and scope criteria allocates the role of the various possible economies, both in internal processes, and between these processes. This will organize and structure the value chain associated with synchronous production.

- For internal plant organization, firms allocate achievable economic criteria. The speed criterion is sought at every level of the process. Economies of scope are managed at the downstream of processes, the cost of product differentiation, thus limiting both in terms of value integration to products and of inventory management. Firms must make the fine trade off between fluidity of product flows, minimal economic size of the production series and variety of their products. Economies of scale are generated in the upstream of the internal process. They are related to modularity of products and basic functions, which reduce the complexity of managing too big a variety of peripheral options (Fouque, 1997).
- In inter-firm relationships, the principle of late product differentiation remains valid, mainly through achieving peripheral variety. It focuses on maintaining zones of economies of scale and speed towards advanced

levels of the downstream inter-industrial process. Also, the first-rank synchronous suppliers (such as specialized plastic transformers) mainly manage economies of scope related to external peripheral variety, as they produce differentiated functions.

Figure 13.2. Inter-firm organization of the synchronous process

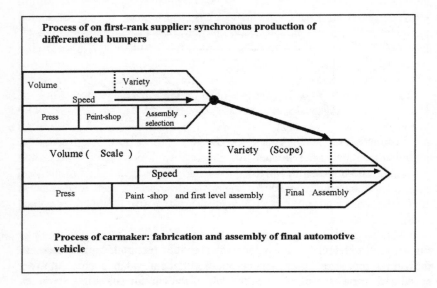

Defining synchronous procedures:

We define synchronous procedures using Just-In-Time procedures as a basis for production and delivery. Just-In-Time consists of delivering a fine standardized component to the final assembly line with a logic linked to flow tightening that reduce production delays and inventory levels through better flow coordination.

Synchronous delivery is the means to deliver differentiated and individualized functions whose coherence must be perfect with the final product. The delivery is made from a picking and selection inventory. Synchronous delivery is also defined as "delivering a fine product, at the right time and in the right order, to the final assembly line of the carmaker". It focuses on function individualization and coherence with the final car, at the logistical level.

Synchronous production relocates the management of economies of scope upstream, within the process of the synchronous supplier, according to two main issues:

- Issue 1 is to limit the requisition time needed (time included between command and assembly of the options). This integrates the production cycles of the carmaker and his supplier even more, by capturing synchronous information, identifying the final product and the associated function upstream in the production process.
- Issue 2 is to limit the costs of differentiating products (inventorying finished products and functions) by relocating the level of individualization before customization. Customizing activities are made under maximal flow tension so as to reduce the inventory value of finished functions and accelerate its turnover.

We also define synchronous production as constructing complex, individualized and differentiated functions, using flow tightening according to the unit rate imposed by the final assembly line. Synchronous production means "producing a fine product (product quality), in the right time (intense flow tightening), and in the right unit order (individualization and coherence of final, differentiated products)".

Organizing such a process rests on much asset specificity and implies that the firms get into close, longer-term contractual relationships and commit themselves to coordinating their investment strategies. Firms do so in order to improve their procedures and also to get and share profitability from co-specific assets.

3. COORDINATING COMPLEMENTARY ACTIVITIES AND INVESTMENT

Firms must shrewdly coordinate their production contracts, and must articulate their complementary activities, in order to achieve economies of scale and of learning (Loasby, 1996, 1998). They must also manage coherent investment policies at the level of the entire value chain and cooperate to improve the profitability of co-specific assets in the mid or long term. To analyze how to articulate complementary activities firms must characterize a way of coordinating production contractually (organizing the triplet coordination-cooperation-competition) and study policies of complementary investment, over a longer period (organizing coordination-cooperation).

Contractual Coordination and Organization of Cooperation-Competition tradeoffs

Managing synchronous production requires specific assets so as to improve productive and logistical efficiency: those assets, both physical and organizational, are allocated between firms to facilitate specialization and improve bilateral coordination. These assets are dedicated (Teece, 1986), and specific to one relation or to a serial of successive industrial relations. They structure productive relationships in an "industrial architecture" (Monateri and Sapina, 1999) which is stabilized for the commercial life of the car. The carmaker uses production contracts as a means to articulate competition and cooperation in the value chain of his final product: a car model.

Two competitive orientations in the inter-industrial value chain

To get into lasting contractual relationships, carmakers organize competition according to two main orientations, in the industrial architecture.

First, the horizontal orientation relates to the competition occurring between firms owning comparable competencies and located on similar activities (Richardson, 1972), on a same "level" in the inter-industrial value chain for one final car: second-rank supplier, first-rank supplier and first-rank synchronous suppliers.

The carmaker coordinates and impulses competition between similar firms according to tradeoffs between market power and incentives for his suppliers to improve their own products and processes, through technical and organizational innovation. Competition at each level determines the market share of the competitors. Such market share is strongly linked to the attribution of production contracts. Production contracts refer to integrating specialized, differentiated functions in the final products. Carmakers use "parallel-sourcing" (Richardson, 1993) as a means to combine the advantages of both coordination ways (competition and cooperation). Parallel-sourcing specializes suppliers and value chains according to final products (car models), and production contracts. A plastic transformer, such as Peguform supplies a complete and complex function (the "bumper function" made or delivered synchronously for the Peugeot 206 car model). It can even dedicate one plant or one product assembly-line to produce that function during the whole commercial lifetime of the car model (the period associated to the production contract). Another synchronous plastic transformer, such as Plastic Omnium makes the "cockpit function" for that vehicle and actually a bumper function for other car models. Parallel-sourcing and plant focus also allow for stronger plant proximity, which comes in useful when tightening production flows. Suppliers specialize in a plant or a production line

(Skinner, 1974) to achieve economies of scale and learning according to volume and mainly to the time of production. The carmaker profits on a twofold basis: it sets strong competition between its suppliers and provides incentives for them to increase productivity and continuously improve industrial relations. The analysis of such a trade-off is found in Helper's work on "new exit" ways to coordinate production (Helper, 1991; Helper and Levine, 1992).

The second axis of competition occurs "vertically" in the value chain, when firms are to share and allocate competencies and value instead of market share. Firms try to position their activities in order to expand their expertise level and the extent of their expertise domains. A strong expertise in conception and production of integrated technical and differentiated functions generates a twofold competitive advantage. Suppliers validate the technical innovation derived from their own core competencies (Teece and Pisano, 1994, Teece et al., 1998), they can then integrate activities once made by carmakers. They also turn the increasing tendency to disintegrate production activities to their profit, boosting their value share and market power in the process.

As activities on which core capabilities are based are complementary, modifying their allocation between firms impacts on the articulation of these activities, on the boundaries of the firms (Langlois and Robertson, 1993) and on their core business. This impact influences the nature of exchanged products or functions as well as the specifications for production contracts.

First-rank suppliers combine both expertise in one field and expansion of that field to keep a favorable position with carmakers. First-rank situation suppliers can directly apprehend the needs of the final customer and direct both the nature and pace of the innovation rate to their own suppliers. This guarantees gains in competitive advantage as well as a more stable position in the business relationship because competition occurs on a more informal, innovative basis, and does not only depend on product cost elasticity.

There is a strong interdependence between the horizontal and vertical dimensions of competition in the inter-industrial value chain: a minimal market share is required to get a strong position with competitors at a given level. It becomes essential when acting in production contracts. Simultaneously, being a major actor who produces more and more complex and integrated functions imposes a strong position in the vertical dimension. Vertical strength comes mainly from sustaining and increasing the wide and large expertise level, which keeps competitors behind. Vertical competition then comes near to bargaining with carmakers for value allocation before contracts are signed.

Contractual coordination: ordering competition and cooperation

Synchronous production management uses co-specific assets (procedures, inter-firm information systems) which are subject to market uncertainty (Richardson, 1990) or strategic uncertainty (Williamson, 1985). To reduce uncertainty and improve bilateral piloting of their production, firms engage in mid- or long-term contractual relationships. A duration of three to four years is common and relates to the commercial lifetime of car models. Increasing contract duration reduces the industrial partners' production and transaction costs as it stabilizes basic coordination features: global production time, global and annual production volumes, production and logistical rates. This presents a twofold advantage:

Such a lasting contractual relationship means a superior production volume is attributed to the supplier, so that he can achieve economies of scale and get experience. He is to share some of its productivity gains, according to annual productivity-sharing plans imposed by the carmaker. Determining a global and annual production volume ex ante from the contractual life allows the supplier to improve its organization, as he can rely on stabilized basics for production (volume, rates and immediate variety).

Limiting the number of contract renegotiations reduces transaction costs through economies of scale on transactions (Dyer, 1997). Cost limitation comes from reducing the number of carmakers' potential suppliers, from limiting the close-up risks (shutting activities) associated with increased supplier size, and from a better bilateral knowledge of operations management. Carmakers also select suppliers on the basis of their capability to continuously innovate and improve their organizational and inter-organizational performance. This selection is made effective through the allocation of the upcoming production contracts, elaborated for the next generations of car models.

Differentiated steps of competition and cooperation

Articulating cooperation and competition through coordination of inter-firm relationships relates to a temporal slip between various phases in the industrial relation:

- When organizing competition carmakers focus on selecting suppliers and negotiating the terms of a production contract. Besides elements of price and quantity, firms must deal with the questions of enforcing and monitoring contracts. Firms have to establish the conditions for reliable and efficient inter-firm coordination. Competition centers on quantitative (prices, quantity, duration) as well as qualitative organizational aspects: the carmaker selects the best supplier (and not necessarily the cheapest), according to those elements as well as the importance of that supplier, notably its vertical position in the industrial architecture.

* During the bilateral piloting of the production contract, cooperation occurs between the carmaker's plants and its synchronous suppliers. Firms try to continuously improve their shared organizational efficiency, which drives them to shrewdly collaborate in the piloting of their individual and shared processes. In addition, they must determine ways to improve their individual (internal processes) and common efficiency (synchronous and logistical processes). By so acting, they both create a "relational capability" (Panizzolo, 1997; Sapina et al., 1999), and reinforce their own productive competencies, which are the basis for vertical positioning and strength in contractual negotiation.

Organizing levels of competition and cooperation, and of technical or commercial tradeoffs, are means to increase market share in the final car market. Competition in this "place" comes from direct competitors (carmakers) as well as from the efficient organization of stable and cooperative industrial architectures focused on car assembly.

Industrial architectures compete on mature, unstable markets. When they must engage in complementary investments in the inter-industrial value chains, firms cannot ensure the profitability of their co-specialized assets ex ante.

Sizing Complementary Investment in a Product-Focused Industrial Architecture

Sizing production assets is central to studying coordination in a value chain linked to synchronous processes. It relates to long-term cooperation between firms, and is based on the lifetime of some assets. This goes far beyond the duration of production contracts linked to the commercial life of product models. It drives firms to cope with market and technical uncertainties. Firms share technical and market information, which impact strongly on the structure and dynamics of the inter-firm value chain. This impact is particularly strong for co-dedicated investments, which require much closer productive cooperation.

Product commercial lifetime versus assets lifetime
One can classify assets according to their specific links to one production contract management, or to a much longer-term industrial relationship.

Firms try to get profitability from assets specific to synchronous production contracts by sizing the leanest productive capacities they can. They seek a dead point in the period of the contract when costs equal incomes. They also try to reach that point at the earliest possible moment.

Nonetheless, evaluation of costs and incomes from the contract occur ex ante, that is, before the contract is signed and even well before production starts. It is also influenced by the bargaining conditions, such as the volumes and period of production, the initial price for the functions and the evolution of productivity efforts imposed by the carmaker during the contract period. As before, basic conditions simultaneously induce cooperation and competition (Langlois and Foss, 1998).

Opposed to that are the assets whose lifetime is longer than the period associated with a one-off production contract. These assets are paint-shops, assembly lines, and so on. and they are used during some contracts before replacement, because of attrition or because they become obsolete. Their profitability does not depend on a particular contract but it is allocated to many. This characteristic induces long-term specificity, provided that the firms sustain their business relation for some successive contracts. This poses the question of how to relate specific assets to one-shot contracts or to a long-term industrial and bilateral relationship and how it impacts on inter-firm relationships: partner firms prolong adequate industrial relationships for more than a one-off only contract. Firms can even vary accountability on production, logistics and engineering.

Long-term specific assets favor the expansion of the firms' strategic horizon. Cooperation is also mixed with competition when bargaining in the vertical dimension. Negotiation occurs in order to determine precisely on which activities core capabilities and peripheral, shared ones will be constituted. Firms cooperate to set and coordinate their long-range planning horizon so as to reduce the uncertainty about their shared investment policies.

Time and uncertainty in the inter-firm value chain
Sizing industrial investment refers to the twofold nature of information available to firms: technical information and market information (Richardson, 1990; Foss, 1994, 1996).

- Technical information relates to the technical level reached by partners when the production contract is signed. Carmakers allocate contracts on an ex ante basis and according to their expectations of the orientation and speed of technical innovation during the contractual duration (production management): specific and co-specific assets generate sufficient importance not to stop the production of a car model, even if commercial success is not totally there. Carmakers and their suppliers improve their capabilities gradually so as not to damage the profitability of assets specific to one contract. When the lifetime of assets exceeds a one-off contract, the issue is even more critical: firms must find margins in the initial sizing of their shared and individual investments, so as to make initial investment profitable and make it evolve over longer periods. Such requirements induce firms to determine and implement long-term devices focused on coordination and cooperation. They must articulate issues linked to synchronous production management in the short-term and tackle the medium-term issues relating to coordinating competition and cooperation, in order to develop and sustain a durable and shared competitive advantage, which covers successive generations of products.

- Market information refers to the competitive positions of firms at a similar level in the value chain. Two sorts of uncertainty are involved: uncertainty of the commercial success of final products (car models), which is unknown when investments are made, and even when production starts; uncertainty about delays, the nature and intensity of the competitors' reaction to the decision of investing. "Horizontal" as well as "vertical" competitors are concerned. When firms cooperate actively in articulating activities closely, they limit market uncertainty since they can set the industrial architecture in a leading innovative position (this was demonstrated by the Toyota group and its industrial Keiretzu).
- The first type of market uncertainty (sold volume of products) impacts severely on product and dedicated assets' profitability, acting at every level of the inter-firm value chain. To cover it, firms must also choose how far they can tolerate over-investment, how to allocate and where to set productive over-capacity.
- Uncertainty about competitors' reactions depends on the gestation period, which follows three steps (Richardson, 1990): (1) competitors capture relevant information; (2) competitors assess and understand the information; (3) competitors make the needed investment or specify productive capacities. When industrial structures are divided amongst firms, these steps coincide with the periods needed by suppliers to negotiate contracts and implement complementary investment. This impacts on the profitability and on the gestation period too.

When they invest, firms must cope with both technical and market uncertainty, at every level of the industrial architecture. Because the value chain specific to one product reduces technical uncertainty at the expense of increasing market uncertainty, a strong increase or decrease in market share or global volume renders market information obsolete and irrelevant for the production cycle organization.

Information obsolescence forces firms to re-examine their initial sizing of physical and organizational assets, or even to rethink the relationships inside the industrial architecture. According to MacDuffie and Helper (1995), this issue hinges on tradeoffs between long-term cooperation and competition organization.

If it is to arbitrate simultaneously between hedging technical and market uncertainty the industrial value chain must be structured around lasting contractual relationships, inside which carmakers share risks with their suppliers, to a certain extent. This implies a cooperative policy (Brousseau, 1996), which determines strong and durable common competitive advantage along with harsh bargaining so this competitive advantage, as well as the associated profits, can be shared.

4. CONCLUSION

We characterized the synchronous production system as a set of bilateral industrial relationships, based on the efficient implementation of co-specific assets, within an industrial architecture. Our contribution was then to describe and analyze the relation between production management and inter-industrial organization, through the firms' shared contractual and investment-related policies.

The industrial architecture described here is specific to one industrial relationship or to more successive industrial relations established between stable long-standing partners. On a long-term basis we use it as a framework for coordinating tradeoffs between cooperation and competition in the field of industrial relations. In the shorter term, the industrial architecture rests on complementary activities and procedures which pilot synchronous production efficiently in the interindustrial value chain.

Focusing the analysis on relationships between carmakers and synchronous first-rank suppliers highlights two phases in organizing industrial relationships. First is the time for production management, when firms make the structure of their exchange and the production of complex products evolve. Their goal is to match reduced costs with the constraints of the variety required and the flow tightening constraints. Second, firms coordinate both hybrid contractual forms and complementary investment policies.

When determining durable industrial architectures, coordination and cooperation aim at perpetuating a piloting model coherent on a short-term and medium-term basis. Such industrial systems reduce uncertainty and stabilize contractual relationships, so that profitability of production and coordination investments can be ensured.

Synchronous production is then considered as a durable "contractual arrangement" (Brousseau and Quelin, 1996), established between firms located at various levels of the inter-industrial value chain. Its goals are to ensure permanent coherence between production management and complementary investment policies.

REFERENCES

Brousseau, E. (1996), "Contrats et comportements coopératifs", in J.L. Ravix (ed), *Coopération entre les entreprises et organisation industrielle*, CNRS Édition, Paris.

Brousseau, E. and Quelin, B., (1996), "Asset specificity and organizational arrangements: the case of the new telecommunications services market", *Industrial and Corporate Change*, **5** (4), 1205-1229.

Dyer, J. H. (1997), "Effective interfirm collaboration: how firms minimize transaction costs and maximize transaction value", *Strategic Management Journal*, **18**, 535-556.

Dyer, J. H. (1995), "Specialized suppliers networks as a source of competitive advantage: evidence from the auto industry", *Strategic Management Journal*, **17**, 271-291

Fisher, M., Jain, A., and MacDuffie, J.P. (1995), "Strategies for Product Productivity ; lessons from the auto industry ", in E. Bowman and B. Kogut *Redesigning the firm*, Oxford University Press, 270 pages.

Foss, N.J. (1996), "Capabilities and the theory of the firm", *Revue d'Economie Industrielle*, **77**, 7-28.

Foss, N.J (1994), "Cooperation is competition: G.B. Richardson on coordination and interfirm relations", *British Review of Economic Issues*, **16** (40), October, 25-49.

Fouque, T. (1997), "Impact de la réduction de la diversité des produits sur les stocks", Thèse de doctorat en Gestion, Paris X, Paris, 230 pages.

Fujimoto, T. (1999), *"The evolution of a manufacturing system at Toyota"*, Oxford University Press, Oxford, New York, 380 pages.

Helper, S.R. (1991), "Strategy and irreversibility in supplier relations: the case of the US automobile industry", *Business History Review*, **65**, winter, 781-824.

Helper SR. and Levine D. (1992), "Long term supplier relations and product-market structure", *Journal of Law, Economics and Organization*, **8** (3), 561-581.

Langlois, R.N. and Foss, N.J (1998), "Capabilities and Governance: the Rebirth of Production in the Theory of Economic Organization", DRUID Working Paper, 97-2, January, 39 pages.

Langlois, R.N., Robertson, P. L. (1993), "Business organization as a coordination problem: towards a dynamic theory of the boundaries of the firm", *Business and Economic History*, **22** (1), 31-41.

Loasby, J. (1998), "The organization of capabilities", *Journal of Economic Behaviour and Organization*, **35**, 139-160.

Loasby, J. (1996), "Competition and imperfect knowledge: the contribution of G. B. Richardson", *Scottish Journal of Political Economy*, **33** (2), 145-158.

MacDuffie, P. and Helper, S. R. (1997), "Creating lean suppliers: diffusing lean production through the supply chain", *California Management Review*, **39** (4), 118-151.

Haurat, A. and Monateri, J.-Ch. (1999), "Dymanique des relations durables entre entreprises, architectures industrielles, coordination, pilotage performance", in A. Langevin, D. Riopel and P. Ladet, 3ième Congrès International De Génie Industriel, Presses Polytechniques, Montréal, Canada, **1**, 505-517.

Monateri, J-Ch. and Sapina, M. (1999), "Dynamique des relations interentreprises, stratégies manufacturières et arrangements contractuels durables" », in A.Langevin, D. Riopel ad P. Ladet, 3ième congrès international de Génie Industriel, Presses Polytechniques, Montréal, Canada, **1**, 273-282.

Panizzolo, R. (1998), "Applying the lessons learned from 27 lean manufacturers. The relevance of relationships management", *International Journal of Production Economics*, **55**, 223-240.

Richardson, G.B. (1972), "The Organisation of Industry", *The Economic Journal*, September, 883-896.

Richardson, G.B. (1990), *Information and Investment: a study in the working of the competitive economy*, Oxford University Press, Clarendon press, 2nd edition.

Richardson, J. (1993), "Parallel sourcing and supplier performance in the Japanese automobile industry", *Strategic Management Journal*, **14**, 339-350.

Sapina, M., Berrah, L., Haurat, A. and Monateri, J.-Ch. (1999), "Piloter-coordonner les relations interentreprises : une approche combinée technique économique", Mosim99, 6-8 Octobre, 7 pages.

Shimizu K. (1999), *Le Toyotisme* , Coll. Repères, La Découverte, 125 pages.

Skinner W. (1974), "The focused Factory", *Harvard Business Review*, **52**, (3), 113-121.

Spiller T. and Zelner B. A. (1997), "Product complementarities, capabilities and governance: a dynamic transaction cost perspective", *Industrial and Corporate Change*, **6** (3), 561-594.

Teece, D.J. (1986), "Profiting from technological innovation", *Research Policy*, **15** (6), 285-305.

Teece, D.J. (1986b), "Firm boundaries, technological innovation and strategic management", in L.G. Thomas, (ed), *The economics of strategic planning*, Lexington Books, Lexington, Mass., 187-199.

Teece, D.J. and Pisano, G. (1994), "The Dynamic Capability of Firms : an Introduction", in *Industrial and Corporate Change*, **3** (3).

Teece, D.J., Pisano, G. and Schuen, A., (1997), "Dynamic capabilities and strategic management", *Strategic Management Journal*, **18** (7), 509-533

Van Hoeck, R. and Weken, H. (1998), "The impact of modular production on the dynamics of supply chains", *International Journal of Logistics Management*, **9** (2), 35-50.

Williamson, O. (1985), *The economic institutions of capitalism*, Free Press, New York, 450 pages.

14. Cooperation and the Organisation of Industry

Joël Thomas Ravix

1. INTRODUCTION

In 1972, R.H. Coase noticed that "what is curious about the treatment of the problems of industrial organisation is that it does not exist" (Coase, 1972, p. 60). This paradox lies in the observation that "we all know what is meant by the organisation of industry. It describes how the activities undertaken within the economic system are divided up between firms. As we know, some firms embrace many different activities; while for others, the range is narrowly circumscribed. Some firms are large; others, small. Some firms are vertically integrated; others are not. This is the organization of industry or – as it used to be called – the structure of industry" (ibid.). That is why he emphasises the necessity to "make progress in understanding the forces which determine the organization of industry" (ibid., p. 59).

The same year, G.B. Richardson made a similar remark: "our simple picture of the capitalist economy was in terms of a division of labour between the firm and the market, between co-ordination that is planned and co-ordination that is spontaneous. What then is the principle of this division? ... It is a matter upon which our standard theories, which merely assume but do not explain a division between firm and market, throw little light" (Richardson, 1972, p. 883). Richardson also specifies that "the dense network of co-operation and affiliation by which firms are inter-related" (ibid.) is left out of account by the traditional dichotomy between firm and market.

The problem emphasised by Coase and Richardson is based on the fact that "'industry' is often used as a synonym for 'market'" (Nightingale, 1978, p. 31). Therefore, an industry is generally defined as a grouping of firm, which operate similar processes and could produce identical products. Consequently, buying and selling are the only inter-firms relationships and they make up, at best, a partial approach to the diversity of industrial relationships, as described by Coase and Richardson.

By contrast, the diversity of inter-firm relationships does tally with a division of labour between different 'business institutions' which encompass not only business organisations like business firms, but also "encompass a wide variety of structures, including those institutions generally described as markets" (Langlois and Robertson, 1995, p. 1). These business institutions can contribute towards the understanding of "the institutional structure of production" (Coase, 1992) because they can explain how firms organise their productive activities.

The first part of this chapter is devoted to an investigation of the theoretical background supporting the institutional organisation of production. The idea is that the time dimension of production leads firms to organise their productive process in different ways. They set up cooperative relationships, the modalities of which might assume various forms. In the second part, this approach is applied to an analysis of the structure of French industry based on special statistics from the French Ministry of Industry (SESSI). These statistics focus on productive relationships between firms, and help to describe the variety of the institutional structure of production in French industry.

2. THE INSTITUTIONAL ORGANIZATION OF PRODUCTION

According to Richardson, when analysing the organisation of production, "the point is not that production is dependent on the state of the art but that it has to be undertaken (as Mrs. Penrose has so very well explained) by human organisations embodying specifically appropriate experience and skill" (Richardson, 1972, p. 888). Consequently, to understand the institutional organisation of production, it is necessary to explain the way in which production is organised within the firm before analysing the productive relationships between firms. In this respect, as suggested by Richardson, it is useful to adopt Edith Penrose's point of view because she considers that "in a private enterprise industrial economy the business firm is the basic unit for the organization of production" (Penrose, 1959, p. 9).

The Organization of Production within the Firm

The originality of the Penrose approach is that the nature of the firm does not depend on the working of the economic system. In contrast, "the very nature of the economy is to some extent defined in terms of the kind of firms that compose it, their size, the way in which they are established and grow, their methods of doing business, and the relationships between them" (ibid.). In this perspective, she states that "the primary economic function of an industrial firm is to make use of productive resources for the purpose of supplying goods and services to the economy in accordance with plans developed and put into effect within the firm" (ibid., p. 15). However, she adds that the firm is also "a collection of productive resources the disposal of which between different uses and over time is determined by administrative decision" (ibid., p. 24). It follows, therefore, that if we define the industrial firm with reference to the administrative framework within which its industrial activities are coordinated, we can be concerned with the way in which this coordination proceeds.

Penrose bases her analysis on a conception where the time dimension of production is central. She establishes a sharp distinction between the physical or human productive resources and the services that the resources can generate. This distinction is close to Georgescu-Rogen's (1971) analysis in terms of *flows* and *funds*. Thus,

"strictly speaking, it is never *resources* themselves that are the 'inputs' in the production process, but only the *services* that the resources can render. The services yielded by resources are a function of the way in which they are used – exactly the same resources when used for different purposes or in different ways and in combination with different types or amounts of other resources provide a different service or set of services. The important distinction between resources and services is not their relative durability: rather it lies in the fact that resources consist of a bundle of potential services and can, for the most part, be defined independently of their use, while services cannot be so defined, the very word 'service' implying a function, an activity" (ibid., p. 25).

Penrose avoids the use of the term 'factor of production' because "it makes no distinction between resources and services" (ibid., p. 25, footnote 1), and that is why she prefers the notion of "productive opportunity" of a firm, which comprises "all of the productive possibilities that its 'entrepreneurs' see and can take advantage of" (ibid., p. 31).

The notion of productive opportunity leads Penrose to adopt an unusual definition of the market. In her analysis, the market appears as a specific part of the firm's activities. It is identified with selling programmes or the commercial activities of the firm since "the 'demand' with which an entrepreneur is concerned when he makes his production plans is nothing more nor less than his own ideas about what he can sell at various prices with varying degrees of selling effort" (ibid., p. 81). More accurately Penrose considers that "at all time a firm has a foothold in certain types of production and in certain types of market", which are called "areas of specialization of the firm" (ibid., p.109). In order to build its "areas of specialization", each firm has to determine its own "market areas", including the customer group which the firm hopes to influence by the same sales programme, "regardless of the number of products sold to that group" (ibid., p. 110). The result is that "the appropriate criteria for the delimitation of market areas are different for different firms; the significance of the boundaries lies in the fact that a movement into a new market area requires the devotion of resources to the development of a new type of selling programme and a competence in meeting a different type of competitive pressure" (ibid.). The idea according to which the firm builds its own market is the consequence of how the firm estimates its potential outlets "for demand from the point of view of the firm is highly subjective – the opinion of the firm's entrepreneur" (ibid., p. 85).

The market areas of the firms are closely connected to their production bases. According to Penrose, "each type of productive activity that uses machines, process, skills, and raw materials that are all complementary and closely associated in the process of production we shall call a 'production base' or 'technological base' of the firm, regardless of the number or type of products produced" (ibid., p. 109). This notion of productive base, dissociated from the product notion, is very important to Penrose's analysis. It comprises the whole technological and managerial knowledge that the firm must mobilise to produce. Penrose indicates that firms differentiate from one another because of their productive opportunity, which induces development of different production bases and different market areas, so that they have different areas of specialisation. As Penrose emphasises, "a movement into a new base requires a firm to achieve competence in some significantly different areas of technology" (ibid., p. 110). This means that the firm must acquire or develop new knowledge to create new competencies.

This more realistic approach of the firm's activity leads to the idea that the organisation of production within the firm takes the form of a process which is divided into various stages, from conception or design operation to the marketing operation, as illustrated in Figure 14.1.

Figure 14.1. The firm's productive process

Activities processed by the firm					
Conception	Provisioning	Manufacturing	Assembling	Finishing	Marketing
PRODUCTIVE BASE					MARKET AREA

In this perspective, the organisation of production articulates three levels of coordination. First, temporal co-ordination of elementary processes relative to one activity. It is a technical co-ordination, which obeys to a workshop logic. It is specific to each stage of the productive process of the firm. Secondly, the productive organisation of the firm requires temporal coordination between activities for assuring consistency with the productive process of the firm. Thirdly, the working of the productive process also requires that the firm coordinates relationships with its customers and providers. These relationships can take up different forms.

In accordance with the firm's technological choices, different modalities of organising inter-firms relationships can be set up. These modalities condition the institutional organisation of production.

Inter-firms Relationships and the Organization of Production

The organisation of production leads to a variety of inter-firm relationships which perfectly fits the network of cooperation by which firms are inter-related, as described by Richardson: "Firm A is a joint subsidiary of firms B and C, it has technical agreements with D and E, sub-contracts work to F, it is in marketing association with G – and so on" (Richardson, 1972, p. 884). This complex and ramified network of cooperative arrangements is analysed by Richardson with the aid of three institutional forms of coordination: the *direction* within the firm, the *cooperation* between firms, and *market transactions*. To explain the principles of division of labour between the three ways in which co-ordination can be effected, Richardson introduces a new distinction between the "similarity" and "complementarity" of industrial activities. *Similar activities* are "activities which require the same capability for their undertaking" (ibid., p. 888). Activities are *complementary* when "they represent different phases in a process of production and require in some way or another to be coordinated" (ibid., p. 889).

Like Penrose, Richardson refers to *activities* rather than products, and to *capabilities* rather than productive factors. Activities are distinct from products because they are "related to the discovery and estimation of future wants, to research, development and design, to the execution and co-ordination of process of physical transformation, the marketing of goods and so on"; while capabilities are associated with knowledge, experience and skills because "the capability of an organisation may depend upon command of some particular material technology, ..., or may derive from skills in marketing or knowledge of and reputation in a particular market" (ibid.).

On this basis, Richardson can explain that when activities are both similar and complementary, they are co-ordinated by the direction within a firm; while activities are closely complementary but dissimilar they have to be co-ordinated by ex ante cooperation, because "coordination is achieved through co-operation when two or more independent organisations agree to match their related plans in advance" (ibid., p. 890). Conversely, Richardson specifies that other activities which are not closely complementary are coordinated by market transactions.

Following Penrose's and Richardson's analysis, it is possible to distinguish among the cooperative arrangements' different types of inter-firm productive relationships. SESSI's typology of activity sharing between a firm and its customer gives such possibility, as is suggested in the Table 14.2.

In this typology, modalities 1 to 4 describe different forms of subcontracting relationships in which the firm performs some productive activities for its customer. The specificity of these modalities is that the customer keeps strategic activities like conception and/or marketing. Therefore, it is necessary that the firm and its customer coordinate their plans in advance. On the contrary, in self-production and service furnishing, the whole productive process is performed within the firm, and the product or service is sold to the customer on a market. This variety of inter-firm relationships which encompasses not only productive arrangements but also market transactions can be used to describe the institutional structure of industry.

Table 14.2. SESSI's typology of activity sharing between a firm and its customer

ACTIVITIES \ MODALITIES	Conception	Provisioning	Manufacturing Assembling Finishing	Marketing
1. Made-to-measure production			▨	
2. Production under specifications		▨	▨	
3. Conception and production supplying	▨ (partial)	▨	▨	
4. Conception supplying	▨			
5. Licensed production		▨	▨	▨
6. Production under the trademark of a distributor	▨	▨	▨	
7. Self-production	▨	▨	▨	▨
8. Service supplying	▨	▨	▨	▨

☐ What the customer does   ▨ What the firm does

Source: Hannoun and Guerrier, (1996).

3. THE INSTITUTIONAL STRUCTURE OF FRENCH INDUSTRY

The previous typology was used in 1994 to analyse the structure of French industry. It appeared that market transactions dominated the whole industry. Yet, this is not the case when the typology is applied to specific industrial sectors. The main reason for this phenomenon is that, over the last ten years, large firms have progressively abandoned strategies of vertical integration to focus on a small number of strategic activities in which they have specific competencies. For technological reasons, this disintegration process is not the same in all industrial sectors.

Inter-firm Relationships in French Industry

The relative part of inter-firms relationship in the whole industry can be evaluated by the business turnover that firms realise in each form of relationship. Table 14.3 contains some interesting information. The most important relationship is market transaction because self-production and service supplying represent over 70% of business turnover in the whole industry. This table also shows that subcontracting is a relationship that needs close consideration.

Table 14.3. Inter-firm relationships in the whole industry

	Distribution of the whole industry turnover	Distribution of firms making no less than 80% of their turnover in one relationship
Made-to-measure production	4.0	14.2
Production under specifications	9.0	16.3
Conception and production supplying	7.8	10.0
Conception supplying	0.2	0.3
Whole subcontracting	*21.1*	*40.8*
Licensed production	4.5	1.4
Production under the trademark of a distributor	3.6	3.8
Self-production	64.5	46.2
Service supplying	6.3	7.6
Total	*100*	*100*

Source: SESSI.

However it is necessary to emphasise that most firms do not carry out their activities within one single relationship. On the contrary, each firm pursues several activities, among which self-production has more or less importance. So, when we look at the firms that make no less than 80% of their turnover in one relationship, the results are very different. It is possible to observe that 40.8% of those firms are subcontractors, while firms which perform only self-production represents 46.2% of all firms.

The structure of inter-firm relationships becomes clearer when the size of the firms is taken into account.

Table 14.4. Inter-firms relationships by firm size

Size of firm	20 to 49 employees	50 to 199 employees	200 to 499 employees	More than 499 employees
Made-to-measure production	9.7	7.3	4.0	1.8
Production under specifications	13.3	13.8	9.8	6.6
Conception and production supplying	9.5	9.5	7.8	7.0
Conception supplying	0.5	0.5	0.2	0.1
Whole subcontracting	*33.0*	*31.2*	*21.8*	*15.6*
Licensed production	1.4	3.2	3.7	5.8
Production under the trade mark of a distributor	3.9	5.3	4.9	2.7
Self-production	52.4	53.8	63.9	70.2
Service supplying	9.3	6.6	5.6	5.7
Total	*100*	*100*	*100*	*100*

Source: SESSI

Table 14.4 confirms that subcontracting activities are principally made by small and medium firms, but it also shows that large firms undertake subcontracting for other firms. In the diversity of subcontracting relationships the made-to-measure production and the production under specifications are chiefly fulfilled by small firms, while conception and production supplying is the area in subcontracting relationship where large firms are mainly concerned. However, Table 14.4 is over-aggregated so that it gives no specific information about the different structure for the organisation of production.

The Diversity of French Industry Organization

The study of inter-firm relationships within different industries shows that industries do not have the same structure and, consequently, the organisation of productive activities can take up various forms. To give a clear indication of this phenomenon it is possible to analyse the structure of inter-firms relationships in some industries.

In particular, two traditional and complementary industries, like wood pulp, the paper and cardboard industry and the paper or cardboard products industry, do not have the same structure of inter-firm relationships. In the first case, large and very small firms are specialised in self-production, while only small firms take a large part in subcontracting relationships. For the last firms, industrial subcontracting represents more than 50% of their activity, as shown in Table 14.5 (see Appendix).

On the contrary, in the paper or cardboard products industry the organisation of production is different. Only large firms are not concerned with subcontracting. Small and medium firms are widely specialised in industrial subcontracting. Table 14.6 indicates that production under specifications is the main mode of inter-firms relationship after market transactions. However, it is essential to emphasise that these productive relations do not necessary characterise the industry's structure of production as far as firms which belong to it generally supply other industries. It is therefore difficult to know whether such relationships are specific to the industry or to inter-industrial relationships.

Although the textile and clothing industries are also traditional, their productive structures are very different from those of the paper and cardboard industries. As is shown in Table 14.7, subcontracting plays a significant role in the textile industry. Whatever the firms' sizes in the textile industry, subcontracting adds about 20% of firms' activities, except for small firms, which also carry out production under the trademark of a distributor and under licence. In this case, production sharing takes place between firms within the industry. The phenomenon is more pronounced in the clothing industry where traditionally subcontracting firms are also purchasers for other firms. Therefore, as Table 14.8 shows, it is not surprising to observe some extensive division of labour in this industry. In particular, very small and small firms are specialised in made-to-measure production, and subcontracting is their main activity.

In intermediate products industries, cooperation takes up a much more significant place. The best example of this situation is the electronic components industry. Table 14.9 indicates that in this industry overall subcontracting adds up to about 50% for very small and medium firms, and about 30% for small and large firms. Such result can be explained by the fact that firms are simultaneously suppliers and purchasers for other firms within and without this industry. But this network of inter-firms co-operation is not only specific to the electronic components industry. The table 10 shows that such productive organisation can also be observed in the aerospace industry. In this case, subcontracting relationships represent more than 50% of small and very small firms' activities, and more than 20% of medium and large firms' activities. The extent of inter-firm cooperation in the aerospace industry is the result of a specific industrial organisation in which it is necessary for firms with different knowledge and different competencies to gather together to produce an aeroplane or a satellite. Therefore it is not surprising that the main activity of small firms is performed in conception and production supplying. Institutional and technological constraints require the sharing the process of production between firms endowed with specific capabilities, the coordination of which implies that firms cooperate from the conception or design stage (Ravix, 2000).

This phenomenon of close cooperation takes a different form in the automobile industry. To emphasise such organisation of production it is necessary to establish a distinction between the motor vehicles industry and the motor vehicle equipment industry. For the first one, Table 14.11 shows that subcontracting is relatively limited; the maximum is for medium firms, which make about 30% of their activity in subcontracting relationships. In motor vehicle equipment industry, on the contrary, Table 14.12 shows that all firms make more than 40% of their activities in subcontracting relationships. Conception and production supplying appears as the prevailing relationship for very small firms and large firms. The distinguishing feature of this industry is that self-production makes up less than 50% of firms' activity, whatever their size. Although the automobile industry may be compared with aerospace the industry, it has not the same organisation of production. In the automobile industry, carmakers maintain direct or indirect control over the entire process of production, while in the aerospace industry, firms group together to design and produce different complementary parts of the same product. This (characteristic) explains why in the aerospace industry large firms make more than 20% of their activities in subcontracting. This is not the case in the motor vehicles industry.

4. CONCLUSION

Two main implications follow from the diversity of inter-firm relationships observed in French industries. The first implication relates to the make or buy approach by which the structure of industry is traditionally analysed. In this approach there is no place for cooperation. However, firms do not have to choose between make or buy, because they can also establish different forms of cooperative arrangements, which have an effect upon the working of the industry. The result is that all industries are not structured in the same way, according to the role played by cooperation or market transactions in the organisation of production.

The second implication is the necessity to reconsider the definition of an industry. The conventional definition of an industry as "a group of competitors producing products or services that compete directly with each other" (Porter, 1990, p. 33), cannot be used to give an understanding of the organisation of production. The term "sector" as defined in French statistics seems much more adapted to name grouping of firms which produce the same products or services. On the other hand, the term "industry" should be reserved for a group of firms sharing different stages of a productive process, and which consequently are not direct competitors in the same market. In other words, competition among suppliers is different from competition between suppliers and purchasers. This raises a new issue: what elements determine industry boundaries?

The distinction between self-production or service supplying and subcontracting as previously defined can help us to determine such boundaries. This distinction based on the necessity to co-ordinate activities *ex post* or *ex ante* allows us to determine the activities belonging to one industry and those belonging to other industries. In this perspective, subcontracting relationships may be used to define industry boundaries, while inter-industries relationships are described by self-production or service supplying because they relate to market transactions. This embryonic solution does not resolve all problems involved in the necessity of a new definition of industry. In particular, it does not explain what elements influence industry structures. However, it shows that Penrose's and Richardson's analysis lead the way to a better understanding of the productive structure of industry.

REFERENCES

Coase, R. (1972), "Industrial organization: a proposal for research", in V.R. Fuchs (ed.), *Policy Issues and Research Opportunities in Industrial Organization*, Columbia University Press, NBER, New York.

Coase, R. (1992), "The Institutional structure of production", *American Economic Review*, **82** (4).

Hannoun, M. and Guerrier G. (1996), *Le partenariat industriel*, Chiffres clés, SESSI, Paris.

Langlois, R.N. and Robertson, P.L. (1995), *Firms, Markets and Economic Change, A Dynamic Theory of Business Institutions*, Routledge, London.

Georgescu-Roegen, N. (1971), *The Entropy Law and the Economic Process*, Harvard University Press, Cambridge, Ma.

Nightingale, J. (1978), "On the definition of 'industry' and 'market'", *The Journal of Industrial Economics*, **XXVII**, (1), pp. 31-40.

Penrose, E.T. (1959), *The Theory of the Growth of the Firm*, Oxford: Basil Blackwell.

Porter, M. (1990), *The Competitive Advantage of Nations*, Free Press, New York.

Ravix, J.T. (2000), *Les modes de coopération interentreprises dans l'industrie aéronautique et spatiale*, Paris: La Documentation Française, forthcoming.

Richardson, G.B. (1972), "The Organisation of industry", *Economic Journal*, **82** (327).

APPENDIX

Table 14.5. Wood pulps, paper and cardboard industry

Size of firm	20 to 49 employees	50 to 199 employees	200 to 499 employees	More than 499 employees
Made-to-measure production	0.9	0.6	0.0	0.0
Production under specifications	12.7	40.4	8.1	0.7
Conception and production supplying	0.0	13.8	0.0	0.0
Conception supplying	0.0	0.0	0.0	0.0
Whole subcontracting	*13.6*	*54.8*	*8.1*	*0.7*
Licensed production	0.0	1.3	1.5	0.5
Production under the trademark of a distributor	0.0	2.4	8.4	1.5
Self-production	86.4	41.0	81.7	96.6
Service supplying	0.0	0.5	0.3	0.4
Total	*100*	*100*	*100*	*100*

Source: SESSI.

Table 14.6. Paper or cardboard products industry

Size of firm	20 to 49 employees	50 to 199 employees	200 to 499 employees	More than 499 employees
Made-to-measure production	11.0	1.5	2.7	0.0
Production under specifications	20.3	38.8	21.1	0.0
Conception and production supplying	6.9	8.1	8.0	0.0
Conception supplying	4.3	0.0	0.0	0.0
Whole subcontracting	*42.5*	*48.4*	*31.8*	*0.0*
Licensed production	0.0	0.4	12.1	0.0
Production under the trademark of a distributor	1.8	6.1	3.9	7.5
Self-production	55.6	42.4	49.8	91.3
Service supplying	0.2	2.7	2.4	1.3
Total	*100*	*100*	*100*	*100*

Source: SESSI

Table 14.7. Textile industry

Size of firm	20 to 49 employees	50 to 199 employees	200 to 499 employees	More than 499 employees
Made-to-measure production	13.4	2.8	1.4	1.2
Production under specifications	6.0	0.7	10.8	0.3
Conception and production supplying	6.8	7.5	4.4	19.2
Conception supplying	0.0	0.0	0.0	0.0
Whole subcontracting	*26.3*	*11.0*	*16.6*	*20.8*
Licensed production	0.0	14.9	0.2	2.5
Production under the trademark of a distributor	1.8	14.7	1.7	3.1
Self-production	70.6	56.9	81.3	73.5
Service supplying	1.3	2.5	0.3	0.1
Total	*100*	*100*	*100*	*100*

Source: SESSI.

Table 14.8. Clothing industry

Size of firm	20 to 49 employees	50 to 199 employees	200 to 499 employees	More than 499 employees
Made-to-measure production	44.1	32.7	17.8	6.3
Production under specifications	5.4	4.9	0.6	0.5
Conception and production supplying	1.2	0.7	1.6	9.4
Conception supplying	0.0	0.2	0.0	0.0
Whole subcontracting	*50.8*	*38.4*	*20.0*	*16.1*
Licensed production	0.1	0.6	1.8	0.9
Production under the trademark of a distributor	3.2	5.8	11.5	3.0
Self-production	44.2	51.2	65.9	78.4
Service supplying	1.7	4.0	0.8	1.5
Total	*100*	*100*	*100*	*100*

Source: SESSI.

Table 14.9. Electronic components industry

Size of firm	20 to 49 employees	50 to 199 employees	200 to 499 employees	More than 499 employees
Made-to-measure production	5.2	4.3	2.3	0.2
Production under specifications	29.5	18.1	31.0	12.4
Conception and production supplying	5.9	5.8	18.3	16.5
Conception supplying	0.1	1.2	1.1	0.1
Whole subcontracting	*40.6*	*29.3*	*52.6*	*29.3*
Licensed production	8.0	0.8	1.7	1.8
Production under the trademark of a distributor	0.0	0.2	4.9	0.3
Self-production	29.6	64.9	35.9	59.9
Service supplying	21.7	4.7	4.8	8.7
Total	*100*	*100*	*100*	*100*

Source: SESSI.

Table 14.10. Aerospace industry

Size of firm	20 to 49 employees	50 to 199 employees	200 to 499 employees	More than 499 employees
Made-to-measure production	26.7	3.2	0.4	0.8
Production under specifications	17.0	13.2	2.6	1.3
Conception and production supplying	5.9	50.6	20.8	19.3
Conception supplying	0.6	0.4	2.0	1.3
Whole subcontracting	*50.4*	*67.5*	*25.9*	*22.6*
Licensed production	0.0	9.2	0.3	0.5
Production under the trademark of a distributor	0.9	0.4	18.0	0.1
Self-production	22.9	10.9	12.1	63.8
Service supplying	25.9	12.1	43.7	12.9
Total	*100*	*100*	*100*	*100*

Source: SESSI

Table 14.11. The motor vehicle industry

Size of firm	20 to 49 employees	50 to 199 employees	200 to 499 employees	More than 499 employees
Made-to-measure production	3.7	0.2	2.7	0.4
Production under specifications	2.3	1.2	16.1	10.5
Conception and production supplying	16.4	13.4	14.9	2.3
Conception supplying	0.0	0.0	0.0	0.0
Whole subcontracting	*22.4*	*14.9*	*33.7*	*13.2*
Licensed production	0.0	0.1	0.2	1.7
Production under the trademark of a distributor	8.8	22.7	12.4	1.6
Self-production	58.6	58.3	52.6	80.5
Service supplying	10.2	4.1	1.1	3.0
Total	*100*	*100*	*100*	*100*

Source: SESSI

Table 14.12. Motor vehicle equipment industry

Size of firm	20 to 49 employees	50 to 199 employees	200 to 499 employees	More than 499 employees
Made-to-measure production	2.5	2.4	2.7	0.2
Production under specifications	6.8	23.0	16.1	13.5
Conception and production supplying	46.3	22.2	21.8	30.9
Conception supplying	0.0	2.4	0.0	0.0
Whole subcontracting	*55.6*	*49.9*	*40.6*	*44.6*
Licensed production	1.3	0.2	13.8	3.8
Production under the trade mark of a distributor	0.2	2.8	4.3	4.8
Self-production	40.3	46.1	40.4	40.6
Service supplying	2.6	1.0	0.9	6.2
Total	*100*	*100*	*100*	*100*

Source: SESSI

Index